THE KAMA SUTRA

The Kama Sutra of Vatsyayana is regarded as a classic on the skills and art of sex and love. The book dates from the third century A.D. and analyses sexual techniques whilst commenting on the situations in which men and women of that period might have found themselves. In advising on how these should be dealt with, *The Kama Sutra* sought to discover in what ways happiness and enjoyment could be best achieved.

The book shares the Indian attitude to love as an ecstatic experience, but assumes that sexual happiness is founded on scientific knowledge and it, therefore, includes a series of chapters based on the practical experience of sex.

The Kama Sutra is a basis for all later Indian writings on love including Sanskrit love poetry and is a classic contribution to Indian culture.

This paperback edition is a reprint of the first 'popular' edition of the book available in England, which appeared in 1963. It includes a Preface by the late W. G. Archer, who provides fascinating background material on the circumstances of the original translation, the roles of the translators and·the place of *The Kama Sutra* in Western studies of Indian culture.

THE KAMA SUTRA OF VATSYAYANA

Translated by SIR RICHARD BURTON and F. F. ARBUTHNOT

Edited with a Preface by
W. G. Archer

Introduction by K. M. Panikkar

This edition publish 1993 by
Diamond Books
77–85 Fulham Palace Road,
Hammersmith, London W6 8JB

This edition first published by
George Allen and Unwin 1963
This paperback edition first published by
Unwin Hyman Ltd 1981

Printed in Great Britain by
HarperCollinsManufacturing Glasgow

FOREWORD

THE 'Richard Burton' translation of the *Kama Sutra* has long been recognised as a classic of Victorian writing. Not only did it introduce to the West an ancient Indian treatise, but its crisp and dignified style set a new standard in translation from the Sanskrit. Although supplemented by later studies and translations, it remains the best interpretation in English of an early Indian writer's treatment of the science and art of love.

The present edition is based on the translation as it appeared in 1883 and includes the translators' preface, introduction, foot-notes and concluding remarks. It follows the second, and more definitive, impression which appeared the same year, a little after the first. The setting style has been adjusted to modern use and in certain cases printers' literals have been amended. 'Aimiability', for example, is corrected to 'amiability', 'mangoe' to 'mango', 'acquaintaince' to 'acquaintance', 'repuired' to 'required', 'buddish' to 'Buddhist'. Many numerals and 'viz.'s with which the original is studded have also been removed. Apart from such minor changes, I have not attempted to alter the language and matter of the original or to modernise spelling, whether of Indian or English words. 'Ajanta' accordingly reads 'Ajunta', the 'Ananga Ranga' 'Anunga Runga', 'Sanskrit' 'Sanscrit', 'Hindu' 'Hindoo', 'Jaipur' 'Jeypoor'. In a similar way, 'shampoo', employed by the translators in its Victorian sense of kneading or massage, has been scrupulously retained.

In the case of foot-notes, it was tempting to correct or amplify various references and delete the more obsolete or irrelevant. To have done this, however, would have been to mar the book's flavour and in the process destroy something of its value as a Victorian study. For the reader unacquainted with Indian history, art and culture, a short bibliography has been added.

For generous co-operation in preparing the present new edition, grateful acknowledgments are given to the President and Council, Royal Asiatic Society, London.

W. G. A.

CONTENTS

PREFACE BY W. G. ARCHER

THE present translation of the *Kama Sutra* was first printed in 1883. It was called 'The Kama Sutra of Vatsyayana, Translated from the Sanscrit. In Seven Parts, with Preface, Introduction and Concluding Remarks.' No names of translators were given and the book, printed on thick paper and bound in white vellum with gold rules, bore the intriguing imprint 'Cosmopoli: 1883: for the Kama Shastra Society of London and Benares, and for private circulation only'. It was the first publication of the society and between 1883 and 1885 was twice reprinted.

The 'Council' of the Kama Shastra Society followed it in 1885 with the 'Ananga-Ranga or the Hindu Art of Love. Translated from the Sanscrit and annotated by A.F.F. and B.F.R.' Their third issue, in 1886, was 'The Perfumed Garden of the Sheik Nefzaoui or the Arab Art of Love, sixteenth century. Translated from the French Version of the Arabian M.S.' In 1887 came an English version of the Persian classic, the *Beharistan* or *Abode of Spring* by Jami, and in 1888, the *Gulistan* or *Rose Garden* by Sadi.

This exhausted the Society's own publications but between 1885 and 1888 the sixteen volumes of Sir Richard Burton's monumental translation, *The Arabian Nights*, were issued. They were headed 'Benares: printed by the Kama Shastra Society for private subscribers only'. The costs of printing and binding were met by Burton and the edition of 1,000 copies realised 16,000 guineas. Burton died in 1890 and with his death the Society ended.

The enigma of the Kama Shastra Society—its Sanskrit name, its imaginary headquarters (as elusive as Erewhon), its connection with Benares, its hidden translators (anonymous save, in one case, for initials, mystifyingly reversed)—

can be quickly resolved. It consisted of only two members—Richard F. Burton (B.F.R.) and Forster Fitzgerald Arbuthnot (A.F.F.), a retired Indian civil servant. To these we might add the name of Richard Monckton Milnes, from 1865 Lord Houghton and centre of 'the Fryston set', as romantic in its day as 'the Cliveden set' in ours. Milnes died in 1885 and Burton prefaced the third volume of his *Arabian Nights* with the words 'Inscribed to the memory of a friend who during a friendship of twenty-six years ever showed me the most unwearied kindness, Richard Monckton Milnes, Baron Houghton'. Milnes was no active participator in the Kama Shastra Society. He was rather its unseen patron, whose passion for erotica sustained Burton in his studies in sex.

The scope of the Society is suggested by its name. In Sanskrit, 'Kama' meant 'love, pleasure, sensual gratification', 'Shastra', 'scripture or doctrines'. The term 'Kama Shastra' therefore included any Hindu book on sex and love. Burton and Arbuthnot had earlier called the *Ananga Ranga* the 'Kama Shastra' but later abandoned the title as too generic. The term, so common in India, however, had stuck in Arbuthnot's mind and as he strove to implement a long-cherished project—the publication of certain Eastern classics—it served to define his aims and give them a pseudo-Indian air of alien scholarship, remote, un-British and beyond the law. On August 5, 1882, Burton wrote to his friend, the great Arabic scholar, John Payne: 'I hope you will not forget my friend, F. F. Arbuthnot and benefit him with your advice about publishing when he applies to you for it. He has undertaken a peculiar branch of literature—the Hindu erotic, which promises well.' Payne was already publishing his own translation of the *Arabian Nights*—a version which Arbuthnot later described as 'suited to cultured men and women'. Its firm adhesion to a frank original 'made Mrs Grundy roar' and no one, in Burton's view, was therefore more suited to advise on how best to publish its Indian counterpart. On December 23rd Burton told Payne: 'My friend Arbuthnot writes to me that he purposes calling upon you. He has founded a society consisting of himself and myself.' On January 15, 1883, he asked Payne: 'Has Arbuthnot sent you his Vatsyayana? He and I and the Printer have started a Hindu Kama Shastra (Ars Amoris) Society. It will make the British Public stare. Please encourage him.'[1]

In such circumstances, the *Kama Sutra* was first printed in England. Its prime sponsor was Arbuthnot. It was he who saw the book through the press, he who paid for its printing, he who supervised its distribution. In May 1883, he wrote with mock solemnity to his friend Bellaney: 'My dear Bellaney, The *Kama Sutra* of Vatsyayana is being printed by some learned Brahmins who are interested in the humanities and concerned about the happiness of man and the comfort of woman. Quaritch in Piccadilly has some copies to sell, but I have some spare copies by me. I shall be happy to present you with half-a-dozen of them for your perusal and for circulation.'

Further copies were sent to H. S. Ashbee, the bibliophile who forwarded one to J. Knight, the writer and reviewer. Knight was greatly impressed and wrote to Ashbee in April 1884: 'My dear Ashbee, Very many thanks indeed for the *Kama Sutra*. It is indeed, as you say, a work of great erudition and a curious contribution to our knowledge of Indian thought. Naturally I have read it through, the task being equally pleasant and profitable. The things that are said in it about women are marvellously fine and the book is more charged with suggestion than any work I have read. I am extremely indebted to you for including me in the list of those who may on so advantageous terms as simple acceptance come into its enviable possession.'

The book, as its dedication declared, was meant only for that 'small section of the British public which takes enlightened interest in studying the manners and customs of the olden East'. Arbuthnot himself expected little. Yet almost at once the *Kama Sutra* aroused notice. It was pirated in India. In 1885 it was re-translated into French and although it is only now being publicly printed in England, its importance for Indian studies was quickly realised. The quiet initiative of the modest Arbuthnot had discovered for the West one of the great Indian classics and thus made possible a new approach to Indian culture.

How, then, was the translation conceived? Who made it? What caused Burton and Arbuthnot to found the Kama Shastra Society—a society which, in fact, was only a friendly alliance, hardly even a legal fiction? What led them to study this 'peculiar branch of literature—the Hindu erotic'? Who prompted whom?

Arbuthnot had been born at Belgaum, near Bombay, in India in 1833, the second son of Sir Robert Arbuthnot, a member of the Bombay Civil Service. His mother was daughter of Field-Marshal Sir John Forster Fitzgerald. He was educated privately at Anhalt and Geneva and in 1851 went to Haileybury after entering the Bombay Civil Service. He reached Bombay in 1853 and from then until 1879, when he retired, he lived continuously, except for three furloughs, in India. In late-life he was known for several traits—amiability, quiet determination, kindness, liberal views on marriage, unassertive modesty, fondness for Balzac, allergy to poetry. In Bombay he enjoyed driving his private coach and team of four and even wrote an article in *Baily's Magazine* (April 1883) where he ranked driving with drawing, painting and music. We are left with the impression of a sweet-natured man who yet had a mind of his own, who was quietly purposive, who was never brazenly unconventional but did not shrink from taking his own line. It was on a youthful Arbuthnot, twenty years old, drawn to India from his birth and preparing to take up an Indian career, that Richard Burton impinged in 1853.[2]

Burton was then aged thirty-two. In appearance he was

strikingly magnetic. Lesley Blanch, in her recent study, has described him as 'a darkling Heathcliff, indescribably alluring to the Victorian miss'. Arthur Symons in an earlier account sensed the same adventurous charm:

'He was Arab in his prominent cheek-bones. He was gypsy in his terrible magnetic eyes—the sullen eyes of a stinging serpent. He had a deeply bronzed complexion, a determined mouth, half-hidden by a black moustache which hung down in a peculiar fashion on both sides of his chin. His face has no actual beauty in it; it reveals a tremendous animalism, an air of repressed ferocity, a devilish fascination. There is an almost tortured magnificence in his huge head, tragic and painful, with its mouth that aches with desire, with those dilated nostrils that drink in I know not what strange perfumes.'

Wilfrid Blunt had a somewhat similar impression when he met Burton in 1867:

'His dress and appearance were those suggesting a released convict rather than anything of more repute. He reminded me by turns of a black leopard, caged but unforgiving, and again with his close cut poll and iron frame of that wonderful creation of Balzac's, the ex-gallérien Vautrin, hiding his grim identity under an Abbé's cassock. He wore, habitually, a rusty black coat with a crumpled black silk stock, his throat destitute of collar, a costume which his muscular frame and immense chest made singularly and incongruously hideous, above it a countenance the most sinister I have ever seen, dark, cruel, treacherous, with eyes like a wild beast's. . . . In his talk he affected an extreme brutality, and if one could have believed the whole of what he said, he had indulged in every vice and committed every crime. . . . He had a power of assuming the abominable which cannot be exaggerated. I remember once his insisting that I should allow him to try his mesmeric power on me and his expression as he gazed into my eyes was nothing less than atrocious. . . . [Nevertheless] the ferocity of his countenance gave place at times to more agreeable expressions, and I can just understand the infatuated fancy of his wife that in spite of his ugliness he was the most beautiful man alive.'

These accounts were written after Burton had endured nerve-wracking adventures, but they are sufficiently close to the Burton of 1853 to explain how Arbuthnot may have reacted. Himself about to go to India, he had met a man whose very personality seemed oriental.

Burton was not merely oriental to look at. He was oriental in thought. Following a rough education first on the continent and later at Oxford, he had gone to Bombay in 1842 as an ensign in the Indian army. From Bombay he had moved to Baroda in Gujarat and in 1844 he had been posted to Sind. There he was seconded from the army to do survey work and this had brought him into daily touch with Indian life. For this he had quickly developed a deep relish. He threw himself into languages. He learnt Hindustani, Sindi, Marathi, Gujarati, Sanskrit, Arabic and Persian and in 1844, aided by two Persian tutors, he began moving in Indian society in disguise. He also opened three shops in Karachi, the better to glean information. Burton went Indian, and, as a result, came to know Indian life with startling intimacy. His sexual adventures need not detain us—he had followed the usual practice of his time and installed an Indian girl as semi-permanent mistress—and there are passages in his fragments of autobiography which list the pros and cons of such an arrangement. What is significant is his general interest in sex, in Indian attitudes and practices, in the whole place of sex in Indian life. He believed that to understand an alien culture, certainly an oriental one, it was necessary to know how a people lived and this could only be done by discovering their intimate concerns. Writing much later in the *Terminal Essay* to his *Arabian Nights*, he said:

'To assert that such lore is unnecessary is to state, as every traveller knows, an "absurdam". Few phenomena are more startling than the vision of a venerable infant, who has lived half his long life in the midst of the wildest anthropological vagaries and monstrosities, and yet who absolutely ignores all that India and Burmah enacts under his very eyes. . . . Against such lack of knowledge my notes are a protest; and I may claim success despite the difficulty of the task. . . . In this matter I have done my best, at a time too when the hapless English traveller is expected to write like a young lady for young ladies, and never to notice what underlies the most superficial stratum. And I also maintain that the free treatment of topics usually taboo'd will be a national benefit to an "empire of Opinion" whose very basis and buttresses are a thorough knowledge by the rulers of the ruled.'

Such a view strikes us today as plain and obvious. We know Malinowski's *The Sexual Life of Savages*, Geoffrey Gorer's *Himalayan Village*, Verrier Elwin's *The Baiga*—works which describe with intimate detail the place of sex in village life. In the India of 1845, no one had done this before. Burton discovered Indian sex. He came to know every aspect of life in Muslim Sind and the very completeness of his knowledge led to a special mission, the 'Karachi enquiry'.

'The "execrabilis familia pathicorum" [he wrote] first came before me by a chance of earlier life. In 1845, when Sir Charles Napier had conquered and annexed Sind . . . the veteran began to consider his conquest with a curious eye. It was reported to him that Karachi, a townlet of some 2,000 souls and distant not more than a mile from camp, supported no less than three bordels in which not women but boys and eunuchs, the former (i.e. the boys) demanding nearly a double price, lay for hire. [This detail especially excited the veteran's curiosity. The reason proved to be that the scrotum of the unmutilated boy could be used as a kind of bridle for directing the movements of the animal.] Being then the only British officer who could speak Sindi, I was asked indirectly to make enquiries and report upon the subject; and I undertook the task on the express condition that my report should not be forwarded to the Bombay Government, from whom supporters of the Conqueror's policy could expect scant favour, mercy or justice. Accompanied by a Munshi, Mirza Muhammed Hosayn of Shiraz, and habited as a merchant, Mirza Abdullah the Bushiri (i.e. Burton) passed many an evening in the townlet, visited all the porneia and obtained the fullest details which were duly dispatched to Government House. . . . This found its way with sundry other reports to Bombay and produced the expected result. A friend in the Secretariat informed me that my summary dismissal had been formally proposed by one of Sir Charles Napier's successors but this excess of outraged modesty was not allowed.'

Whether the Bombay Government's reactions had followed Burton to England in 1849 is not clear. It would be tempting to regard him as a character whose unseemly adventures had already given him a vicious aura, to see him as a mystery man, a kind of T. E. Lawrence but with something of the sinister smear of a Roger Casement. For the young Arbuthnot, Burton's general personality was probably more important. Burton had shown how fascinating Indian life was. He had proved that life itself could be enhanced by understanding India. Burton's capacity for adventure, his original and spirited gusto must all have left their mark. Arbuthnot's character had not the same flamboyant vigour, the frenzied abandon, the anarchic daring which later appeared in Burton. But he can hardly have failed to be impressed.

Burton, for his part, may have sensed that Arbuthnot, his feeling for India already developed, was instinctively sympathetic. He may have seen in Arbuthnot a young civilian who over the years might continue the explorations of Indian life which he himself had started. He may also have responded to Arbuthnot's youthful admiration. In assessing Burton's later career, we have constantly to bear in mind the 'Karachi enquiry' and its possible effects on his character. Burton's preference for Arab society, his obsessional studies of pederasty, the very thoroughness of the Karachi report, his friendship with Swinburne, his long absences from society, even his mania for fencing and weapons (itself at times a symptom of the crypto-homosexual), suggest that behind his investigation of sex in all its forms lay a need to placate, defend or justify a latent homosexuality. Arbuthnot himself may have shared none of these traits and yet have drawn Burton to him by his mild, serene temperament.

Such a friendship, established in 1853, continued throughout Burton's life. In 1885, when dedicating the fourth volume of the *Arabian Nights* to Arbuthnot, Burton referred to a friendship which by then had 'lasted nearly a third of a century'. In 1890, Burton died and his widow wrote saying that she was keeping for Arbuthnot Burton's gold chain as a memorial since he was 'his best friend'. Wright records that, alone of all his friends, Burton called Arbuthnot by a pet-name, 'Bunnie'. It is clear, therefore, that despite Burton's severance from India—he left it finally in 1856 (to return for only one short visit in 1876)—Burton and Arbuthnot had a strong feeling of identity. This was possibly cemented in 1854 when for a few months Burton was in Bombay after returning from Mecca and before going to Harar. They may also have met in 1856. For the rest, until Arbuthnot's own retirement, it can only have been during his first and last furloughs—1859–60 and 1872–4—that the two can have seen each other. Until 1879, when Arbuthnot retired to Guildford and at last married, their friendship depended on letters.

Tenuous though this basis may seem, it served as a creative stimulus and there are two ways in which Burton may have influenced Arbuthnot during the first part of his life in India. As Burton explored Africa and Brazil, we can see certain traits developing—his zeal for extended knowledge, his determination to publish accounts of sex, to put on record foreign customs and ways of living. In 1863 he founded the Anthropological Society of London with a membership of eleven. 'Each', wrote Burton, 'had his own doubts and hopes and fears touching the vitality of the new-born. Still, we knew that our cause was good. . . . We all felt the weight of a great want. As a traveller and a writer of travels, I have found it impossible to publish those questions of social economy and those physiological observations, always interesting to our common humanity, and at times so valuable.' The *Memoirs of the Anthropological Society*, Wright explains, met this difficulty. By 1865—the year when Burton's experiment in 'learned debauchery', the Cannibal Club, was founded—the society had 500 members. It continued to grow and in 1871 it united with the Ethnographical Society and formed the Anthropological Institute of Great Britain. Its publications, however, do not seem to have satisfied Burton for in 1873 certain members of the old society, including Burton himself, founded the London Anthropological Society and issued a periodical called *Anthropologia*. 'My motive', Burton wrote 'was to supply travellers with an organ which would rescue their observations from the outer darkness of manuscript and print their curious information on social and sexual matters out of place in the popular book intended for the Nipptisch, and indeed better kept from public view.' Even a scientific journal, however, could not be safely printed and Burton records, 'Hardly had we begun when "Respectability", that whited sepulchre full of all uncleanness, rose up against us. "Propriety" cried us down with her brazen, blatant voice and the weak-kneed brethren fell away.' Burton must certainly have kept Arbuthnot in touch with these developments and their gathering friendship ensued that in a matter so vital to Burton's heart Arbuthnot would co-operate. We must see in Burton's experiments the germs of the Kama Shastra Society and the quickening of a desire in Arbuthnot to make his own records of exotic customs. Publication he could see would be problematic. It would have peculiar difficulties. But records must be made.

The second influence was literary. In exciting and fascinating Victorian society, Burton had appeared as the ardent traveller, the pilgrim to Mecca, the explorer of the Nile, the penetrator of dense tropical highlands, the grim adventurer fighting his way out of ambushes, the savage outsider. It was a Burton who communicated a frisson, an almost surrealist shock. His travels may well have fulfilled some private need. They may also have been the working out of the supposed Arab or gypsy strain in his blood. With them, however, had gone an equally strong form of self-expression—writing. Each visit to a country drove Burton to write a travel book, to record in words his journeys and experiences. His books were sometimes roughly, even awkwardly written, but they also contained passages of vivid description or brilliant rhythmical prose. The extracts we have already quoted hardly flatter Burton. The following passage from the Foreword to the *Arabian Nights* does him more justice:

'This work, laborious as it may appear, has been to me a labour of love, an unfailing source of solace and satisfaction. During my long years of official banishment to the luxuriant and deadly deserts of Western Africa, and to the dull and dreary half-clearings of South America, it proved itself a charm, a talisman against ennui and despondency. Impossible even to open the pages without a vision starting into view; without drawing a picture from the pinacothek of the brain; without reviving a host of memories and reminiscences which are not the common property of travellers, however widely they may have travelled. From my dull and commonplace and "respectable" surroundings, the Jinn bore me at once to the land of my predilection, Arabia, a region so familiar to my mind that even at first sight, it seemed a reminiscence of some by-gone metempsychic life in the distant Past. Again I stood under the diaphanous skies, in air glorious as aether, whose every breath raises men's spirits like sparkling wine. Once more I saw the evening star hanging like a solitaire from the pure front of the western firmament; and the after-glow transfiguring and transforming, as by magic, the homely and rugged features of the scene into a fairy-land lit with a light that never shines on other soils or seas. Then would appear the woollen tents, low and black, of the true Badawin, mere dots in the boundless waste of lion-tawny clays and gazelle-brown gravels, and the camp-fire dotting like a glow-worm the village centre. Presently, sweetened by distance, would be heard the wild weird song of lads and lasses, driving or rather pelting, through the gloaming, their sheep and goats; and the measured chant of the spearsmen gravely stalking behind their charge, the camels, mingled with the bleating of the flocks and the bellowing of the humpy herds; while the rere-mouse flitted overhead with his tiny shriek, and the rave of the jackal resounded through deepening glooms, and—most magical of music—the palm-trees answered the whispers of the night-breeze with the softest tones of falling water.'

It is the Burton of the *Arabian Nights*, the deliberate writer, the Burton with a flair for style and rhythm who was now to prove significant.

In perhaps the year 1869 or 1870, Arbuthnot agreed to translate with Burton a well-known Indian treatise on the art of love, the *Ananga Ranga*. This had been composed in Sanskrit by the poet Kalyan Mall for the delectation of a certain Lada Khan, a scion of the Lodi dynasty. It was probably written in the sixteenth century but had since acquired wide popularity in India through numerous translations. Burton himself possessed Hindi, Marathi and Gujarati versions. Arabic, Persian and Turkish editions also existed and in Bombay itself there were many lithographed copies. As an account of Indian sex, it not only seemed to sum up previous writings but to be itself 'a part of the national life'.

To Arbuthnot, the book was particularly sympathetic. In Burton's case there is a kind of ferocious interest in sex, a fascination with every possible variety. Burton, it was said, had no comprehension of women. He did not understand the feminine temperament. Arbuthnot, on the other hand, was consistently humane. He was acutely aware of women's needs and had come to deplore the state of Victorian marriage. In discussing with Ashbee the publications of the Kama Shastra Society, he wrote:

'The first impression on roughly running through the writings of the old Indian sages is that Europeans and modern society generally would be greatly benefited by some such treatises. It is difficult to get Englishmen to acknowledge that matrimonial happiness may in many cases be attained by a careful study of the passions of a wife, that is to say admitting that a wife be allowed to feel passion. Many a life has been wasted and the best feelings of a young woman outraged by the rough exercise of what truly become the husband's "rights", and all the innate delicate sentiments and illusions of the virgin bride are ruthlessly trampled on when the curtains close round the couch on what is vulgarly called the "first night". The master either swoops down on his prey like a vulture or what is just as bad, sins by ignorance, appearing to the trembling creature either as a cruel brute or a stupid bungling fool. The French nation, certainly more refined in love matters than the English, know this well, and have founded many novels upon the danger arising from the folly of husbands not knowing how to woo their wives delicately. Unfortunately, continental marriages are no more made in heaven than are those of the "nation of shopkeepers" as what is the use of all the husband's art, gentle kindness and soothing endearments, when his courtship begins only *after* marriage and not *before*? The summum bonum is the

English system of free choice and mutual engagement without "go-betweens", and the husband to possess all the philosophy and knowledge of conjugal arts peculiar to the people who dwell under a hotter sun than we do. Such ideas, however, are quite foreign to insular minds, and those daring to give them utterance are put down as paradoxical philosophers or simply obscene wretches. The Englishman who would advise "those about to marry" to read Balzac, would probably be rated as a madman, and if he continued would be told that there is nothing to be learnt from "dirty foreigners" but debauchery and vice. The same reproach cannot apply to the work under notice, written many thousands of years ago, and which has obtained the consecration of time.'

The *Ananga Ranga* dealt precisely with this problem—how to ensure marital happiness. What was more, it approached it from exactly the same angle—the need of understanding woman and satisfying her passions. Its author conceded that 'no joy in the world of mortals can compare with that derived from the knowledge of the Creator'. But he went on to assert:

'Second, however, and subordinate only to this, are the satisfaction and pleasure arising from the possession of a beautiful woman. Men, it is true, marry for the sake of undisturbed congress, as well as for love and comfort, and often they obtain handsome and attractive wives. But they do not give them plenary contentment nor do they themselves enjoy their charms. The reason of which is that they are purely ignorant of the Scripture of Cupid, the Kama Shastra; and despising the difference between the several kinds of women, they regard them only in an animal point of view. Such men must be looked upon as foolish and unintelligent; and this book is composed with the object of preventing lives being wasted in similar manner and the benefits to be derived from its study are set forth in the following verses:

' "The man who knoweth the Art of Love and who understandeth the thorough and varied enjoyment of woman;

' "As advancing age cooleth his passions, he learneth to think of his Creator, to study religious subjects and to acquire divine knowledge:

' "Hence he is freed from further transmigration of souls; and when the tale of his days is duly told, he goeth direct with his wife to the Svarga (heaven)."

'And thus all you who read this book shall know how delicious an instrument is woman, when artfully played upon; how capable she is of producing the most exquisite harmony; of executing the most complicated variations and of giving the divinest pleasures.'

Aiming at appreciating woman, the book then describes in detail the physical aspects of sex. It explains how women obtain their rapture, the different days and different times of day when different women enjoy sex most, the varieties of love-play which husbands can use and the various kinds of posture which give most enjoyment. As, at length, he completes his survey the author declares:

'No one yet has written a book to prevent the separation of the married pair and to show them how they may pass through life in union. Seeing this I felt compassion and composed this treatise, offering it to the god Pandurang.

'The chief reason for the separation between the married couple and the cause which drives the husband to the embraces of strange women and the wife to the arms of strange men is the want of varied pleasures and the monotony which follows possession. There is no doubt about it. Monotony begets satiety, and satiety distaste for congress, especially in one or the other; malicious feelings are engendered, the husband or the wife yields to temptation, and the one follows, being driven by jealousy. For it seldom happens that the two love each other equally, and in exact proportion, therefore is the one more easily seduced by passion than the other. From such separations result polygamy, adulteries, abortions, and every manner of vice, and not only do the erring husband and wife fall into the pit, but they also drag down the manes of their deceased ancestors from the place of beatified mortals, either to hell or back again upon this world. Fully understanding the way in which such quarrels arise, I have in this book shown how the husband, by varying the enjoyment of his wife, may live with her as with thirty-two different women, ever varying the enjoyment of her and rendering satiety impossible. I have also taught all manner of useful arts and mysteries, by which she may render herself pure, beautiful and pleasing in his eyes. Let me therefore conclude with the verse of blessing:

'"May this treatise, Ananga Ranga, be beloved of man and woman, as long as the Holy River Ganges springeth from Shiva with his wife Gauri on his left side; as long as Lakshmi loveth Vishnu; as long as Brahma is engaged in the study of the Vedas, and as long as the earth, the moon and the sun endure."'

Such passages have all the style and mannered ease of Burton at his best and the question arises as to what precise part was played in the translation by Arbuthnot and what part by Burton. Arbuthnot, Ashbee states, was the 'chief translator' and from a note by Arbuthnot referring to 'translating with the pundits' it would seem that his method was the same as that employed by most British scholars in India. This was to engage an Indian pundit or scholar and reach the meaning by close discussion with him. Jones, Tod, Prinsep, even Burton himself, had retained scholars or teachers and a well-known picture shows Tod sitting with his pundit. Much depended on how well the Indian scholar knew English. If he knew only the vernacular, translation would proceed by day-to-day sessions—the British scholar conferring with his Indian adviser and writing out a draft as they went along. If the Indian scholar knew enough English, he would sometimes prepare an English draft and this would then be discussed, revised and re-done by his employer. In either case, translation involved much arduous and intricate discussion since however good might be the Indian scholar's English, the precise equivalents might elude him. The problem for the British scholar was to see beyond the Indian pundit's English to the realities of the Sanskrit or Indian text. It was only then that a version could have pretence of accuracy. Finally when the plain meaning had been got, the whole would have to be re-cast so as to read smoothly and well. It would have to be given style.

The English of the *Ananga Ranga* implies this arrangement. For Arbuthnot, the main consideration was sense. His own books—*Early Ideas* (1881), *Persian Portraits* (1887), *Arabic Authors* (1890)—reveal a plain and simple style. He was not literary. He did not claim to be a writer. He produced no travel books. He was even anti-poetry. He was well aware of these traits and, in introducing his *Persian Portraits*, wrote: 'The work, however much it may be wanting in style and language, will be found to contain a good deal of information collected and collated from the works of various authors.' In all his books, Arbuthnot was less concerned with style than with matter. Burton, on the other hand, he realised, had a flair for 'style and language', and their joint version reflects this division. The more eloquent passages are almost certainly by Burton. Phrases such as 'amatory blandishments', 'cold concupiscence' are probably his. So we may assume is much of the firmly written preface. The rest is Arbuthnot, 'translating with the pundits' and producing a straightforward draft in plain, direct English.

The *Ananga Ranga* was probably completed by 1871 and Arbuthnot now considered publication. He was on furlough from 1872 to 1874. Printing could therefore be started. Burton, however, was finding matters far from easy. His attempts at scientific publication were failing. Prudence was needed. Could their English version in fact stand?

'It was at first our intention, after rendering the "Kama Shastra" into English, [they wrote in their preface] to dress it up in Latin, that it might not fall into the hands of the vulgar. But further considerations satisfied us that it contains nothing essentially immoral and much matter deserving of more consideration than it receives at present. The generation which prints and reads literal English translations of the debauched Petronius Arbiter and the witty indecencies of Rabelais, can hardly be prudish enough to complain of the devout and highly moral Kalyana Malla. At least, so think the Translators.'

Arbuthnot, who was paying for the printing, decided to proceed. He found a printer and the translation was duly set up. The fact that both Burton and Arbuthnot were concerned was declared on the title page by including their initials but cautiously reversing them. The phrase ran 'Translated from the Sanscrit and Annotated by A.F.F. and B.F.R.' They further protected themselves by including the words 'For private use of the Translators only in connection with a work on the Hindoo religion and on the manners and customs of the Hindoos'.

Yet despite their caution, the work miscarried. Did they lose their nerve? Did the printer refuse? Ashbee, in his *Index Librorum Prohibitorum* published in 1877, noted that 'the talented translators are F. F. Arbuthnot and R. F. Burton, the celebrated African traveller; the initials of their names being reversed'. He added, 'Only four copies (proofs) exist, for the printer, on reading the proofs, became alarmed at the nature of the book, and refused to print off the edition.' Ashbee himself made his notes from a corrected proof copy. Yet was it the printer or Arbuthnot who grew alarmed? When at last the *Ananga Ranga* was printed in 1885, the translators added the following postscript to their preface:

'P.S. In the *Index Librorum Prohibitorum*, the translation appears under the generic name of "Kama Shastra" which we first adopted and the reader is told that only four copies exist for reasons best known to the printer. This is so far true that the limited supply has hitherto prevented the public deriving any benefit from our labours. We now take advantage of an offer made by a well-known house in Cosmopoli, and produce a reprint FOR PRIVATE CIRCULATION ONLY, with many additions and emendations.'

In the preface to the *Kama Sutra* (1883) a somewhat different account had been given. Referring to the *Ananga Ranga*, it noted, 'It contains ten chapters, and has been translated into English but only six copies were printed for private circulation.' Is it possible that Ashbee was wrong and that faced with the work in proof Arbuthnot himself decided to have only six copies printed, deeming it better to postpone full publication until some later date?

Despite this set-back, Arbuthnot's enthusiasm was unaffected. His interest had been aroused. He would explore still further the 'Hindu erotic'. He wanted to get a full view of its place in Indian culture. He believed that in due time his and Burton's endeavours would be successful Their work would be reprinted and British understanding of India would be improved. In working with his pundits he had been intrigued by references in the *Ananga Ranga* to a work called the *Kama Sutra*. He decided to find out what this text was like and when he returned to India in 1874 he made his plans.

What happened has been described in two notes. The first was included in the Introduction to the *Kama Sutra* when it eventually appeared in 1883.

'It may be interesting to some persons to learn how it came about that Vatsyayana was first brought to light and translated into the English language. It happened thus. While translating with the pundits, the "Anunga Runga, or the stage of love", reference was frequently found to be made to one Vatsya. The sage Vatsya was of this opinion, or of that opinion. The sage Vatsya said this, and so on. Naturally questions were asked who the sage was, and the pundits replied that Vatsya was the author of the standard work on love in Sanscrit literature, that no Sanscrit library was complete without his work, and that it was most difficult now to obtain in its entire state. The copy of the manuscript obtained in Bombay was defective, and so the pundits wrote to Benares, Calcutta and Jeypoor for copies of the manuscript from Sanscrit libraries in those places. Copies having been obtained, they were then compared with each other, and with the aid of a Commentary called "Jayamangla" a revised copy of the entire manuscript was prepared, and from this copy the English translation was made. The following is the certificate of the chief pundit:

' "The accompanying manuscript is corrected by me after comparing four different copies of the work. I had the assistance of a Commentary called 'Jayamangla' for correcting the portion in the first five parts, but found great difficulty in correcting the remaining portion, because, with the exception of one copy thereof which was tolerably correct, all the other copies I had were far too incorrect. However, I took that portion as correct in which the majority of the copies agreed with each other."

'This commentary (of Jayamangla) was most useful in explaining the true meaning of Vatsyayana, for the commentator appears to have had a considerable knowledge of the times of the older author and gives in some places very minute information.

'A complete translation of the original work now follows. It has been prepared in complete accordance with the text of the manuscript and is given, without further comments, as made from it.'

In this note, several points are significant. No names are mentioned—neither those of the pundits, Arbuthnot nor

Burton. The discovery of the text is emphasised but not its nature. Its importance is not discussed. Even the name of the person, Arbuthnot, who, 'while translating with the pundits', noticed the references to the sage Vatsya, is suppressed. We are given a few dark hints but in fact we are told very little.

We must remember, however, that the *Kama Sutra* was the first translation of the 'Hindu erotic' to be sponsored by the Kama Shastra Society. Arbuthnot and Burton could not tell how far their device would protect them. In his book, *Early Ideas* (1881), Arbuthnot had included a summary account of part of the *Kama Sutra* but had omitted all mention of its strongly sexual character. He had also taken descriptions of the four types of woman from the *Ananga Ranga* but had drastically altered one sentence. The original said 'Her yoni resembles the opening lotus-bud and her love-seed is perfumed as the lily which has newly burst.' In *Early Ideas*, this became 'Her mouth resembles the opening lotus-bud and her perfume is as a lily that has newly burst.' To print the *Kama Sutra* in its entirety was, therefore, to be far more robust. He would be holding nothing back. But, equally, he could not tell how it would be received. He dared not compromise anyone. He therefore gave only a very general idea of how the *Kama Sutra* was 'first brought to light and translated into the English language'.

Two years later, he felt bolder. The *Kama Sutra* had safely appeared and had been twice reprinted. The translation of the *Ananga Ranga*, jettisoned in 1873, was on the point of coming out. He was pressed by Ashbee to give a fuller account and he agreed. Yet even now he was reticent and cautious. Although his note would be included in a book designed for private circulation—*Catena Librorum Tacendorum* (1885)—it would none the less be printed. It might be seen by the authorities. Anything he said might be used against him. He could not safely divulge his own part in the translation neither could he involve Burton. Burton was smarting under the attacks levied by Mrs Grundy against his co-Arabist, Payne. 'I don't care a button about being prosecuted and if the matter comes to a fight, I will walk into court with my Bible and my Shakespeare and my Rabelais under my arm, and prove to them that, before they condemn me, they must cut half of *them* out, and not allow them to be circulated to the public.'

None the less in issuing his own *Arabian Nights* he enclosed the following circumspect memorandum:

'In issuing this first volume of "The Nights" Captain Burton begs to remind all who have honoured him by subscribing to it, that the work is intended only for those who wish to study the peculiarities of Moslem life and Arabo-Egyptian manners, customs and language. It is emphatically a book for men and students; and nothing could be more repugnant to the translator's feelings than the idea of these pages being placed in any other hands than the class for whose especial use it has been prepared. In this essential matter the writer trusts confidently to the good faith of his subscribers.'

Arbuthnot did not have quite so confident a faith. He decided therefore to suppress once more his own share in the translation and make it seem that it was the work of two Indian pundits and of them alone. As a result he gave Ashbee the following note:

'*The Kama Shastra*, or the *Hindoo Art of Love* (*Ars Amoris Indica*), was printed in London in 1873. In this work, at pages 46 and 59, references were made to the holy sage *Vatsyayana* and his opinions. On my return to India in 1874, I made enquiries about Vatsyayana and his works. The pundits informed me that the *Kama Sutra* of Vatsyayana was now the standard work on love in Sanscrit literature and that no Sanscrit library was supposed to be complete without a copy of it. They added that the work was now very rare, and that the versions of the text differed considerably in different manuscripts, and the language in many of them was obscure and difficult. It was necessary then first to prepare as complete and as correct a copy of the work as possible in Sanscrit and after this had been accomplished, then to get it properly translated. The first thing then to be done was to find a man competent to prepare the Sanscrit text, and after that a competent translator. After some enquiry Dr Buhler, now Sanscrit Professor in Vienna, but then employed in the Educational Department in Bombay, recommended to me the Pundit Bhugwuntlal Indraji. This Pundit had already been frequently employed by Mr James Fergusson and Mr James Burgess, in copying and translating for them writings found on copper plates, on stone boundaries and in temples in many parts of India. Not only had he been useful to the above named gentlemen, but to many others engaged in Indian archaeology and antiquities. Last year he submitted a paper to the Oriental Congress held at Leyden in Holland and the University there conferred on him the degree of Doctor of Letters, while the Royal Asiatic Society of London elected him as an honorary member. The Pundit himself was unable to speak English fluently but understood it sufficiently, and after an interview I set him to work to compile a complete copy of the *Kama Sutra of Vatsyayana* in Sanscrit. The copy of the text he had procured in Bombay being incomplete, the pundit wrote for other copies from Calcutta, Benares and Jeypoor, and from these he prepared a complete copy of the work. With the aid then of another Brahmin, by name Shivaram Parshuram Bhide, then studying at the University of Bombay and well acquainted both with Sanscrit and English, and now employed in the service of His Highness the Guicowar at Baroda, a complete translation of the above text was prepared, and it is this translation which has now been printed and published in London, with the impress of Benares 1883. The pundits obtained great assistance in their translation from a commentary on the original work, which was called *Jayamangla* or *Sutrabashya* and which is fully alluded to in the introduction to the *Kama Sutra*.

'Without this commentary the translation would have been most difficult, if not impossible. The original work is written in very old and difficult Sanscrit and without the aid of the commentary it would have been in many places unintelligible.

'The above information will be found in a less detailed form and without mention of names, in the introduction to the work itself.'

Such a note takes us a great deal further but even so it still leaves much unexplained. Compared with the *Ananga Ranga*, the *Kama Sutra* is in every way a more accomplished and finished piece of translation. In their concluding remarks the translators observe:

'As a collection of facts, told in plain and simple language, it must be remembered that in those early days, there was apparently no idea of embellishing the work, either with a literary style, a flow of language or a quantity of superfluous padding. The author tells the world what he knows in very concise language, without any attempt to produce an interesting story. From his facts how many novels could be written!'

Like the original, the translation of the *Kama Sutra* has no 'superfluous padding' but in two respects—'literary style' and 'flow of language'—it departs superbly from it. It uses short clear words and is simple and direct. It reads well. Every paragraph has an air of easy assurance.

'The following are the men who generally obtain success with women:

Men well versed in the science of love.
Men skilled in telling stories.
Men acquainted with women from their childhood.
Men who have secured their confidence.
Men who send presents to them.

Men who talk well.
Men who do things that they like.
Men who have not loved other women previously.
Men who act as messengers.
Men who know their weak points.
Men who are desired by good women.
Men who are united with their female friends.
Men who are good looking.
Men who have been brought up with them.
Men who are their neighbours.
The lovers of the daughters of their nurse.
Men who have been lately married.
Men who like picnics and pleasure parties.
Men who are liberal.
Men who are celebrated for being very strong.
Enterprising and brave men.
Men whose dress and manner of living are magnificent.'

It is hardly possible that English-knowing pundits—Bhugwuntlal Indraji and Shivaram Parshuram Bhide—could have produced English of this kind. Indeed Arbuthnot's touch is everywhere apparent—in the clear sentences, the unerring preference for simple words, the lean and muscular English. We can only explain this on one assumption—that, while the pundits, especially Bhide, may have prepared a draft version, Arbuthnot himself also grappled with the original and moulded the translation.

That a pundits' version existed is clear for, apart from Arbuthnot's statement that 'the pundits obtained great assistance in their translation', there are occasional hints or traces of 'pundits' English' in the final version. 'Moon-lit nights', for example, reads 'moonlight nights', 'playing at dice' is 'playing with dice', 'men showing love towards women and attracting love to themselves' reads 'attracting love to himself'. Arbuthnot could scarcely have made these mistakes in English but in working with a pundits' draft he might easily have overlooked them. Without belittling the pundits' vital role as Arbuthnot's collaborators, it would seem more accurate, then, to regard them as preliminary advisers and assistants rather than as ultimate translators.

Yet if the English, at least in draft, was Arbuthnot's, the final translation can hardly have been his alone. Burton was later to call the *Kama Sutra* 'Arbuthnot's Vatsyayana' and basically that is what it was. In particular, the preface and introduction bear all the impress of Arbuthnot's character. But the text is another matter. Left to himself, Arbuthnot could not have given it rhythmical vigour and assured style. These are Burton's contribution. We know that Burton visited India in 1876 and that he stayed at Bandora, Arbuthnot's country house outside Bombay. By then, the translation was either far advanced or already finished. Burton could have seen the Sanskrit original, checked Arbuthnot's version and suggested alterations. In their earlier book, the *Ananga Ranga*, they had learnt how to work together. After leaving India, Burton might well have revised the draft still further. The *Kama Sutra* was not published in final form until 1883 and during these seven years much could still have been done. It is suggested that after checking sense and meaning, Burton gave it literary form. Using Arbuthnot's plain and simple language, he made it read well. He added no embellishments. He avoided rich phrases. He smoothed it out. But smoothing out was essential. Without Burton's aid, Arbuthnot's version would have lacked brilliance. By intervening, Burton gave it style.

There is one further way in which he may have helped. Impressed by its stature as an ancient classic, Arbuthnot must have felt that some tribute to Vatsyayana was needed. The book had greatness. A few prosaic remarks would not do. They must end on a fitting note. Burton was clearly the man to do this and the last paragraph of the book's concluding remarks is almost certainly his:

'In a beautiful verse of the Vedas of the Christians it has been said of the peaceful dead, that they rest from their labours and that their works do follow them. Yes indeed; the works of men of genius do follow them, and remain as a lasting treasure. And though there may be disputes and discussions about the immortality of the body or the soul, nobody can deny the immortality of genius, which ever remains as a bright and guiding star to the struggling humanities of succeeding ages. This work, then, which has stood the test of centuries, has placed Vatsyayana among the immortals, and on This and on Him no better elegy or eulogy can be written than the following lines:

'So long as lips can kiss, and eyes shall see
So long lives This and This gives life to Thee.'

Since its first appearance in English in 1883, the *Kama Sutra* has increasingly affected Indian studies. To Arbuthnot, it may have seemed important less as a clue to Indian culture than as a tract for the times, a manual for Victorian husbands. There was only one work in the English language which seemed at all comparable—'Kalogynomia: or the Laws of Female Beauty'. It was by a certain Dr T. Bell and had been printed in 1821 with twenty-four plates. It treated of 'Beauty, of Love, of Sexual Intercourse, of the Laws regulating that Intercourse, of Monogamy and Polygamy, of Prostitution, of Infidelity, ending with a *catalogue raisonnée* of the defects of female beauty'. Other works—'The Elements of Social Science or Physical, Sexual and Natural Religion' by a Doctor of Medicine, London, 1880, and 'Every Woman's Book' by a Dr Waters, published in 1826—also entered 'into great details of private and domestic life'. 'To persons interested in the above subjects', Arbuthnot wrote, 'these works will be found to contain such details as have been seldom before published and which ought to be thoroughly understood by all philanthropists and benefactors of society.'

The *Kama Sutra*, he believed, was in this class.

'After a perusal of the Hindoo work, and of the English works above mentioned, the reader will understand the subject, at all events from a materialistic, realistic and practical point of view. If all science is founded more or less on a stratum of facts, there can be no harm in making known to mankind generally certain matters intimately connected with their private, domestic and social life.

'Alas! complete ignorance of them has unfortunately wrecked many a man and many a woman, while a little knowledge of a subject generally ignored by the masses would have enabled numbers of people to have understood many things which they believed to be quite incomprehensible, or which were not thought worthy of their consideration.'

Arbuthnot, in fact, would have subscribed to Bertrand Russell's definition—'The good life is one inspired by love and guided by knowledge.' But he might have gone still further and maintained that knowledge of love was as important as love itself, that only through education in love and sex was the good life possible.

Today there is something grotesque in treating the *Kama Sutra* as a British marriage manual, though not perhaps stranger than using ancient Jewish history, as purveyed in the Old Testament, as a guide to modern life and morals. The *Kama Sutra* introduces the Western reader to coital postures, ways of making love and sexual techniques, some of which are either too acrobatic or too adjusted to Indian physiques and temperaments to be capable of general adoption. Whatever instructional value the book may have had has long since lapsed and though its contents may have administered a salutory shock to certain Victorians and enormously widened ideas of the possibilities of sex, no one today would solemnly turn to the *Kama Sutra* for serious instruction. Van der Velde's *Ideal Marriage* contains much more information relevant to contemporary Western life than Vatsyayana's ancient classic.

It is rather as an expression of fundamental Indian attitudes that the book is important. Burton and Arbuthnot did not stress this aspect but to widen Western knowledge of Eastern culture was their professed aim. Having discovered the *Kama Sutra*, Arbuthnot realised that far from being an aberration, it was in fact a crucial part of the Indian tradition. A sensuous element in Indian culture had been recognised by earlier writers. Sir William Jones had written, 'That anything natural can be offensively obscene never seems to have occurred to the Indians or to their legislators; a singularity pervading their writings and conversation but no proof of moral depravity.' Yet in translating Jayadeva's *Gita Govinda*, he had shrunk from putting into English the more literal descriptions of Radha and Krishna's love-making. The marvellous climax of the poem—a page in George Keyt's recent translation—shrinks in Jones's version to the following few lines:

'In the morning she rose disarrayed, and her eyes betrayed a night without slumber; when the yellow-robed God, who gazed on her with transport, thus meditated on her charms in his heavenly mind: "Though her locks be diffused at random, though the lustre of her lips be faded, though her garland and zone be fallen from their enchanting stations, and though she hide their places with her hands, looking towards me in bashful silence, yet even thus disarranged she fills me with extatick delight." '

Jones may well have thought that the readers of *Asiatick Researches* might have found the original too frank but, in electing to suppress Jayadeva's exact meaning, he was, in fact, distorting and falsifying an Indian attitude.

This attitude, expressed in the *Kama Sutra* and reinforced in subsequent writings, regarded love as nothing if not sexual. It was as whole-hearted as Donne's

> 'I wonder by my troth what thou and I
> Did till we loved?'
> 'Who ever loves, if he do not propose

The right true end of love, he's one that goes
To sea for nothing but to make him sick.'

Indians did not shrink from 'the physical fact'. Sex, they believed, could be the finest thing in life. They knew that sex with anyone and everyone was not possible. They conceded that other considerations must sometimes operate. They recognised morals. But this did not affect their main contention. Sex was life at its most intense and, confronted by this intensity, other values lost much of their force. Their attitude, in fact, was not so different from that expressed in the Chinese classic, the *Chin Ping Mei* or *Golden Lotus*, the Arab classic *The Perfumed Garden*—the third book to be published by the Kama Shastra Society—and even in that eighteenth-century classic, *The Memoirs of Fanny Hill*. John Cleland, its author, had lived in India and it can hardly be coincidence that in relating his heroine's adventures, he should stress what Vatsyayana himself would have stressed—the supreme delight of sex:

'How often when the rage and tumult of my senses had subsided after the melting flow, have I, in a tender meditation, ask'd myself coolly the question, if it was in nature for any of its creatures to be so happy as I was? Or, what were all fears of the consequence, put in the scale of one night's enjoyment of a thing so transcendently the taste of my eyes and heart, as that delicious, fond, matchless youth?'

It is this conception which makes the *Kama Sutra* so essential a part of the Indian tradition and so great a classic of Indian writing. As its author, writing at the dead-end of life, looks back on life as he has known it, his angle constantly shifts. He looks at every situation. It is not for nothing that he commences with 'the man about town', describes his elegant routine of cultured luxury, but at no point introduces or refers to his wife. Sex at this point is something extra-marital—to be essayed with utter abandonment, to be most enjoyed when most free. In a similar way, with a cool air of calm detachment, Vatsyayana describes how women should be seduced. He suggests that certain women should be avoided, but mainly on grounds of inconvenience. His angle shifts again and now he is recording the behaviour of courtesans and how best they can practise their profession. He is a kind of camera neither praising nor blaming but surveying the whole field of sex. The courtesan, he takes it, often does enjoy sex and in turn gives great enjoyment. His angle shifts once more. He describes married life, how a young wife should be wooed, how fidelity should be ensured. Of sex from mere carnal desire he seemingly disapproves. From time to time he mentions duty. Then it is as if these qualifications are either dropped or forgotten. Sex is there and, whether right, wise or prudent, life is nothing if it is not enjoyed. For this reason he constantly reverts to skill, technique and knowledge. He analyses in detail the physical conditions on which sexual rapture depends. He emphasises the need for variety. He lists the most intricate of small refinements. How extensive was this stock of Indian knowledge, how careful had been its analysis, how erudite its codification had not been realised before.

Burton and Arbuthnot's translation of the *Kama Sutra*, Arbuthnot's discovery that such a text existed, revolutionised the Western approach to Indian culture. It showed how central and natural to Indian thought and life was sex. Indian art, poetry and religion had all reflected this basic concern. It is not too much to claim that from this classic translation in 1883 the modern understanding of Indian art and culture derives.

NOTES

[1] Thomas Wright, *The Life of Sir Richard Burton* (1906). For facts concerning Arbuthnot—his character, career and share in the Kama Shastra Society—I have drawn on Wright (the first biographer to stress Arbuthnot's role), the *Dictionary of National Biography* (Second Supplement, Volume I), Arbuthnot's own books, especially *Early Ideas* (1881) and *Persian Portraits* (1887), his notes on the *Ananga Ranga* and *Kama Sutra* contributed to H. S. Ashbee (Pisanus Fraxi), *Index Librorum Prohibitorum* (1877) and *Catena Librorum Tacendorum* (1885) and certain autograph letters preserved in a copy of the *Kama Sutra* in the Department of Oriental Printed Books and Manuscripts (British Museum). This copy is said to have belonged to Arbuthnot (N. M. Penzer, *An Annotated Bibliography of Richard Burton*, 1924). The provenance and character of the letters suggest, however, that it was more probably Ashbee's.

[2] For details of Burton, I have used Francis Hitchman, *Richard F. Burton: his Early, Private and Public Life* (1887), Isabel Burton, *The Life of Captain Sir Richard F. Burton* (1893), Georgiana M. Stisted, *The True Life of Capt. Sir Richard Burton* (1896), Wright's *Life* (1906), Jean Burton, *Sir Richard Burton's Wife* (1942) and Lesley Blanch, *The Wilder Shores of Love* (1954). Among Burton's own writings, I have referred, in particular, to *Scinde or The Unhappy Valley* (1851), *Personal Narrative of a Pilgrimage to El-Medinah and Meccah* (1856), *Sind Revisited* (1877), *The Arabian Nights* (*The Thousand Nights and One Night*, translated by Richard F. Burton, Foreword, Terminal Essay, Text, 1885–8), passages of autobiography in Isabel Burton's *Life*. Passages on Burton by Wilfrid Blunt (*My Diaries*) and Arthur Symons (*Dramatis Personae*) are quoted from Jean Burton and Lesley Blanch.

INTRODUCTION BY K. M. PANIKKAR

I

'THE *Kama Sutra* was composed, according to the precepts of the Holy Writ, for the benefit of the world by Vatsyayana, while leading the life of a religious student and wholly engaged in the contemplation of the Deity.'

Thus states our author at the end of his work. It may sound strange—if not blasphemous—to Westerners that Vatsyayana should make the claim that it was while he was 'wholly engaged in contemplating the Deity' a work on the science of Kama or love was written by a religious student. And yet traditionally in India Vatsyayana's claim was never disputed and he was always alluded to with reverence as Vatsyayana Maharshi—or Vatsyayana the Great Seer. In justification of this attitude we may quote Vatsyayana himself as to the object he had in view in undertaking this study. 'He who is acquainted with the true principles of this science (of Kama) pays regard to Dharma (religious duty), Artha (worldly welfare), Kama (the life of the senses) and to his own experiences, as well as to the teachings of others, and does not act simply on the dictates of his own desire. . . . An act is never looked upon with indulgence for the simple reason that it is authorized by the science, because it ought to be remembered that it is the intention of the science that the rules which it contains should only be acted upon in particular cases. . . . This work is not intended to be used merely as an instrument for satisfying our desires. A person, acquainted with the true principles of this science, and who preserves his Dharma, Artha and Kama, and has regard for the practices of the people, is sure to obtain the mastery over his senses.

'In short, an intelligent person, attending to Dharma

and Artha, and attending to Kama also, without becoming the slave of his passions, obtains success in everything that he may undertake.'

Vatsyayana was well aware of the objection that might be raised on the ground of his having dealt with habits and practices which morality would condemn and his reply to this criticism is illuminating. 'As for the errors in the science of love which I have mentioned in this work, on my own authority as an author, I have, immediately after mentioning them, carefully censured and prohibited them.' The *Kama Sutra* is, thus, essentially a didactic work, where the moralist condemns certain practices which as a scientific observer he has to observe and record. This didactic character derives from the fact that Kama or the life of the senses is considered by the Hindus as a necessary and integral part of man's life, as much entitled to study as all other aspects of life.

The Hindu conception of a full life postulates the harmony of three activities: Dharma, Artha and Kama. Dharma meant, in this connection, a life of religious obligation, Artha, social welfare (economic and political activity) and Kama, the life of the senses. Each of these is to have its legitimate place, though the life in righteousness has always been accorded primacy. But it was emphasised that neither Artha nor Kama was to be neglected by the normal man. A verse in the *Mahabharata* emphasises this point by saying that while life in pursuit of Artha and Kama, to the neglect of Dharma, should be shunned by man, a life which neglects Artha and Kama could not also be considered as the right way. These three departments of human activity were, therefore, considered from the beginning to be fit objects of careful study. A vast literature dealing with each one of these aspects thus became a feature of Sanskrit. In each sphere in due course one writer came to be considered as authoritative: Manu in the literature of Dharma, Kautilya in the literature of Artha, and Vatsyayana in the literature of Kama. Before

Vatsyayana wrote his *Kama Sutra* there were other pioneers in the field and we shall say something about them later. But his own work came to be accepted as authoritative so that earlier writers are now known only by allusion to their views in our text.

The Hindu view of sex differs fundamentally from that of most other civilisations. It is not only considered normal and necessary but almost sacramental. It is conceived as the human counterpart of creation and the religious symbolism of the Hindus emphasises this at all levels. It is the union of Purusha (or matter) with Prakriti (or energy) symbolised as the union of Shiva and Shakti, that is said to create the world. The symbol of Shiva is the lingam or phallus, the symbol of Shakti is the yoni. It is for this reason that every aspect of godhead in Hinduism is represented with a female counterpart.

The doctrine of the godhead being a combination of both the male and the female principles is carried to its logical conclusion in the conception of Shiva as Ardha-narishwara, the God who is half-woman. This representation of Shiva in sculpture and painting shows half his body with feminine characteristics, while the other half preserves the male aspects. Everything, in fact, is considered in this dual aspect. The clouds, for example, have as their Shakti the lightning. The sun has the chaya or shadow which always follows him. Briefly, the Hindu view of nature itself is that it embodies both the male and the female principles.

Nor is this attitude to be considered a later or 'decadent' aspect of Hindu thought. In the earliest literature of the Hindus, in the *Rig Veda*, in the *Hymn of Creation*, it is stated:

> Desire, then arose, at first within it
> Desire which was the earliest seed of spirit,
> The bond of being, in non-being sages,
> Discovered searchings in their heart with wisdom.

In the *Atharva Veda* there are mantras or formulae which cover every aspect of sexual relationship.

Nor do the *Upanishads*, which deal with pure philosophic thought, neglect the problem. In the *Chandogya Upanishad*, the sexual act is compared to a sacred sacrifice. There it is stated, 'The woman is the fire, her womb the fuel, the invitation of man the smoke. The door is the flame, entering the ember, pleasure the spark. In this fire gods form the offering. From this offering springs forth the child.' In the *Brihadaranyaka Upanishad*, it is stated, 'In the embrace of his beloved a man forgets the whole world—everything both within and without. In the same way he who embraces the Self knows neither within nor without.' The Hindu view of salvation being that of the union of the individual soul with the universal, the utter merging of one in the other, the union of man and woman in which the duality is lost becomes in the Hindu view the perfect symbol of liberation.

With the development of tantric religion, or the worship of the Mother Goddess, this aspect of Hindu thought attained even greater prominence. In the tantric form of worship, the female principle as symbolising the process of birth is considered more important. The great Sankaracharya begins his *Hymn to the Devi* with the verse. 'Shiva is capable of creation only when united with Shakti: otherwise he is only inert matter.' The Shiva Shakti samyoga or the union of Shiva and Shakti or matter and energy is that which creates the world. It is not only in the tantric form of worship that this union is considered orthodox. Every Hindu sect, in one form or another, accepts this as a fundamental as may be seen from Krishna's statement in the Gita, 'I am the Kama that procreates'.

When this was the orthodox attitude of Hinduism to the man-woman relationship—as the human counterpart of the cosmic union between matter and energy which creates the world—it is but natural that Hindu thinkers had none of the inhibitions of Western writers in studying matters relating to sex. To the Hindus it was important and necessary to approach the study of this subject with reverence and objectivity and not treat it as something obscene or secret.

Though early Buddhism also seems to have shared the view that women were a source of temptation, in the doctrines of Mahayana the original Hindu ideas seem to have asserted themselves. The wide acceptance of tantric practices in the Mahayana is evidence of this development.

Kama thus became a regular subject of study and in due course produced what seems immediately to have become a classic. The *Kama Sutra* of Vatsyayana, from the time of its writing, acquired the position of an authoritative text which no later writer has even ventured to question.

II

The author, whose personal name was Mallanaga, belonged to the Vatsyayana gotra or sept and is thus known by that name.

The *Kama Sutra* seems to have been composed between the first and fourth centuries A.D. The upper limit for this date is fixed by Vatsyayana's allusion to an incident relating to the king Kuntala Satakarni who reigned in the first years of the Christian era. The lower limit is provided by the fact that Kalidasa who lived in any case not later than the fifth century has in his work numerous allusions which indicate his detailed knowledge of the text of the *Kama Sutra*. Again in Subandhu's *Vasavadatta* (fifth century A.D.) there is a passage which mentions the *Kama Sutra* by name: 'It [the mountain which the poet was describing] was filled with elephants and was fragrant with the perfume of its jungles just as the *Kama Sutra* written by Mallanaga contains the delight and enjoyment of mistresses.' In a work of the third century, Kama is enumerated along with grammar, Dharma and Artha as essential subjects of study. Though, as in the case of most early Indian authors, it is difficult to assign an exact date for the work, it is clear that Vatsyayana lived sometime before Kalidasa and after the reign of Kuntala Satakarni, perhaps before the fourth century A.D.

The work is written, as the name indicates, in sutra form, i.e. in aphorisms. The early literature of thought in Sanskrit, as distinct from the literature of imagination, developed a form known as the Sutras—or compressed expressions, using the minimum of words. Originally this form of composition seems to have been meant to enable students to memorise the text. It was no doubt devised at a time when writing was not widely prevalent and continued to be popular even at a later time because it provided a kind of useful shorthand. Also a technique had been developed by which even complicated doctrines could be compressed into aphoristic statements through the use of symbols which could easily be committed to memory. The most famous works of Indian philosophy, grammar, logic, etc., are written in the sutra form. The *Brahma Sutra* on which the whole structure of advaita philosophy is based, *Patanjali Sutras* on which the yoga is reared, Panini's grammar on which both ancient and to a large extent even modern philology is founded—to mention only a few of the most notable examples—are in the sutra form. The *Kama Sutra*, as the name itself shows, follows this traditional method.

It is obvious that the sutra form of writing involves a system of detailed explanatory commentaries. In most cases the commentary, known as Vykhayana or Bhashya, is as important as the original text. Thus, for example, the *Mahabhashya* or the great commentary of Patanjali is what makes Panini's grammar understandable to the ordinary student. Most of the very extensive grammatical literature of Sanskrit consists of further commentaries on Panini's sutras in the light of the *Mahabhashya*. In the same way all the philosophical systems of India are in the nature of commentaries on sutra texts.

The model that Vatsyayana used for his *Kama Sutra* was the celebrated *Artha Shastra* (Science of Polity) of Kautilya. Jolly, in his study of the *Artha Shastra*, has pointed out how the author of the *Kama Sutra* modelled his work on that of Kautilya, which had by the time of Vatsyayana achieved an authoritative position in the complementary field of Artha (economics and politics).

By keeping to the sutra form Vatsyayana makes his text altogether bare. It was left to the commentator to explain the implications. For the *Kama Sutra* to have achieved the authoritative position which it did at least by the fourth century, there must have been many authoritative commentaries. But none of the earlier bhashyas have come down to us. The most authoritative commentary now generally in use is Jayamangala, also known as the *Sutra Bhashya*, or commentaries on the Sutras. This work is not earlier than the eleventh century, as the text contains a quotationfrom a work on rhetoric known as *Kavya Prakasha* or *Light on Poetry*, written in the tenth century. Other commentaries have also been discovered but Jayamangala is the most comprehensive of the bhashyas available.

Vatsyayana himself gives a fanciful history of the science of sex. He says in the prologue that in the beginning 'Prajapati—the Lord of Beings—created men and women and in the form of commandments in 100,000 chapters laid down rules regulating their existence with regard to Dharma, Artha and Kama.' Those that related to Dharma were discussed by Manu, those relating to Artha by Brihaspati, and those that referred to Kama were expounded by Nandi (the attendant on Shiva) in 1,000 chapters. So far obviously the statement is entirely mythological. The procedure is traditional and is meant to give the science the status of semi-divine origin.

Nandi's 1,000 chapters were condensed into a work of 500 chapters by Svetaketu. This Svetaketu appears to have been a rather prominent figure in the stabilisation of social relationships in ancient times. Svetaketu's story appears without much variation both in the *Chandogya Upanishad* and in the *Brihadaranyaka Upanishad*, both very ancient texts (perhaps earlier than the seventh century B.C.). The story briefly is as follows. Svetaketu, a young Brahmin scholar, went to an Assembly of the Kuru-Panchalas, a people inhabiting the area around Delhi and was there defeated in argument by Pravahana Jaivali, a scholar of the Kshatriya caste. Mortified at this discomfiture he sought instruction from his father, Uddalaka, himself a renowned Vedic scholar, who was unable to give him satisfaction. Thereupon Uddalaka, the father, approached Jaivali. Among the subjects Jaivali taught him was the Kama Shastra or the science of love. This Uddalaka is specially mentioned in the *Brihadaranyaka Upanishad* as a great teacher of the relations between the sexes. His son Svetaketu whose curiosity was the cause of Uddalaka's own interest in the subject is claimed to be the real founder of Kama Shastra or the science of man-woman relationships. Vatsyayana himself quotes the opinion of Svetaketu—alluded to as the son of Uddalaka—in at least three places in the text.

The next writer mentioned by our author is Babhravya, also a resident of the Kuru-Panchala country. He is said to have made an abstract of Svetaketu's large work. Vatsyayana admits that his own studies on the subject were based mainly on Babhravya's work. This is how he ends the *Kama Sutra*: 'After reading and considering the works of Babhravya and other ancient authors, and thinking over the meaning of the rules given by them, the *Kama Sutra* was composed by Vatsyayana.' It is difficult to say who this Babhravya was, but there is some reason to identify him with the Babhravya Panchala, the author of the *Kramapatha* of the *Rig Veda*. Whether it be the same sage or some later scholar of the same family, Vatsyayana's debt to him is undoubted and is gratefully acknowledged.

Some of the other earlier writers on the subject mentioned by our author deserve notice. Dattaka is the author of a special treatise on courtesans. He is supposed to have written the work at the request of the courtesans of Pataliputra. The courtesans of this great capital were celebrated all over India for their education and culture. The work of Dattaka, now lost, was well known in the tenth century, for we have a statement in a very interesting work by Damodara Gupta, the Kashmir poet, that a young man visiting a courtesan should show his knowledge of these subjects by quoting from Dattaka, while a commentator on this poem has actually quoted a sutra from Dattaka's work. Vatsyayana's section on courtesans is said to be only an abstract of Dattaka's work. Another writer alluded to by Vatsyayana is Kushamara who was the author of a book on *Upanishadika* which is mentioned in Rajasekhara's *Kavyamimamsa*. Other authors, like Gonikaputra and Ghotamukha, are only known to us by name, though their works seem to have been in circulation at least as late as the twelfth century. It is more than probable that the wide popularity and the authority which Vatsyayana's work had attained led to the neglect of the earlier writers, which through lack of demand ceased to be copied and preserved.

III

Vatsyayana's approach to the problem of Kama may now be considered. A certain amount of opprobrium has come to be attached to the work in modern times as Kama in the popular mind is identified with desire, lust or physical love. Hence the *Kama Sutra* has been generally considered as a book on erotics—something unworthy of serious study. But this is far from the case. Our author himself describes Kama as the enjoyment of appropriate objects by the five senses of hearing, seeing, feeling, tasting and smelling assisted by the mind together with the soul. In the context of the book it is used to cover the whole range of man-woman relationships, education, courtship, marriage, and conjugal life considered as one of the three aspects of life. Vatsyayana's approach, therefore, is not *essentially* on the erotic plane. In fact the first part of the *Kama Sutra* does not deal with matters of sex at all, but about the ideals and accomplishments of a nagarika (or dweller in the city), a man about town, and about characteristics of different types of women. Part II no doubt deals with sexual unions, but Part III again is headed the acquisition of a wife, and Part IV deals with family life.

It is in this respect that the Kama Sutra differs from such works as Ovid's *Art of Love*. Ovid is a kind of text book on the art of seduction and of pleasure. He makes no pretence of dealing with the subject as a science, and indeed disclaims all ethical considerations. The conquest of women and the retention of their affections are his main themes. These and similar subjects—apart of course from the different forms of union—are discussed by Vatsyayana also, but the major portion of the work as we have noticed above deals with courtship, marriage and wifely duties. Ovid writes to initiate his pupils into the course of illicit love, and he proudly proclaims 'I am the teacher of Love' and the course he prescribes is stated thus: 'First remember to choose carefully the woman you will set your heart upon; second you must secure her submission; third you must perpetuate her attachment to you. This is my entire syllabus and text.' This is indeed very different from the syllabus and text of Vatsyayana.

Again, Ovid is exclusively writing for men, to instruct them in the ways of the world of love. Vatsyayana, it will be noticed, devotes a good portion of his book to women, advising them on their wifely duties and how to ensure conjugal happiness.

But in the area common to them there are many points of similarity between the two writers. See, for example, the importance attached to the maid or female companion. Ovid bluntly advises the young man 'The best thing to do is to make friends with the maid. . . . This is very important, you must win the maid.' Vatsyayana makes the same point in a different way. He advises the young man to take under his care 'the daughter of the nurse', the traditional maid and companion of young women of good family and teach her the different forms of pleasure.

Again, Ovid says 'Another thing, my fellow citizens, acquaint yourself thoroughly in the fine arts but not merely be the mouth piece of some protégé.' We have already seen the importance that Vatsyayana attaches to education in Arts. There are in this way many points of similarity between Ovid and our author when they discuss questions of a similar nature. But Ovid's work is limited in character, and has but little importance from the general point of view of man-woman relationship.

Nor is the *Kama Sutra* to be compared in any manner with the writings of later authors like the Marquis de Sade. Sade had a whole philosophy on the question of sex; but it was a philosophy of libertinage which he preaches in numerous volumes. While Sade was no doubt a powerful thinker, his approach to the man-woman relationship was devoid of any sense of ethics. His one serious contribution—the element of pain in sex relationships—is something which Vatsyayana also does not neglect, though he does not give it the same prominence. Also Sade writes for the 'sovereign' individual who defies moral codes and it may be said that Sade estimated the degree of pleasure by the enormity of the defiance of social values. Sade enunciates his doctrine in one place in the following words. 'They have convinced me that through vice alone is man capable of experiencing this moral and physical vibration which is the source of the most delicious voluptuousness.' This is an attitude totally opposed to that of Vatsyayana whose object in writing the book is a thoroughly moral one—that of instructing men and women in the legitimate pleasures of the senses.

In fact the readers who approach this work in the hope of reading a pornographic book will be greatly disappointed, for throughout it Vatsyayana keeps up the attitude of a moralist. Even in the passages which are devoted to describing various phases of physical love, he is careful to point out that though particular practices are described in books there is no reason why they should be actually tried. 'The taste and the strength and the digestive qualities of the flesh of dogs', he says, 'are mentioned in works on medicine, but it does not, therefore, follow that it should be eaten by the wise. In the same way there are some men, some places and some times with respect to which such practices can be made use of. A man should, therefore, pay regard to the place, to the time and to the practice which is to be carried out, as also as to whether it is agreeable to his nature and to himself, and then he may or may not practise these things according to circumstances.'

This emphasis on the customs of different places is one of the characteristics of Vatsyayana. He has a proper sociological approach to the problem, and carefully describes the social habits and practices of the different regions of India. What is normal or considered permissible in one area may be considered a vice in another. This approach to the study of sex relations—from the point of view of the social habits of different peoples—has become popular only in recent years in the West and Vatsyayana may, therefore, be considered the forerunner of such thinkers as Havelock Ellis, Malinowski, Kraft-Ebbing and others who have written on this subject.

Vatsyayana's approach is basically that of a sociologist and he deals with the most intimate questions in an objective and an almost scientific way. As he himself affirms, 'this work is not to be used merely as an instrument for satisfying our desires. A person, acquainted with the true principles of this science, and who preserves his Dharma, Artha, and Kama and has regard for the practices of the people, is sure to obtain the mastery over his senses.'

The first section of the book is particularly important for an understanding of Vatsyayana's approach to the whole science. At the very start he answers the objection of moralists to the study of Kama as a science:

'Some learned men say that as Dharma is connected with things not belonging to this world, it is appropriately treated of in a book. But Kama being a thing which is practised even by the brute creation, and which is to be found everywhere, does not want any work on the subject.'

To this objection Vatsyayana replies: 'This is not so. Sexual intercourse being a thing dependent on man and woman requires the application of proper means by them and these means are to be learnt from the Kama Shastra. The non-application of proper means which we see in the brute creation is caused by their being unrestrained . . . and by their intercourse not being preceded by thought of any kind.' Two other objections which Vatsyayana raises and meets are interesting. To those who say that as fate decides human lives why worry about such matter he replies: 'As the acquisition of every object presupposes some exertion on the part of man, the application of proper means may be said to be the cause of gaining all our ends.' Without understanding the proper means, no man can succeed in this or in any other sphere. To the moralists who say that pleasures should not be sought for because history shows that many people who gave themselves up to pleasure had come to grief, Vatsyayana answers: 'This objection cannot be sustained, for pleasures being as necessary for the existence and well-being of the body as food, are consequently equally required. They are, moreover, the results of Dharma and Artha. Pleasures are, therefore, to be followed with moderation and caution.'

After thus disposing of the objections to the study of Kama Shastra, Vatsyayana emphasises that it should be integrated with other studies necessary for the development of one's culture. He lays down that a man should study the Kama Sutra and the arts and sciences subordinate thereto *in addition* to the arts and sciences contained in Dharma and Artha. Dharma and Artha are the primary studies, but Kama being equally a part of life, its study is not to be neglected. What are the arts and sciences subordinate to Kama Shastra? These are the sixty-four kalas or arts, which Vatsyayana enumerates. The number is traditional and various authors include different items according to whether the approach is Dharma, Artha or Kama. It is significant that the *Lalitha Vistara*, the biography of the Buddha, in enumerating the subject that the young Siddhartha—the future Buddha—studied mentions the qualities of woman and the art of attraction among the kalas. The *Artha Shastra* as it deals with the education of princes has a different list. So far as Vatsyayana is concerned, his list is of special interest as showing what cultivated men and women were expected to know. In this list apart from such subjects as chemistry and mineralogy, carpentry, the art of war, arms and armies, mines and quarries, etc., and such curiosities as arithmetical recreations, knowledge of dictionaries and vocabularies, the teaching of parrots and starlings to speak, the emphasis is on general culture. Those who desire success in the life of Kama are enjoined to study singing, dancing, playing on musical instruments, writing and drawing, scenic representations and amateur acting, gardening, adornment of body, composing poems, skill in youthful sports, knowledge of the rules of society and how to pay respects and compliments to others. Literature, art, dance and music are especially emphasised as necessary studies. Vatsyayana considers that a man should have a cultivated mind and body, with intellectual and artistic interests, if he is to lead a proper and disciplined life of enjoyment.

The ideal life that Vatsyayana visualised was that of a nagarika, or a city dweller, a man of leisure and culture. It is to the nagarika he addresses himself. The development of great cities in India, at least from the eighth century B.C., is a fact of great social significance. We know now that the Mahenjodaro and Harappa culture which extended over most of Hindustan was predominantly urban and though the Aryans who displaced the Harappans were originally a pastoral people and were always calling on their gods to destroy the 'towns' of their enemies, they also developed a town life once they entered the fertile Gangetic Valley. Great cities like Hastinapura and Benares came into existence which created a tradition of urban life. In the time of the Buddha in the sixth century B.C. we have evidence of a flourishing and highly organised urban life in great cities like Rajgir, Vaisali, Benares and Taxila. The story of Ambapali, the courtesan of Vaisali, who was rich, powerful and cultivated is evidence enough of the position that courtesans had achieved in city life at that time. With the founding of Pataliputra as a great imperial capital in the fifth century B.C., and the emergence of Magadha as a great empire in the time of the Nandas and the Mauryas, a tradition of city life, courtly, refined and devoted to pleasure seems to have developed and achieved recognition among the higher classes. As already mentioned, it was at the request of the courtesans of Pataliputra that Dattaka wrote his treatise on the life of a courtesan.

The conception of the nagarika or leisured man about town was central to Vatsyayana's teachings. There is a general misconception in the West that the Hindu ideal of life was renunciatory and emphasised other-worldliness, that conceptions such as maya led to a general acceptance of the illusoriness of the world. This idea became prevalent in the West by the identification of the ideas of certain philosophical schools with the Hindu view of life. The works of schoolmen and philosophers represented the outcome of speculation and while they were important, they did not in any way represent the general Hindu approach to life. The doctrine of the four ashramas (or phases of life) which was universally accepted among all classes of Hindus provided for the renunciation of worldly life only after the other three phases had been completed—those of the student, the householder, and the detached participant in worldly affairs. Only at the end of a man's life, when he had led a life of useful activity and normal enjoyment, was he supposed to renounce the world. The necessity of life in the world in the full and legitimate enjoyment of Artha and Kama was always emphasised in Hindu thought. Not only is this taught in secular books. The *Bhagavad Gita*, considered by the generality of Hindus as one of the most authoritative texts, says as follows: 'The painless yoga is his who has appropriate food, reasonable recreation, is active in works which are appropriate to him, and enjoys himself appropriately.' That is what Sri Krishna lays down as the yoga for active men. The fact that renunciation, after fulfilment of one's duties, is preached should not lead us to the notion that Hinduism was renunciatory in its ideal of life.

Nor is there any justification for the view that Hinduism preached a life of austerity or simplicity as an ideal. Of course for saints and holymen, as in all other religions, a life of austerity was enjoined, but for the man in the world —the grihasta, the householder—the ideal proclaimed was by no means austere. This is clear from the sacred books themselves. Neither Rama nor Krishna, the two great incarnations popularly worshipped in India, lived a life of austerity. In Ayodhya, Rama led the life of a great king. Krishna is depicted as having lived a life of great luxury. All the heroes of Indian mythology—even Yudhisthira who is pictured as the ideal monarch—lived a life of disciplined pleasure. The doctrine of a simple life of limited wants was what those who renounced the world accepted for themselves and not what Hindu thinkers considered right for the ordinary man. It would in fact be more correct to say that the conception of the nagarika is more in keeping with Hindu life than that of the sannyasin.

Vatsyayana describes the ideal life of a nagarika in Chapter IV of Part I of the *Kama Sutra.* Though the word 'nagarika' means a city dweller, in ordinary use it had acquired the meaning of a cultivated man of leisure. The nagarika is pictured as a man of education and of easy means. He is advised to take a house in a city or in a large village. The locality should be carefully chosen: it should be in the vicinity of good men, and must have an adequate supply of water. Our author devotes considerable attention to the conveniences which a nagarika should provide for himself. The house should be divided into a number of apartments meant for different purposes. The inner apartments should be reserved for ladies, a practice which is still common all over India. The nagarika's own apartment should be elegantly furnished, with a bed 'soft, agreeable to the sight' and 'covered with a clean white cloth' with a canopy over it. There should also be a sofa or couch. Other furnishings and appointments in the nagarika's rooms are also significant as indicating the life that he is expected to lead. There should be a place for his lute and for his books, a separate place for artistic diversions like carving. The importance of having a flower garden attached to the house is emphasised. There should be swings, bowers of flowering creepers with suitable seats where the nagarika could enjoy himself.

Housed in this elegant manner, the nagarika should live a life of cultured leisure. But he is not to neglect his duties. After getting ready for the day and dressing himself decently and attractively he should devote attention to *his normal business.* A householder's duties cannot be neglected.

After a short rest at midday, he should spend the afternoon in the company of friends.

The emphasis that Vatsyayana places on the elegance of a nagarika's dress and toilet is interesting. In the morning after his daily bath the nagarika should apply 'a limited quantity of ointments and perfumes to his body, put some ornaments on his person and collyrium on his eyelids and below his eyes and colour his lips with alaktaka'. He is in fact not to be dressed like a popinjay, but elegantly, with a moderate use of ornaments and perfumes. The use of collyrium on the eyelids is a practice which is still prevalent in some parts of India, more as a protection against the glare of the sun than as an element of personal adornment. The use of alaktaka (a reddening substance) for lips was general among women. The poet Kalidasa in describing the marriage toilet of Parvati speaks of its use even in the case of the goddess. Nor is it omitted in the offerings of worship for the goddess, but it was unusual among men. The use of betel along with other fragrant things to give taste to the mouth is also enjoined.

The nagarika as befits his condition should eat three meals, in the forenoon, afternoon and at night. The drinking of wine was not only not prohibited but recognised as a friendly social custom. It was a general habit in India and drinking festivities are described in great detail in literature. Vatsyayana even says that men should drink wine only after women have been served.

Many kinds of social diversions are suggested for the nagarika, riding in public gardens, mixed bathing in rivers and swimming pools, moon-light picnics, gambling in night clubs, etc. 'These and similar other amusements should always be carried on by citizens.'

That the nagarika was not merely a creature of Vatsyayana's imagination or an ideal presented to young men may be seen from widespread allusions in literature. Kalidasa, who pictures cultivated Indian society best, in describing Vidisha, a capital city in Central India, says that the less accessible areas of the hills near it were fragrant with the amorous dalliances of nagarikas and courtesans. Again in the famous play, *The Toy Clay Cart*, the life described is that of nagarikas.

We come across allusions to many sports mentioned by Vatsyayana in other works of the time even as late as the eleventh century.

The counterpart of the nagarika is the nayika. In the sense in which the Kama Shastra uses the word she is a woman enjoyment with whom is not prohibited by Dharma.

Ex-communicated women, wives of other men of respectability and wives of relations and friends are excluded from the category of nayikas. The proper nayikas are maidens, twice married women, and courtesans. Vatsyayana especially emphasises that a nagarika should find his enjoyment only with those who are suitable for him.

To understand the position of women as described in Vatsyayana, it is necessary to remember that he makes a clear distinction between wives and nayikas. He follows strictly the rules of orthodoxy in his conception of an ideal wife. The wife enjoys a certain amount of freedom; but the emphasis is on duties and on decorum. An elaborate code of conduct is prescribed for her: but her relationship with the husband was not one of inferiority. That the wife should present herself properly dressed and with ornaments before the husband is one of the oldest ideas of Hindu domestic life. Vatsyayana's own advice to a wife is never to present herself without some ornaments on her person even when she is alone with her husband. It is interesting to note that one of the boons which Sita received from a saint while she was sharing the exile of her husband Rama in the forest was the she would appear in his eyes at all times as if dressed with jewels, etc., as for a festive occasion.

The position of nayikas or women in society was different. They were much freer. They accompanied men to public places, took part in sports and amusements. They were also much better educated. The daughters of kings and ministers and courtesans are required to educate themselves in science and Vatsyayana gives as one of the reasons that 'if a wife becomes separated from her husband and falls into distress, she can support herself easily, even in a foreign country, by the knowledge of these arts. Even the bare knowledge of them gives attractiveness to a woman.'

The physiological aspect of love with its descriptions of innumerable postures and poses would seem to be no more than a schematic statement, and therefore unimportant in the general context of the work. But it has had a very great influence on Sanskrit literature and Indian painting and deserves study from this point of view.

There is one aspect of Vatsyayana's teaching which deserves attention and that is the section which he devotes to physical violence in the practice of love. There are special chapters devoted to striking, biting, scratching, etc. —in fact the methods of inflicting pain. He also mentions striking with instruments, which, however, he disapproves as barbarous and base. But he emphasises the connection between pain and pleasure. The difference between the treatment of pain as an ingredient of pleasure in Vatsyayana's *Kama Sutra* and in the works of the Marquis de Sade lies in the fact that, while the Marquis sees in it the essence of refined pleasure, Vatsyayana declared, 'A horse having once attained the fifth degree of motion goes on with blind speed, regardless of pits, ditches, and posts in his way; and in the same manner a loving pair become blind with passion in the heat of congress, and go on with great impetuosity, paying not the least regard to excess. For this reason, one who is well acquainted with the science of love and knowing his own strength, as also the tenderness, impetuosity and strength of the young women, should act accordingly. The various modes of enjoyment are not for all times or for all persons but should be used at the proper time and in the proper countries and places.' In fact Vatsyayana recognises pain as an element of pleasure, but takes up a position totally different from Sade who finds in the infliction of pain the essential ingredient of pleasure.

More important in every way is Vatsyayana's treatment of courtship, marriage, and other social institutions in Part III. The Hindu conception of a wife is one with whom Dharma is practised. The results of union, Vatsyayana says, 'are the acquisition of Dharma and Artha, offspring, affinity, increase of friends and untarnished love'. The bride to be chosen should be of good family and well connected. She should also be good looking, of a cheerful disposition, with good hair, nails, teeth, ears, eyes and breasts and not troubled with a sickly body. Among the kinds of women whom one should not marry it is interesting to note that our author includes 'one who is kept concealed'.

Marriage, of course, is to be negotiated but strange as it may appear Vatsyayana gives his support to the view of earlier writers that 'no other girl than one who is loved should be married'. Since such love cannot blossom unless there are opportunities for social contact, our author prescribes that 'when a girl becomes marriageable', she should be provided with such opportunities under of course suitable guidance and care. 'Every afternoon, having dressed her and decorated her in a becoming manner, they (the parents) should send her with her female companions to sports, sacrifices and marriage ceremonies, and thus show her to advantage in society.' According to our author proper marriage is possible only where there is free social intercourse and men and women respect each other.

Vatsyayana's views on the treatment of women deserve to be specially noted. In a remarkable passage dealing with the creation of mutual confidence after marriage he says 'women, being of a tender nature, want tender beginnings.

. . . The man should therefore approach the girl according to her liking and should make use of those devices by which he may be able to establish himself more and more into her confidence.' Vatsyayaṇa's hints for courtship show that in this matter the world has not changed greatly during the last 2,000 years. When a boy has begun to woo the girl he loves, he should spend his time with her, amuse her with various diversions, fitted for their age and acquaintanceship, such as picking and collecting flowers, and playing various kinds of games. He should show friendship to her friends. He should do whatever the girl takes most delight in and give her presents. After having gained her attention he should arrange for a private rendezvous where he should amuse her by stories and songs, take her out to moonlight fairs—in fact gain her love by active courtship. It is also interesting to note that our author does not subscribe to the view that women, if they fall in love, make no effort to win for themselves the object of their affections but wait patiently to be taken. Such a view he characterises as foolish.

Young women should be modest, but they should not hide their love. Vatsyayana lays down the appropriate forms under which a maiden may show her preferences and this passage in Chapter III of Part III has had an immense influence on the poetic and dramatic literature of India—not only of Sanskrit but of all the languages derived from it. The actions of a maiden in love as prescribed by Vatsyayana have been followed almost to the letter in the poetry of India.

I have already emphasised the fact that the *Kama Sutra* is less a book on the art of love than a treatise on sex relationships. The chapters dealing with the duties of a wife, of her life in the family, where there might be many women bring this out very clearly. The wife should take upon herself the whole care of the family. She should keep the house well cleaned, arrange flowers in appropriate places and take special care of the floor. She should surround the house with a garden and arrange everything for the appropriate rites. The kitchen garden is not to be neglected but the emphasis is on the pleasure garden which should have seats and must have aromatic plants.

The functions and amusements that our author prescribes for a dutiful wife are also interesting. As for meals the wife should always consider what the husband likes and dislikes, and what things are good for him and what are injurious to him. She should avoid the company of doubtful people, fortune tellers, and beggars. She should neither accept nor extend invitations without the consent of her husband. If she wants to engage in any games or sport she should not do it against his will. When the husband is away she should look after her household affairs, sleep near the elder women of the house, should not overdecorate herself, and should look after and keep in repair things that are liked by her husband. These and similar functions may perhaps be unsuited to a society based on the absolute equality of men and women, but in the normal conditions where man is the bread-winner and the head of the family, these injunctions would seem to be more than useful for the development of harmonious conjugal relations.

The section in the *Kama Sutra* dealing with courtesans is a fascinating study of a very important subject, which has interested mankind from the earliest times. In India the courtesan enjoyed at all times a special position and was not to be confused with ordinary prostitutes. In the time of the Buddha (sixth century B.C.) we hear of famous courtesans like Ambapali who held a high position in the great city of Vaisali. It was in her mango grove that the Blessed One stayed during his visit to the city and she not only entertained him but made a gift of the garden to the Buddha. In the jataka tales there are many stories which indicate that learned and accomplished courtesans were held in respect and esteem. Kautilya's *Artha Shastra* (circa 300 B.C.) bears witness to the fact that courtesans held high positions near the person of the king and held over him the royal umbrella and the yak fans—both emblems of sovereignty. These courtesans were generally women of high education and culture and were held in honour for their accomplishments. Kautilya prescribes that those who teach these women arts such as singing, playing on musical instruments, reading, dancing, acting, writing and painting shall be endowed with maintenance by the State. This tradition of learning has been a continuous one in India as we can see from Domingo Paes's description of their position in the court of Vijayanagar in 1522. 'These women', he says, 'live in the best streets that are in the city, their streets have the best rows of houses. They are much esteemed and are classed among those honoured ones who are the mistresses of captains. These women are allowed to enter even in the presence of the wives of the king and they stay with them and eat betel with them, a thing which no other person may do whatever their rank may be.' At the end of the eighteenth century the famous Abbé Dubois, who wasnaturally a prejudiced observer, noted however that the courtesans enjoy 'the privilege of learning to read, to dance and to sing'. Indeed they were at one time considered models of deportment, courtly behaviour and politeness and young princes and nobles were sent to elderly courtesans to be instructed in manners.

That courtesans were not always immoral but were capable of loyalty and honourable living is the theme of many stories. In the *Katha Sarit Sagara* of Soma Deva (tenth century A.D.) there is an interesting story dealing with the relations of Madanamalla with King Vikramaditya specially meant to prove this. In a famous poem entitled *Kuttinimatam* (or *The Opinions of a Go-Between*) by Damodara Gupta (eighth century A.D.), which in itself may be considered a poetic commentary on Vatsyayana, the theme again is developed with great skill that a courtesan can show the qualities of a devoted wife. It will be noticed that there is a special chapter in Vatsyayana's section on courtesans entitled 'Of living like a wife'.

Hindu theorists always made distinctions between ganikas (cultured courtesans) and kalutas (mere prostitutes). Vatsyayana himself makes this distinction. He says that one who is versed in arts obtains the name of a ganika or woman of society, of high quality, and receives a seat of honour in the assemblage of men. She is moreover always respected by the king and praised by learned men and her favour being sought by all she becomes an object of universal regard. It is significant that there is a whole section of dramatic literature in Sanskrit (known as bhana) of which the heroines are courtesans, and the scenes are laid in the streets of pleasure. The courtesans are always shown as ladies of culture and refinement, in honourable love with someone and devoted to music and dances, though carrying on their profession. This kind of literature seems to have existed from very early times, for in the *Kuttinimatam* (eighth century), already alluded to, there is a reference to a bhana by Dhenuka. In the famous play, *The Toy Clay Cart*, the heroine Vasanta Sena is a courtesan, and her love for a poor but noble Brahmin is held up in honour.

Nor is the tradition entirely dead in India today. There are well-known cases even at the present time of courtesans who are notable scholars and women of refinement and culture. One such lady in Madras was famed for her interpretation of Sanskrit musical compositions and in her later years gave away her wealth to endow a temple.

The life of courtesans, their training and accomplishments seem to have been studied at some length, for apart from Dattaka's classic which is now lost, and general works on Kama Shastra, there are in existence handbooks known as Vaisika tantra, or the Science of Attraction, which deal with the training and practices of courtesans. Of the general training given to these courtesans the *Dasa Kumara Charita* or *The Story of the Ten Princes* gives a short description. The mother of a young courtesan describes the trouble she had taken to train her daughter:

'From earliest childhood I have bestowed the greatest care upon her, doing everything in my power to promote her health and beauty. As soon as she was old enough, I had her carefully instructed in the art of dancing, acting, playing on musical instruments, singing, painting, preparing perfumes and flowers, in writing and conversation and even to some extent in grammar, logic and philosophy.'

With such an educational background, it is not surprising that the courtesan played an important part in society. The nearest approach to the Indian ganika was of course the Greek hetera. Vatsyayana's chapter dealing with this subject is a very interesting one and fully justifies the observation that 'the subtlety of women, their wonderful perceptive powers, their knowledge and their intuitive appreciation of men and things are all shown in the following pages, which may be looked upon as a concentrated essence that has since been worked up into detail by many writers in every quarter of the globe'.

IV

From this brief description of the contents of the book it is easy to see how the *Kama Sutra* came to have an immense influence on the general literary and artistic life of India. Indeed it would not be too much to say that from at least the fourth century A.D. it became almost a canonical text in the artistic world in literature, sculpture and painting, where love had to be treated. This may indeed look surprising, but anyone with the least knowledge of Sanskrit poetry, especially kavyas (epics) and drama, will agree that no single work has influenced the treatment of love themes as Vatsyayana's *Kama Sutra* has done. This is so, to a lesser extent, even with the Indian regional languages of today.

The earliest direct evidence of Vatsyayana is in Kalidasa's epics and dramas. Canto XIX of the *Raghuvamsa*, where Kalidasa portrays the life of degraded vice into which king Agnivarna had fallen, could in many places be fully understood only by reference to the *Kama Sutra*. Not only does the poet use the technical phraseology of Vatsyayana in many places, but at least in one passage he closely follows the *Kama Sutra*, taking the first part wholesale from one of the sutras in the text. Again, Vatsyayana says that when the bridegroom's hand touches that of the bride, the hairs on her forearm stand on end, while the fingers of the bride become wet with perspiration. Kalidasa incorporates this in a sloka in the *Raghuvamsa* describing the marriage of Aja and Indumati. Numerous other instances can be quoted, but two are particularly interesting. In the famous drama *Sakuntala*, Kalidasa takes care to follow the text carefully in describing the evidence of love in young maidens—not speaking directly, and turning away the face and so on—and the hero notes all this and narrates them to his friend, in a manner which leaves no doubt that the author is following the injunctions of Vatsyayana. The significance of this particular passage requires to be emphasised for, following Kalidasa, all later poets in dealing with the signs of love have consciously described the actions and behaviour of maidens as laid down in the *Kama Sutra*. The second instance is even more interesting. There is a very famous verse in *Sakuntala* where the heroine is given solemn paternal advice about her conduct in her husband's house. It says: 'Serve your elders: be like friends with the other wives of your husband. Do not, out of anger as a result of neglect, act in a manner unfriendly to your husband. Be gracious and friendly to your attendants; do not be elated by pleasures. In this way young women become good wives; otherwise they bring sorrow to the family.' In the *Kama Sutra* are the very words which Kalidasa uses in the poem for two of the admonitions and others also appear elsewhere in the text.

Further in Kalidasa's *Kumara Sambhava*—the epic dealing with the birth of the war-god—in the eighth canto which is devoted primarily to the amorous dalliances of Shiva with Parvati, there is a verse the real significance of which could be interpreted only in terms of Vatsyayana's sutras.

If the influence that Vatsyayana exercised was so direct on the greatest of Sanskrit poets, who became a model for all others afterwards, it can well be imagined how his Sutras came to have almost canonical importance to the later poets who dealt with love. In fact it became a regular practice with all mahakavya (epic) writers to devote at least one canto to the amours of the hero, and this opportunity was utilised to exhibit both directly and by allusion the poet's familiarity with the sutras of Vatsyayana. To have described not merely the love-making but the behaviour of the hero and the heroine except in terms of Vatsyayana would have apparently been considered as unorthodox and perhaps unnatural. Even the most respectable writers—poets who were known for their piety and high morals—did not fail to describe such scenes. To give only two examples, Vastupala—the great minister of Viradhavala—who was a most pious Jain and spent millions in constructing Jain temples, including one of the superbly carved marble temples at Abu—was also the author of a mahakavya entitled *Naranarayaniya* where a whole canto is devoted to what may appropriately be called a poetic commentary on certain portions of Vatsyayana's text. In the fifteenth century, the queen of one of the Vijayanagar kings wrote a heroic poem in many cantos dealing with the conquest of Madura by her husband. Though the author was a woman and a queen, she does not hesitate to describe her husband's loves, closely following in many portions the text of Vatsyayana.

Not only was the influence of Vatsyayana seen in the description of love scenes in poems in the mahakavya style, but it was even more marked in dramas. Vatsyayana devotes a set of sutras in the chapter 'Of creating confidence in the girl', to various early conversations between a man and a girl. 'He should converse with her by means of a female friend: on such an occasion the girl should smile with her head bent down and if the female friend says more on her part than she was desired to do, she should chide her and dispute with her.' Anyone reading the first act of *Sakuntala* will see how closely these directions are followed by Kalidasa. In every one of the Sanskrit dramas which deal with love stories, the beginning of love and its maturing are dealt with on the lines laid down in the *Kama Sutra*. In the first scene where the hero meets the heroine, she is always attended by her friend who speaks for her, while the heroine behaves with due modesty and shows her attitude by such action and gestures as are prescribed by our author.

In the field of love poetry Vatsyayana's influence was naturally supreme in the *Amaru Sataka* or *Century of Amaru* which is the most notable collection of Sanskrit love lyrics. The situations described in many slokas which appear so natural and unaffected are in fact related to some sutra of our text and are so explained by commentators. Also there are a few verses the full meaning of which could not be understood unless one is familiar with the Kama Sutra. On such occasions the poet by merely giving a significant allusion conveys the particular posture or act which is described by our author. Other writers of love-lyrics like Govardhana Charya, the author of *Arya Sapta Sati* or *Seven Centuries*, are even more allusive.

Even religious poetry fell under the influence of Vatsyayana. The most remarkable example of this is the great poem of Jayadeva entitled the *Gita Govinda*, translated into English by Sir Edwin Arnold under the title of *The Indian Song of Songs*. The poem deals with the love of

Radha, the cowherdess, for Krishna and is considered in India to be the supreme example of religious devotional poetry and is even today sung as such regularly in South Indian temples. Radha is here the symbol of the human soul in search for the universal soul Krishna, feeling the tremors of expectation, enjoying the ecstasies of union, suffering the pangs of separation and finally the ineffable joy of ultimate union. The *Gita Govinda* is understood in this symbolic spirit and the text therefore is treated with the greatest reverence and its author is considered not only a great poet but a great saint. But the verses are in terms of carnal love and in many places could only be understood fully in terms of Vatsyayana's text. (Indeed, the standard commentary on this work by Kumbha, the king of Mewar [Udaipur], quotes liberally from the *Kama Sutra* to explain the allusions in the text.) To quote only one example (translation by George Keyt):

O make him enjoy me, my friend, that haughty destroyer
of Keshi, that Krishna so fickle,
Me whose masses of curls were like loose-slipping flowers,
whose amorous words
Were vague as of doves and kokila birds, that Krishna
whose bosom is marked
With scratches, surpassing all in his love that the science
of love could teach.
O make him enjoy me, my friend, that haughty destroyer
of Keshi, that Krishna so fickle,
To whose act of desire accomplished the anklets upon my
feet bejewelled
Vibrated sounding, who gave his kisses seizing the hair of
the head,
And to whom in his passionate love my girdle sounded in
eloquence sweet.
O make him enjoy me, my friend, that haughty destroyer
of Keshi, that Krishna so fickle,

Whose lotus eyes had closed a little, and who had drowsily grown—
Having tasted in bodily pleasure with me the shattering thrill in the end,
With me whose vine-like body collapsed, unable to bear any more.

All these lines of verse, it will be seen, follow closely the sutras of Vatsyayana. More especially the full significance of the second stanza could only be understood in terms of our text for expressions like 'feet bejewelled vibrated sounding', 'who gave his kisses seizing the hair of the head' and 'girdle sounded in eloquence sweet' are direct allusions to the sutras and are interpreted by reference to them.

It may also be noticed that Vatsyayana's influence was not confined to any particular part of India but pervaded it from Kashmir to Cape Comorin and from Bengal to Gujarat. We have already alluded to Damodara Gupta, the Kashmir poet. Jayadeva the author of the *Gita Govinda* was a Bengali. Gangadevi came from the Deccan; Vastu Pal came from Gujerat. In fact his influence was felt everywhere in India. It also spread wherever Indian civilisation spread. In the Kavi literature of Java, Vatsyayana and his teachings are often alluded to. That was perhaps not a matter of surprise as Kavi poetry was modelled on the Kavyas of Sanskrit. In Cambodia, Vatsyayana is directly alluded to by name as an authority on the science of love. In an inscription of Yaco Varman (889–900 A.D.) published by Auguste Barth occurs the following verse:

'experts in the art of love, as if they have been taught by Vatsyayana and others'.

Nor was the dominance of the *Kama Sutra* confined to Sanskrit poetry. With the growth of the regional languages of the eleventh century, the *Kama Sutra* had become so standard a work, that it could be said to have shaped the early love poetry in these languages. Vidyapati writing in Maithili sang of the loves of Radha and Krishna and the Vaishnava lyrics which became the fashion in the period following described the love-scenes of Krishna in terms of Vatsyayana. Notably in songs by the great Bengali poet Chandidas, the influence of our text is clearly visible. In Hindi, the sringara poetry that developed from the sixteenth to the eighteenth centuries again bore unmistakable marks of the *Kama Sutra.* In south Indian languages also this influence could be seen in the love poetry of the time. Until the growth of new ideas in lyrical and love poetry under the influence of the West, Vatsyayana continued to exercise directly a remarkable influence on Indian literature.

The influence of the *Kama Sutra* on the sculpture of India has attracted wide attention. To Westerners it was formerly a matter of some curiosity why some of the most famous Hindu temples should have sexual practices of different kinds sculptured on their walls. The most notable examples of such maithuna, or union sculptures, are at Konarak, Khajuraho, Belur, Halebid and other famous medieval temples. Nor is this a feature only of medieval temples. There are Bacchanalian scenes in the Ajanta caves which are predominantly of Buddhist inspiration. In Nagarjunikonda, a most remarkable centre of Buddhist architecture and sculpture, there are many panels depicting maithuna scenes. Many of them could be identified as sculptural versions of Vatsyayana's sutras—sometimes as interpreted by poets. On the walls of Jain temples nude women are also found sculptured.

It cannot be that these builders of religious edifices were either themselves morally degenerate individuals or were merely pampering to the taste of a decadent public. Obviously they expressed some fundamental aspect of Indian religious beliefs. As we have emphasised earlier the union of man and woman is conceived as the symbol of divine creation and is not looked upon as a base or unworthy act but as a transformation from duality into unity. This principle is clearly brought out not only in Hindu tantric worship, but in certain developments of Buddhism represented by the Guhya Samaj. Maithuna or the act of union has thus come to represent symbolically a basic religious doctrine in Hinduism. What the Hindu sculptors endeavoured to realise is this mystic union and the figures on the temple walls, voluptuous as they are in the poses, convey an idea of serenity even more than of enjoyment. The influence of Vatsyayana on these sculptured forms can be seen in their attitudes and poses. A careful study of the sculptures at Konarak, Khajuraho and other famous temples will show how closely the artist in most cases has followed the sutras of our text.

In the field of painting the influence of Vatsyayana is not so obvious. But it is necessary to remember that the Radha-Krishna paintings which have contributed so much to the treasury of Indian art draw their inspiration from the *Gita Govinda* and similar works, themselves drawing freely upon Vatsyayana. The classification of different kinds of nayikas, their attitudes, etc., though greatly elaborated by later writers, can be traced to the *Kama Sutra* and here also the paintings of such scenes can be claimed at least indirectly to be derived from Vatsyayana.

The authority of Vatsyayana was so great that at one time the *Kama Sutra* seems to have been taught to young women. Only the portions dealing with wifely duties might have been the subject of study. In a south Indian work of the eighteenth century entitled *Naishadha Champu* occurs the statement that the Princess Damayanti showed unusual ability in studying under proper tutors, kavyas, dramas, epics and the text of Vatsyayana. Vatsyayana himself says that young maids should study the *Kama Sutra* along with its arts and sciences before marriage and after it they should continue to do so with the consent of their husbands.

'Some women', he adds, 'such as daughters of princes and their ministers and public women are actually versed in the *Kama Sutra*.'

It would appear from this that some kind of sex education based on Vatsyayana was given to maidens of high families. Naturally among the more educated courtesans, it was learnt as a manual of their profession. In a Kerala work of the fifteenth century entitled *Chandrotsava* or *The Festival of the Moon* there is described a discussion among some leading courtesans in which Vatsyayana is quoted by them as authority to prove the correctness of the thesis expounded. The inscription from Cambodia quoted above also seems to provide evidence that Vatsyayana was taught as a text book on love to young women in that country.

The state of society in second century India as seen reflected in the *Kama Sutra* cannot fail to strike one as evidencing a high civilisation. Education was widely prevalent both among the men and women of the upper classes. There was considerable freedom of social intercourse and subject to rules of Dharma, there was but little interference with the life of the normal citizen. Widow remarriage was widely prevalent and even among the upper classes there was no custom of child marriage. Vatsyayana even says that a maiden before her marriage should study the Kama Shastra, which would have been impossible if the later custom of child marriage was then prevalent. Life was well ordered and peaceful and economically prosperous. The kind of life prescribed for a nagarika is possible only in a society in which there was a rich middle class which had plenty of leisure. Social gatherings, festivals, gambling establishments, celebrations with different kinds of wine and all other marks of a society which was gay and cultured seem to have been part of the life of India at the time. Music was specially cultivated and so was literature.

Of the rigidity which came to be a feature of Indian society at a later time, there is no evidence in the *Kama*

Sutra. A gay and happy people who worshipped their gods, performed their rituals but enjoyed life with all its refinements to the full is the picture of Indian society which is seen in Vatsyayana. That this was not an idealistic presentation may be seen from other evidence, but is clear from the text itself, because what our author attempts to do is not to describe an ideal society, but to instruct people how to live the life of the senses in society as it existed.

[illegible] A gay and happy people [illegible] quarrels, [illegible]
performed their rituals and enjoyed life with all its re[illegible]
[illegible] the fall of the [illegible] Indian society which is
[illegible]. That this was not an idealistic presenta-
[illegible] from other evidence, but [illegible]

[illegible]

[illegible] The Oxford History of India (3rd edition, ed. [illegible] 1958)

[illegible], ed. J. Campbell, [illegible] Art of Indian Asia [illegible] (New York, 1955)

BIBLIOGRAPHY

ANAND, M. R. *Kama Kala: Some Notes on the Philosophical Basis of Hindu Erotic Sculpture* (Geneva, 1958)

ARCHER, W. G. *The Loves of Krishna* (London, 1957)

—*Indian Miniatures* (London and New York, 1960)

BASHAM, A. L. *The Wonder that was India* (London, 1954)

ELWIN, V. *The Baiga* (London, 1940)

—*The Muria and their Ghotul* (London and Bombay, 1947)

FOUCHER, M.-P. *The Erotic Sculpture of India* (London, 1959)

FREDERIC, L. *Indian Temples and Sculpture* (London, 1959)

KEITH, A. B. *History of Sanskrit Literature* (Oxford, 1928)

KEYT, G. (trans) *Shri Jayadeva's Gita Govinda* (Bombay, 1947)

LIN YUTANG and others (trans) *Wisdom of India* (London, 1949)

MAZUMDAR, R. C. and others. *History and Culture of the Indian People* (London, 1950; Bombay, 1951)

MEYER, J. J. *Sexual Life in Ancient India* (2nd edition, London, 1952)

MOOKERJEE, A. *Art of India* (Calcutta, 1952)

PANDIT, R. S. (trans) *Ritusamhara or The Pageant of the Seasons* (Bombay, 1947)

PEIRIS, H., and VAN GEYZEL, L. C. (trans) *Kalidasa: The Seasons, The Ornament of Love, The Broken Pot* (Colombo, 1961)

RANDHAWA, M. S. *Basohli Painting* (New Delhi, 1959)

—*Kangra Paintings on Love* (New Delhi, 1962)

RAWSON, P. *Indian Painting* (Paris, 1961)

SINGH, M. *India: Paintings from Ajanta Caves* (London and New York, 1954)

SMITH, V. A. *The Oxford History of India* (3rd edition, ed. P. Spear, Oxford, 1958)

UPADHYAYA, S. C. (trans) *Kama Sutra of Vatsyayana* (Bombay, 1961)

ZIMMER, H. (ed. J. Campbell) *The Art of Indian Asia* (New York, 1955)

THE KAMA SUTRA

OF VATSYAYANA

TRANSLATED BY SIR RICHARD BURTON
AND F. F. ARBUTHNOT

DEDICATED

TO THAT SMALL PORTION OF THE BRITISH PUBLIC WHICH TAKES ENLIGHTENED INTEREST IN STUDYING THE MANNERS AND CUSTOMS OF THE OLDEN EAST

PREFACE

IN the literature of all countries there will be found a certain number of works treating especially of love. Everywhere the subject is dealt with differently, and from various points of view. In the present publication it is proposed to give a complete translation of what is considered the standard work on love in Sanscrit literature, and which is called the 'Vatsyayana Kama Sutra', or Aphorisms on Love, by Vatsyayana.

While the introduction will deal with the evidence concerning the date of the writing, and the commentaries written upon it, the chapters following the introduction will give a translation of the work itself. It is, however, advisable to furnish here a brief analysis of works of the same nature, prepared by authors who lived and wrote years after Vatsyayana had passed away, but who still considered him as the great authority, and always quoted him as the chief guide to Hindoo erotic literature.

Besides the treatise of Vatsyayana the following works on the same subject are procurable in India:

The Ratirahasya, or secrets of love
The Panchasakya, or the five arrows
The Smara Pradipa, or the light of love
The Ratimanjari, or the garland of love
The Rasmanjari, or the sprout of love
The Anunga Runga, or the stage of love; also called Kamaledhiplava, or a boat in the ocean of love.

The author of the 'Secrets of Love' was a poet named Kukkoka. He composed his work to please one Venudutta, who was perhaps a king. When writing his own name at the end of each chapter he calls himself 'Siddha patiya pandita', i.e. an ingenious man among learned men. The work was translated into Hindi years ago, and in this the author's name was written as Koka. And as the same name crept into all the translations into other languages in India, the book became generally known, and the subject was popularly called Koka Shastra, or doctrines of Koka, which is identical with the Kama Shastra, or doctrines of love, and the words Koka Shastra and Kama Shastra are used indiscriminately.

The work contains nearly eight hundred verses, and is divided into ten chapters, which are called Pachivedas. Some of the things treated of in this work are not to be found in the Vatsyayana, such as the four classes of women, the Padmini, Chitrini, Shankini and Hastini, as also the enumeration of the days and hours on which the women of the different classes become subject to love. The author adds that he wrote these things from the opinions of Gonikaputra and Nandikeshwara, both of whom are mentioned by Vatsyayana, but their works are not now extant. It is difficult to give any approximate idea as to the year in which the work was composed. It is only to be presumed that it was written after that of Vatsyayana, and previous to the other works on this subject that are still extant. Vatsyayana gives the names of ten authors on the subject, all of whose works he had consulted, but none of which are extant, and does not mention this one. This would tend to show that Kukkoka wrote after Vatsya, otherwise Vatsya would assuredly have mentioned him as an author in this branch of literature along with the others.

The author of the 'Five Arrows' was one Jyotirisha. He is called the chief ornament of poets, the treasure of the sixty-four arts, and the best teacher of the rules of music. He says that he composed the work after reflecting on the aphorisms of love as revealed by the gods, and studying the opinions of Gonikaputra, Muladeva, Babhravya, Ramtideva, Nundikeshwara and Kshemandra. It is impossible to say whether he had perused all the works of these authors, or had only heard about them; anyhow, none of them appear to be in existence now. This work contains nearly six hundred verses, and is divided into five chapters, called Sayakas or Arrows.

The author of the 'Light of Love' was the poet Gunakara, the son of Vechapati. The work contains four hundred verses, and gives only a short account of the doctrines of love, dealing more with other matters.

'The Garland of Love' is the work of the famous poet Jayadeva, who said about himself that he is a writer on all subjects. This treatise is, however, very short, containing only one hundred and twenty-five verses.

The author of the 'Sprout of Love' was a poet called Bhanudatta. It appears from the last verse of the manuscript that he was a resident of the province of Tirhoot, and son of a Brahman named Ganeshwar, who was also a poet. The work, written in Sanscrit, gives the descriptions of different classes of men and women, their classes being made out from their age, description, conduct, etc. It contains three chapters, and its date is not known, and cannot be ascertained.

'The Stage of Love' was composed by the poet Kullianmull, for the amusement of Ladkhan, the son of Ahmed Lodi, the same Ladkhan being in some places spoken of as Ladana Mull, and in others as Ladanaballa. He is supposed to have been a relation or connection of the house of Lodi, which reigned in Hindostan from A.D. 1450–1526. The work would, therefore, have been written in the fifteenth or sixteenth century. It contains ten chapters, and has been translated into English but only six copies were printed for private circulation. This is supposed to be the latest of the Sanscrit works on the subject, and the ideas in it were evidently taken from previous writings of the same nature.

The contents of these works are in themselves a literary curiosity. There are to be found both in Sanscrit poetry and in the Sanscrit drama a certain amount of poetical sentiment and romance, which have, in every country and in every language, thrown an immortal halo round the subject. But here it is treated in a plain, simple, matter of fact sort of way. Men and women are divided into classes and divisions in the same way that Buffon and other writers on natural history have classified and divided the animal world. As Venus was represented by the Greeks to stand forth as the type of the beauty of woman, so the Hindoos describe the Padmini or Lotus woman as the type of most perfect feminine excellence, as follows:

She in whom the following signs and symptoms appear is called a Padmini. Her face is pleasing as the full moon; her body, well clothed with flesh, is soft as the Shiras or mustard flower, her skin is fine, tender and fair as the yellow lotus, never dark coloured. Her eyes are bright and beautiful as the orbs of the fawn, well cut, and with reddish corners. Her bosom is hard, full and high; she has a good neck; her nose is straight and lovely, and three folds or wrinkles cross her middle—about the umbilical region. Her yoni resembles the opening lotus bud, and her love seed (Kama salila) is perfumed like the lily that has newly burst. She walks with swan-like gait, and her voice is low and musical as the note of the Kokila bird, she delights in white raiments, in fine jewels, and in rich dresses. She eats little, sleeps lightly, and being as respectful and religious as she is clever and courteous, she is ever anxious to worship the gods, and to enjoy the conversation of Brahmans. Such, then, is the Padmini or Lotus woman.

Detailed descriptions then follow of the Chitrini or Art woman; the Shankhini or Conch woman, and the Hastini or Elephant woman, their days of enjoyment, their various seats of passion, the manner in which they should be manipulated and treated in sexual intercourse, along with the characteristics of the men and women of the various countries in Hindostan. The details are so numerous, and the subjects so seriously dealt with, and at such length, that neither time nor space will permit of their being given here.

One work in the English language is somewhat similar to these works of the Hindoos. It is called 'Kalogynomia: or the Laws of Female Beauty', being the elementary principles of that science, by T. Bell, M.D., with twenty-four plates, and printed in London in 1821. It treats of Beauty, of Love, of Sexual Intercourse, of the Laws regulating that Intercourse, of Monogamy and Polygamy, of Prostitution, of Infidelity, ending with a *catalogue raisonnée* of the defects of female beauty.

Other works in English also enter into great details of private and domestic life: The Elements of Social Science, or Physical, Sexual and Natural Religion, by a Doctor of Medicine, London, 1880, and Every Woman's Book, by Dr Waters, 1826. To persons interested in the above subjects these works will be found to contain such details as have been seldom before published, and which ought to be thoroughly understood by all philanthropists and benefactors of society.

After a perusal of the Hindoo work, and of the English books above mentioned, the reader will understand the subject, at all events from a materialistic, realistic and practical point of view. If all science is founded more or less on a stratum of facts, there can be no harm in making known to mankind generally certain matters intimately connected with their private, domestic, and social life.

Alas! complete ignorance of them has unfortunately wrecked many a man and many a woman, while a little knowledge of a subject generally ignored by the masses would have enabled numbers of people to have understood many things which they believed to be quite incomprehensible, or which were not thought worthy of their consideration.

INTRODUCTION

It may be interesting to some persons to learn how it came about that Vatsyayana was first brought to light and translated into the English language. It happened thus. While translating with the pundits the 'Anunga Runga, or the stage of love', reference was frequently found to be made to one Vatsya. The sage Vatsya was of this opinion, or of that opinion. The sage Vatsya said this, and so on. Naturally questions were asked who the sage was, and the pundits replied that Vatsya was the author of the standard work on love in Sanscrit literature, that no Sanscrit library was complete without his work, and that it was most difficult now to obtain in its entire state. The copy of the manuscript obtained in Bombay was defective, and so the pundits wrote to Benares, Calcutta and Jeypoor for copies of the manuscript from Sanscrit libraries in those places. Copies having been obtained, they were then compared with each other, and with the aid of a Commentary called 'Jayamangla' a revised copy of the entire manuscript was prepared, and from this copy the English translation was made. The following is the certificate of the chief pundit:

'The accompanying manuscript is corrected by me after comparing four different copies of the work. I had the assistance of a Commentary called "Jayamangla" for correcting the portion in the first five parts, but found great difficulty in correcting the remaining portion, because, with the exception of one copy thereof which was tolerably correct, all the other copies I had were far too incorrect. However, I took that portion as correct in which the majority of the copies agreed with each other.'

The 'Aphorisms on Love' by Vatsyayana contain about one thousand two hundred and fifty slokas or verses, and are divided into parts, parts into chapters, and chapters into paragraphs. The whole consists of seven parts, thirty-six chapters, and sixty-four paragraphs. Hardly anything is known about the author. His real name is supposed to be Mallinaga or Mrillana, Vatsyayana being his family name. At the close of the work this is what he writes about himself:

'After reading and considering the works of Babhravya and other ancient authors, and thinking over the meaning of the rules given by them, this treatise was composed, according to the precepts of the Holy Writ, for the benefit of the world, by Vatsyayana, while leading the life of a religious student at Benares, and wholly engaged in the contemplation of the Deity. This work is not to be used merely as an instrument for satisfying our desires. A person acquainted with the true principles of this science, who preserves his Dharma (virtue or religious merit), his Artha (worldly wealth) and his Kama (pleasure or sensual gratification), and who has regard to the customs of the people, is sure to obtain the mastery over his senses. In short, an intelligent and knowing person attending to Dharma and Artha and also to Kama, without becoming the slave of his passions, will obtain success in everything that he may do.'

It is impossible to fix the exact date either of the life of Vatsyayana or of his work. It is supposed that he must have lived between the first and sixth century of the Christian era, on the following grounds. He mentions that Satakarni Satavahana, a king of Kuntal, killed Malayevati his wife with an instrument called kartari by striking her in the passion of love, and Vatsya quotes this case to warn people of the danger arising from some old customs of striking women when under the influence of this passion. Now this king of Kuntal is believed to have lived and reigned during the first century A.D., and consequently Vatsya must have lived after him. On the other hand, Virahamihira, in the eighteenth chapter of his 'Brihatsanhita', treats of the science of love, and appears to have borrowed largely from Vatsyayana on the subject. Now Virahamihira is said to have lived during the sixth century A.D., and as Vatsya must have written his works previously, therefore not earlier than the first century A.D., and not later than the sixth century A.D., must be considered as the approximate date of his existence.

On the text of the 'Aphorisms on Love', by Vatsyayana, only two commentaries have been found. One called 'Jayamangla' or 'Sutrabashya', and the other 'Sutra vritti'. The date of the 'Jayamangla' is fixed between the tenth and thirteenth century A.D., because while treating of the sixty-four arts an example is taken from the 'Kavyaprakasha' which was written about the tenth century A.D. Again, the copy of the commentary procured was evidently a transcript of a manuscript which once had a place in the library of a Chaulukyan king named Vishaladeva, a fact elicited from the following sentence at the end of it.

'Here ends the part relating to the art of love in the commentary on the "Vatsyayana Kama Sutra", a copy from the library of the king of kings, Vishaladeva, who was a powerful hero, as it were a second Arjuna, and head jewel of the Chaulukya family.'

Now it is well known that this king ruled in Guzerat from 1244 to 1262 A.D., and founded a city called Visalnagur. The date, therefore, of the commentary is taken to be not earlier than the tenth and not later than the thirteenth century. The author of it is supposed to be one Yashodhara, the name given him by his preceptor being Indrapada. He seems to have written it during the time of affliction caused by his separation from a clever and shrewd woman, at least that is what he himself says at the end of each chapter. It is presumed that he called his work after the name of his absent mistress, or the word may have some connection with the meaning of her name.

This commentary was most useful in explaining the true

meaning of Vatsyayana, for the commentator appears to have had a considerable knowledge of the times of the older author, and gives in some places very minute information. This cannot be said of the other commentary, called 'Sutra vritti', which was written about A.D. 1789, by Narsing Shastri, a pupil of a Sarveshwar Shastri; the latter was a descendant of Bhaskur, and so also was our author, for at the conclusion of every part he calls himself Bhaskur Narsing Shastri. He was induced to write the work by order of the learned Raja Vrijalala, while he was residing in Benares, but as to the merits of this commentary it does not deserve much commendation. In many cases the writer does not appear to have understood the meaning of the original author, and has changed the text in many places to fit in with his own explanations.

A complete translation of the original work now follows. It has been prepared in complete accordance with the text of the manuscript, and is given, without further comments, as made from it.

PART I

INTRODUCTORY

CHAPTER I

PREFACE

Salutation to Dharma, Artha and Kama

In the beginning, the Lord of Beings created men and women, and in the form of commandments in one hundred thousand chapters laid down rules for regulating their existence with regard to Dharma,[1] Artha,[2] and Kama.[3] Some of these commandments, namely those which treated of Dharma, were separately written by Swayambhu Manu; those that related to Artha were compiled by Brihaspati; and those that referred to Kama were expounded by Nandi, the follower of Mahadeva, in one thousand chapters.

Now these 'Kama Sutra' (Aphorisms on Love), written by Nandi in one thousand chapters, were reproduced by Shvetaketu, the son of Uddvalaka, in an abbreviated form in five hundred chapters, and this work was again similarly reproduced in an abridged form, in one hundred and fifty chapters, by Babhravya, an inheritant of the Punchala (South of Delhi) country. These one hundred and fifty chapters were then put together under seven heads or parts named severally

1. Sadharana (general topics)
2. Samprayogika (embraces, etc.)
3. Kanya Samprayuktaka (union of males and females)
4. Bharyadhikarika (on one's own wife)

[1] Dharma is acquisition of religious merit, and is fully described in Chapter 5, Volume III, of Talboys Wheeler's *History of India*, and in the edicts of Asoka.

[2] Artha is acquisition of wealth and property, etc.

[3] Kama is love, pleasure and sensual gratification.

These three words are retained throughout in their original, as technical terms. They may also be defined as virtue, wealth and pleasure, the three things repeatedly spoken of in the Laws of Manu.

5. Paradika (on the wives of other people)
6. Vaisika (on courtesans)
7. Aupamishadika (on the arts of seduction, tonic medicines, etc.)

The sixth part of this last work was separately expounded by Dattaka at the request of the public women of Pataliputra (Patna), and in the same way Charayana explained the first part of it. The remaining parts, viz. the second, third, fourth, fifth, and seventh, were each separately expounded by

Suvarnanabha (second part)
Ghotakamukha (third part)
Gonardiya (fourth part)
Gonikaputra (fifth part)
Kuchumara (seventh part), respectively.

Thus the work being written in parts by different authors was almost unobtainable and, as the parts which were expounded by Dattaka and the others treated only of the particular branches of the subject to which each part related, and moreover as the original work of Babhravya was difficult to be mastered on account of its length, Vatsyayana, therefore, composed his work in a small volume as an abstract of the whole of the works of the above named authors.

PART I: INTRODUCTORY

PART V: ABOUT THE WIVES OF OTHER PEOPLE

PART VI: ABOUT COURTESANS

CHAPTER II

ON THE ACQUISITION OF DHARMA, ARTHA AND KAMA

MAN, the period of whose life is one hundred years, should practise Dharma, Artha and Kama at different times and in such a manner that they may harmonize together and not clash in any way. He should acquire learning in his childhood, in his youth and middle age he should attend to Artha and Kama, and in his old age he should perform Dharma, and thus seek to gain Moksha, i.e. release from further transmigration. Or, on account of the uncertainty of life, he may practise them at times when they are enjoined to be practised. But one thing is to be noted, he should lead the life of a religious student until he finishes his education.

Dharma is obedience to the command of the Shastra or Holy Writ of the Hindoos to do certain things, such as the performance of sacrifices, which are not generally done, because they do not belong to this world, and produce no visible effect; and not to do other things, such as eating meat, which is often done because it belongs to this world, and has visible effects.

Dharma should be learnt from the Shruti (Holy Writ), and from those conversant with it.

Artha is the acquisition of arts, land, gold, cattle, wealth, equipages and friends. It is, further, the protection of what is acquired, and the increase of what is protected.

Artha should be learnt from the king's officers, and from merchants who may be versed in the ways of commerce.

Kama is the enjoyment of appropriate objects by the five senses of hearing, feeling, seeing, tasting and smelling, assisted by the mind together with the soul. The ingredient in this is a peculiar contact between the organ of sense and its object, and the consciousness of pleasure which arises from that contact is called Kama.

Kama is to be learnt from the Kama Sutra (aphorisms on love) and from the practice of citizens.

When all the three, viz. Dharma, Artha and Kama, come together, the former is better than the one which follows it, i.e. Dharma is better than Artha, and Artha is better than Kama. But Artha should always be first practised by the king for the livelihood of men is to be obtained from it only. Again, Kama being the occupation of public women, they should prefer it to the other two, and these are exceptions to the general rule.

Objection 1

Some learned men say that as Dharma is connected with things not belonging to this world, it is appropriately treated of in a book; and so also is Artha, because it is practised only by the application of proper means, and a knowledge of those means can only be obtained by study and from books. But Kama being a thing which is practised even by the brute creation, and which is to be found everywhere, does not want any work on the subject.

Answer

This is not so. Sexual intercourse being a thing dependent on man and woman requires the application of proper means by them, and those means are to be learnt from the Kama Shastra. The non-application of proper means, which we see in the brute creation, is caused by their being unrestrained, and by the females among them only being fit for sexual intercourse at certain seasons and no more, and by their intercourse not being preceded by thought of any kind.

Objection 2

The Lokayatikas[1] say: Religious ordinances should not be observed, for they bear a future fruit, and at the same time it is also doubtful whether they will bear any fruit at all. What foolish person will give away that which is in his own hands into the hands of another? Moreover, it is better to have a pigeon today than a peacock tomorrow; and a copper coin which we have the certainty of obtaining, is better than a gold coin, the possession of which is doubtful.

Answer

It is not so. 1st. Holy Writ, which ordains the practice of Dharma, does not admit of a doubt.

2nd. Sacrifices such as those made for the destruction of enemies, or for the fall of rain, are seen to bear fruit.

3rd. The sun, moon, stars, planets and other heavenly bodies appear to work intentionally for the good of the world.

4th. The existence of this world is effected by the observance of the rules respecting the four classes of men and their four stages of life.[2]

5th. We see that seed is thrown into the ground with the hope of future crops.

Vatsyayana is therefore of opinion that the ordinances of religion must be obeyed.

Objection 3

Those who believe that destiny is the prime mover of all things say: We should not exert ourselves to acquire wealth, for sometimes it is not acquired although we strive to get it, while at other times it comes to us of itself without any

[1] These were certainly materialists who seemed to think that a bird in the hand was worth two in the bush.

[2] Among the Hindoos the four classes of men are the Brahmans or priestly class, the Kshutrya or warlike class, the Vaishya or agricultural and mercantile class, and the Shoodra or menial class. The four stages of life are, the life of a religious student, the life of a householder, the life of a hermit, and the life of a Sunyasi or devotee.

exertion on our part. Everything is therefore in the power of destiny, who is the lord of gain and loss, of success and defeat, of pleasure and pain. Thus we see that Bali[1] was raised to the throne of Indra by destiny, and was also put down by the same power, and it is destiny only that can re-instate him.

Answer

It is not right to say so. As the acquisition of every object pre-supposes at all events some exertion on the part of man, the application of proper means may be said to be the cause of gaining all our ends, and this application of proper means being thus necessary (even where a thing is destined to happen), it follows that a person who does nothing will enjoy no happiness.

Objection 4

Those who are inclined to think that Artha is the chief object to be obtained argue thus. Pleasures should not be sought for, because they are obstacles to the practice of Dharma and Artha, which are both superior to them, and are also disliked by meritorious persons. Pleasures also bring a man into distress, and into contact with low persons; they cause him to commit unrighteous deeds, and produce impurity in him; they make him regardless of the future, and encourage carelessness and levity. And lastly, they cause him to be disbelieved by all, received by none, and despised by everybody, including himself. It is notorious, moreover, that many men who have given themselves up to pleasure alone, have been ruined along with their families and relations. Thus, king Dandakya, of the Bhoja dynasty, carried off a Brahman's daughter with evil intent, and was eventually ruined and lost his kingdom. Indra, too, having violated the chastity of Ahalya, was made to suffer for it. In a like manner the mighty Kichaka, who tried to seduce

[1] Bali was a demon who had conquered Indra and gained his throne, but was afterwards overcome by Vishnu at the time of his fifth incarnation.

Draupadi, and Ravana, who attempted to gain over Sita, were punished for their crimes. These and many others fell by reason of their pleasures.[1]

Answer

This objection cannot be sustained, for pleasures, being as necessary for the existence and well being of the body as food, are consequently equally required. They are, moreover, the results of Dharma and Artha. Pleasures are, therefore, to be followed with moderation and caution. No one refrains from cooking food because there are beggars to ask for it, or from sowing seed because there are deer to destroy the corn when it is grown up.

Thus a man practising Dharma, Artha and Kama enjoys happiness both in this world and in the world to come. The good perform those actions in which there is no fear as to what is to result from them in the next world, and in which there is no danger to their welfare. Any action which conduces to the practice of Dharma, Artha and Kama together, or of any two, or even one of them, should be performed, but an action which conduces to the practice of one of them at the expense of the remaining two should not be performed.

[1] Dandakya is said to have abducted from the forest the daughter of a Brahman, named Bhargava, and, being cursed by the Brahman, was buried with his kingdom under a shower of dust. The place was called after his name the Dandaka forest, celebrated in the Ramayana, but now unknown.

Ahalya was the wife of the sage Gautama. Indra caused her to believe that he was Gautama, and thus enjoyed her. He was cursed by Gautama and subsequently afflicted with a thousand ulcers on his body.

Kichaka was the brother-in-law of King Virata, with whom the Pandavas had taken refuge for one year. Kichaka was killed by Bhima, who assumed the disguise of Draupadi. For this story the Mahabarata should be referred to.

The story of Ravana is told in the Ramayana, which with the Mahabarata form the two great epic poems of the Hindoos; the latter was written by Vyasa, and the former by Valmiki.

CHAPTER III

ON THE ARTS AND SCIENCES TO BE STUDIED

MAN should study the Kama Sutra and the arts and sciences subordinate thereto, in addition to the study of the arts and sciences contained in Dharma and Artha. Even young maids should study this Kama Sutra along with its arts and sciences before marriage, and after it they should continue to do so with the consent of their husbands.

Here some learned men object, and say that females, not being allowed to study any science, should not study the Kama Sutra.

But Vatsyayana is of opinion that this objection does not hold good, for women already know the practice of Kama Sutra, and that practice is derived from the Kama Shastra, or the science of Kama itself. Moreover, it is not only in this but in many other cases that, though the practice of a science is known to all, only a few persons are acquainted with the rules and laws on which the science is based. Thus the Yadnikas or sacrificers, though ignorant of grammar, make use of appropriate words when addressing the different Deities, and do not know how these words are framed. Again, persons do the duties required of them on auspicious days, which are fixed by astrology, though they are not acquainted with the science of astrology. In a like manner riders of horses and elephants train these animals without knowing the science of training animals, but from practice only. And similarly the people of the most distant provinces obey the laws of the kingdom from practice, and because there is a king over them, and without further reason.[1] And from experience we find that some women,

[1] The author wishes to prove that a great many things are done by people

such as daughters of princes and their ministers, and public women, are actually versed in the Kama Shastra.

A female, therefore, should learn the Kama Shastra, or at least a part of it, by studying its practice from some confidential friend. She should study alone in private the sixty-four practices that form a part of the Kama Shastra. Her teacher should be one of the following persons: the daughter of a nurse brought up with her and already married,[1] or a female friend who can be trusted in everything, or the sister of her mother (i.e. her aunt), or an old female servant, or a female beggar who may have formerly lived in the family, or her own sister who can always be trusted.

The following are the arts to be studied, together with the Kama Sutra:

Singing

Playing on musical instruments

Dancing

Union of dancing, singing, and playing instrumental music

Writing and drawing

Tattooing

Arraying and adorning an idol with rice and flowers

Spreading and arranging beds or couches of flowers, or flowers upon the ground

Colouring the teeth, garments, hair, nails and bodies, i.e. staining, dyeing, colouring and painting the same

Fixing stained glass into a floor

The art of making beds, and spreading out carpets and cushions for reclining

Playing on musical glasses filled with water

Storing and accumulating water in aqueducts, cisterns and reservoirs

Picture making, trimming and decorating

---

from practice and custom, without their being acquainted with the reason of things, or the laws on which they are based, and this is perfectly true.

[1] The proviso of being married applies to all the teachers.

Stringing of rosaries, necklaces, garlands and wreaths

Binding of turbans and chaplets, and making crests and top-knots of flowers

Scenic representations, stage playing

Art of making ear ornaments

Art of preparing perfumes and odours

Proper disposition of jewels and decorations, and adornment in dress

Magic or sorcery

Quickness of hand or manual skill

Culinary art, i.e. cooking and cookery

Making lemonades, sherbets, acidulated drinks, and spirituous extracts with proper flavour and colour

Tailor's work and sewing

Making parrots, flowers, tufts, tassels, bunches, bosses, knobs, etc., out of yarn or thread

Solution of riddles, enigmas, covert speeches, verbal puzzles and enigmatical questions

A game, which consisted in repeating verses, and as one person finished, another person had to commence at once, repeating another verse, beginning with the same letter with which the last speaker's verse ended, whoever failed to repeat was considered to have lost, and to be subject to pay a forfeit or stake of some kind

The art of mimicry or imitation

Reading, including chanting and intoning

Study of sentences difficult to pronounce. It is played as a game chiefly by women, and children and consists of a difficult sentence being given, and when repeated quickly, the words are often transposed or badly pronounced

Practice with sword, single stick, quarter staff and bow and arrow

Drawing inferences, reasoning or inferring

Carpentry, or the work of a carpenter

Architecture, or the art of building

Knowledge about gold and silver coins, and jewels and gems

Chemistry and mineralogy

Colouring jewels, gems and beads

Knowledge of mines and quarries

Gardening; knowledge of treating the diseases of trees and plants, of nourishing them, and determining their ages

Art of cock fighting, quail fighting and ram fighting

Art of teaching parrots and starlings to speak

Art of applying perfumed ointments to the body, and of dressing the hair with unguents and perfumes and braiding it

The art of understanding writing in cypher, and the writing of words in a peculiar way

The art of speaking by changing the forms of words. It is of various kinds. Some speak by changing the beginning and end of words, others by adding unnecessary letters between every syllable of a word, and so on

Knowledge of language and of the vernacular dialects

Art of making flower carriages

Art of framing mystical diagrams, of addressing spells and charms, and binding armlets

Mental exercises, such as completing stanzas or verses on receiving a part of them; or supplying one, two or three lines when the remaining lines are given indiscriminately from different verses, so as to make the whole an entire verse with regard to its meaning; or arranging the words of a verse written irregularly by separating the vowels from the consonants, or leaving them out altogether; or putting into verse or prose sentences represented by signs or symbols. There are many other such exercises.

Composing poems

Knowledge of dictionaries and vocabularies

Knowledge of ways of changing and disguising the appearance of persons

Knowledge of the art of changing the appearance of things, such as making cotton to appear as silk, coarse and common things to appear as fine and good

Various ways of gambling

Art of obtaining possession of the property of others by means of muntras or incantations

Skill in youthful sports

Knowledge of the rules of society, and of how to pay respect and compliments to others

Knowledge of the art of war, of arms, of armies, etc.

Knowledge of gymnastics

Art of knowing the character of a man from his features

Knowledge of scanning or constructing verses

Arithmetical recreations

Making artificial flowers

Making figures and images in clay

A public woman, endowed with a good disposition, beauty and other winning qualities, and also versed in the above arts, obtains the name of a Ganika, or public woman of high quality, and receives a seat of honour in an assemblage of men. She is, moreover, always respected by the king, and praised by learned men, and her favour being sought for by all, she becomes an object of universal regard. The daughter of a king too as well as the daughter of a minister, being learned in the above arts, can make their husbands favourable to them, even though these may have thousands of other wives besides themselves. And in the same manner, if a wife becomes separated from her husband, and falls into distress, she can support herself easily, even in a foreign country, by means of her knowledge of these arts. Even the bare knowledge of them gives attractiveness to a woman, though the practice of them may be only possible or otherwise according to the circumstances of each case. A man who is versed in these arts, who is loquacious and acquainted with the arts of gallantry, gains very soon the hearts of women, even though he is only acquainted with them for a short time.

CHAPTER IV

THE LIFE OF A CITIZEN

HAVING thus acquired learning, a man, with the wealth that he may have gained by gift, conquest, purchase, deposit,[1] or inheritance from his ancestors, should become a householder, and pass the life of a citizen.[2] He should take a house in a city, or large village, or in the vicinity of good men, or in a place which is the resort of many persons. This abode should be situated near some water, and divided into different compartments for different purposes. It should be surrounded by a garden, and also contain two rooms, an outer and an inner one. The inner room should be occupied by the females, while the outer room, balmy with rich perfumes, should contain a bed, soft, agreeable to the sight, covered with a clean white cloth, low in the middle part, having garlands and bunches of flowers[3] upon it, and a canopy above it, and two pillows, one at the top, another at the bottom. There should be also a sort of couch besides, and at the head of this a sort of stool, on which should be placed the fragrant ointments for the night, as well as flowers, pots containing collyrium and other fragrant substances, things used for perfuming the mouth, and the bark of the common citron tree. Near the couch, on the ground, there should be a pot for spitting, a box containing ornaments, and also a lute hanging from a peg made of the tooth of an elephant, a board for drawing, a pot containing perfume, some books, and some garlands of the yellow

[1] Gift is peculiar to a Brahman, conquest to a Kshatrya, while purchase, deposit, and other means of acquiring wealth belongs to the Vaishya.

[2] This term would appear to apply generally to an inhabitant of Hindoostan. It is not meant only for a dweller in a city, like the Latin Urbanus as opposed to Rusticus.

[3] Natural garden flowers.

amaranth flowers. Not far from the couch, and on the ground, there should be a round seat, a toy cart, and a board for playing with dice; outside the outer room there should be cages of birds,[1] and a separate place for spinning, carving and such like diversions. In the garden there should be a whirling swing and a common swing, as also a bower of creepers covered with flowers, in which a raised parterre should be made for sitting.

Now the householder, having got up in the morning and performed his necessary duties,[2] should wash his teeth, apply a limited quantity of ointments and perfumes to his body, put some ornamants on his person and collyrium on his eyelids and below his eyes, colour his lips with alacktaka,[3] and look at himself in the glass. Having then eaten betel leaves, with other things that give fragrance to the mouth, he should perform his usual business. He should bathe daily, anoint his body with oil every other day, apply a lathering substance[4] to his body every three days, get his head (including face) shaved every four days and the other parts of his body every five or ten days.[5] All these things should be done without fail, and the sweat of the armpits should also be removed. Meals should be taken in the forenoon, in the afternoon, and again at night, according to Charayana. After breakfast, parrots and other birds should be taught to speak, and the fighting of cocks, quails, and rams should follow. A limited time should be devoted to diversions with Pithamardas, Vitas, and Vidushakas,[6] and then should be taken the midday sleep.[7] After

[1] Such as quails, partridges, parrots, starlings, etc.

[2] The calls of nature are always performed by the Hindoos the first thing in the morning.

[3] A colour made from lac.

[4] This would act instead of soap, which was not introduced until the rule of the Mahomedans.

[5] Ten days are allowed when the hair is taken out with a pair of pincers.

[6] These are characters generally introduced in the Hindoo drama; their characteristics will be explained further on.

[7] Noonday sleep is only allowed in summer, when the nights are short.

this the householder, having put on his clothes and ornaments, should, during the afternoon, converse with his friends. In the evening there should be singing, and after that the householder, along with his friend, should await in his room, previously decorated and perfumed, the arrival of the woman that may be attached to him, or he may send a female messenger for her, or go for her himself. After her arrival at his house, he and his friend should welcome her, and entertain her with a loving and agreeable conversation. Thus end the duties of the day.

The following are the things to be done occasionally as diversions or amusements:

Holding festivals[1] in honour of different Deities
Social gatherings of both sexes
Drinking parties
Picnics
Other social diversions

Festivals

On some particular auspicious day, an assembly of citizens should be convened in the temple of Saraswati.[2] There the skill of singers, and of others who may have come recently to the town, should be tested, and on the following day they should always be given some rewards. After that they may either be retained or dismissed, according as their performances are liked or not by the assembly. The members of the assembly should act in concert, both in times of distress as well as in times of prosperity, and it is also the duty of these citizens to show hospitality to strangers who may have come to the assembly.

[1] These are very common in all parts of India.

[2] In the 'Asiatic Miscellany', and in Sir W. Jones's works, will be found a spirited hymn addressed to this goddess, who is adored as the patroness of the fine arts, especially of music and rhetoric, as the inventress of the Sanscrit language, etc. etc. She is the goddess of harmony, eloquence and language, and is somewhat analogous to Minerva. For further information about her, see Edward Moor's *Hindoo Pantheon*.

What is said above should be understood to apply to all the other festivals which may be held in honour of the different Deities, according to the present rules.

Social Gatherings

When men of the same age, disposition and talents, fond of the same diversions and with the same degree of education, sit together in company with public women,[1] or in an assembly of citizens, or at the abode of one among themselves, and engage in agreeable discourse with each other, such is called a sitting in company or a social gathering. The subjects of discourse are to be the completion of verses half composed by others, and the testing the knowledge of one another in the various arts. The women who may be the most beautiful, who may like the same things that the men like, and who may have power to attract the minds of others, are here done homage to.

Drinking Parties

Men and women should drink in one another's houses. And here the men should cause the public women to drink, and should then drink themselves, liquors such as the Madhu, Aireya, Sara and Asawa, which are of bitter and sour taste; also drinks concocted from the barks of various trees, wild fruits and leaves.

[1] The public women, or courtesans (Vesya), of the early Hindoos have often been compared with the Hetera of the Greeks. The subject is dealt with at some length in H. H. Wilson's *Select Specimens of the Theatre of the Hindoos*, in two volumes, Trubner and Co., 1871. It may be fairly considered that the courtesan was one of the elements, and an important element too, of early Hindoo society, and that her education and intellect were both superior to that of the women of the household. Wilson says, 'By the Vesya or courtesan, however, we are not to understand a female who has disregarded the obligation of law or the precepts of virtue, but a character reared by a state of manners unfriendly to the admission of wedded females into society, and opening it only at the expense of reputation to women who were trained for association with men by personal and mental acquirements to which the matron was a stranger.'

Going to Gardens or Picnics

In the forenoon, men having dressed themselves should go to gardens on horseback, accompanied by public women and followed by servants. And having done there all the duties of the day, and passed the time in various agreeable diversions, such as the fighting of quails, cocks and rams, and other spectacles, they should return home in the afternoon in the same manner, bringing with them bunches of flowers, etc.

The same also applies to bathing in summer in water from which wicked or dangerous animals have previously been taken out, and which has been built in on all sides.

Other Social Diversions

Spending nights playing with dice. Going out on moonlight nights. Keeping the festive day in honour of spring. Plucking the sprouts and fruits of the mango trees. Eating the fibres of lotuses. Eating the tender ears of corn. Picnicing in the forests when the trees get their new foliage. The Udakakashvedika or sporting in the water. Decorating each other with the flowers of some trees. Pelting each other with the flowers of the Kadamba tree, and many other sports which may either be known to the whole country, or may be peculiar to particular parts of it. These and similar other amusements should always be carried on by citizens.

The above amusements should be followed by a person who diverts himself alone in company with a courtesan, as well as by a courtesan who can do the same in company with her maid servants or with citizens.

A Pithamarda[1] is a man without wealth, alone in the world, whose only property consists of his Mallika,[2] some

[1] According to this description a Pithamarda would be a sort of professor of all the arts, and as such received as the friend and confidant of the citizens.

[2] A seat in the form of the letter T.

lathering substance and a red cloth, who comes from a good country, and who is skilled in all the arts; and by teaching these arts is received in the company of citizens, and in the abode of public women.

A Vita[1] is a man who has enjoyed the pleasures of fortune, who is a compatriot of the citizens with whom he associates, who is possessed of the qualities of a householder, who has his wife with him, and who is honoured in the assembly of citizens and in the abodes of public women, and lives on their means and on them.

A Vidushaka[2] (also called a Vaihasaka, i.e. one who provokes laughter) is a person only acquainted with some of the arts, who is a jester, and who is trusted by all.

These persons are employed in matters of quarrels and reconciliations between citizens and public women.

This remark applies also to female beggars, to women with their heads shaved, to adulterous women, and to old public women skilled in all the various arts.

Thus a citizen living in his town or village, respected by all, should call on the persons of his own caste who may be worth knowing. He should converse in company and gratify his friends by his society, and obliging others by his assistance in various matters, he should cause them to assist one another in the same way.

There are some verses on this subject as follows:

'A citizen discoursing, not entirely in the Sanscrit

[1] The Vita is supposed to represent somewhat the character of the Parasite of the Greek comedy. It is possible that he was retained about the person of the wealthy and dissipated as a kind of private instructor, as well as an entertaining companion.

[2] Vidushaka is evidently the buffoon and jester. Wilson says of him that he is the humble companion, not the servant, of a prince or man of rank, and it is a curious peculiarity that he is always a Brahman. He bears more affinity to Sancho Panza, perhaps, than any other character in western fiction, imitating him in his combination of shrewdness and simplicity, his fondness of good living and his love of ease. In the dramas of intrigue he exhibits some of the talents of Mercury, but with less activity and ingenuity, and occasionally suffers by his interference. According to the technical definition of his attributes he is to excite mirth by being ridiculous in person, age, and attire.

language,[1] nor wholly in the dialects of the country, on various topics in society, obtains great respect. The wise should not resort to a society disliked by the public, governed by no rules, and intent on the destruction of others. But a learned man living in a society which acts according to the wishes of the people, and which has pleasure for its only object is highly respected in this world.'

[1] This means, it is presumed, that the citizen should be acquainted with several languages. The middle part of this paragraph might apply to the Nihilists and Fenians of the day, or to secret societies. It was perhaps a reference to the Thugs.

CHAPTER V

ABOUT THE KINDS OF WOMEN RESORTED TO BY THE CITIZENS, AND OF FRIENDS AND MESSENGERS

WHEN Kama is practised by men of the four castes according to the rules of the Holy Writ (i.e. by lawful marriage) with virgins of their own caste, it then becomes a means of acquiring lawful progeny and good fame, and it is not also opposed to the customs of the world. On the contrary the practice of Kama with women of the higher castes, and with those previously enjoyed by others, even though they be of the same caste, is prohibited. But the practice of Kama with women of the lower castes, with women excommunicated from their own caste, with public women, and with women twice married,[1] is neither enjoined nor prohibited. The object of practising Kama with such women is pleasure only.

Nayikas,[2] therefore, are of three kinds, viz. maids, women twice married, and public women. Gonikaputra has expressed an opinion that there is a fourth kind of Nayika, viz. a woman who is resorted to on some special occasion even though she be previously married to another. These special occasions are when a man thinks thus:

This woman is self-willed, and has been previously

[1] This term does not apply to a widow, but to a woman who has probably left her husband, and is living with some other person as a married woman, *maritalement*, as they say in France.

[2] Any woman fit to be enjoyed without sin. The object of the enjoyment of women is twofold, viz. pleasure and progeny. Any woman who can be enjoyed without sin for the purpose of accomplishing either the one or the other of these two objects is a Nayika. The fourth kind of Nayika which Vatsya admits further on is neither enjoyed for pleasure or for progeny, but merely for accomplishing some special purpose in hand. The word Nayika is retained as a technical term throughout.

enjoyed by many others besides myself. I may, therefore, safely resort to her as to a public woman though she belongs to a higher caste than mine, and, in so doing, I shall not be violating the ordinances of Dharma.

Or thus:

This is a twice-married woman and has been enjoyed by others before me; there is, therefore, no objection to my resorting to her.

Or thus:

This woman has gained the heart of her great and powerful husband, and exercises a mastery over him, who is a friend of my enemy; if, therefore, she becomes united with me she will cause her husband to abandon my enemy.

Or thus:

This woman will turn the mind of her husband, who is very powerful, in my favour, he being at present disaffected towards me, and intent on doing me some harm.

Or thus:

By making this woman my friend I shall gain the object of some friend of mine, or shall be able to effect the ruin of some enemy, or shall accomplish some other difficult purpose.

Or thus:

By being united with this woman, I shall kill her husband, and so obtain his vast riches which I covet.

Or thus:

The union of this woman with me is not attended with any danger, and will bring me wealth, of which, on account of my poverty and inability to support myself, I am very much in need. I shall therefore obtain her vast riches in this way without any difficulty.

Or thus:

This woman loves me ardently, and knows all my weak points; if therefore, I am unwilling to be united with her, she will make my faults public, and thus tarnish my character and reputation. Or she will bring some gross accusation against me, of which it may be hard to clear myself, and I shall be ruined. Or perhaps she will detach from me her husband who is powerful, and yet under her control, and will unite him to my enemy, or will herself join the latter.

Or thus:

The husband of this woman has violated the chastity of my wives, I shall therefore return that injury by seducing his wives.

Or thus:

By the help of this woman I shall kill an enemy of the king, who has taken shelter with her, and whom I am ordered by the king to destroy.

Or thus:

The woman whom I love is under the control of this woman. I shall, through the influence of the latter, be able to get at the former.

Or thus:

This woman will bring to me a maid, who possesses wealth and beauty, but who is hard to get at, and under the control of another.

Or lastly thus:

My enemy is a friend of this woman's husband, I shall therefore cause her to join him, and will thus create an enmity between her husband and him.

For these and similar other reasons the wives of other men may be resorted to, but it must be distinctly understood that is only allowed for special reasons, and not for mere carnal desire.

Charayana thinks that under these circumstances there is also a fifth kind of Nayika, viz. a woman who is kept by a minister, or who repairs to him occasionally; or a widow who accomplishes the purpose of a man with the person to whom she resorts.

Suvarnanabha adds that a woman who passes the life of an ascetic and in the condition of a widow may be considered as a sixth kind of Nayika.

Ghotakamukha says that the daughter of a public woman, and a female servant, who are still virgins, form a seventh kind of Nayika.

Gonardiya puts forth his doctrine that any woman born of good family, after she has come of age, is an eighth kind of Nayika.

But these four latter kinds of Nayikas do not differ much from the first four kinds of them, as there is no separate object in resorting to them. Therefore, Vatsyayana is of opinion that there are only four kinds of Nayikas, i.e. the maid, the twice-married woman, the public woman, and the woman resorted to for a special purpose.

The following women are not to be enjoyed:

A leper

A lunatic

A woman turned out of caste

A woman who reveals secrets

A woman who publicly expresses desire for sexual intercourse

A woman who is extremely white

A woman who is extremely black

A bad-smelling woman

A woman who is a near relation

A woman who is a female friend

A woman who leads the life of an ascetic

And, lastly the wife of a relation, of a friend, of a learned Brahman, and of the king

The followers of Babhravya say that any woman who has been enjoyed by five men is a fit and proper person to be enjoyed. But Gonikaputra is of opinion that even when this is the case, the wives of a relation, of a learned Brahman and of a king should be excepted.

The following are of the kind of friends:

One who has played with you in the dust, i.e. in childhood

One who is bound by an obligation

One who is of the same disposition and fond of the same things

One who is a fellow student

One who is acquainted with your secrets and faults, and whose faults and secrets are also known to you

One who is a child of your nurse

One who is brought up with you

One who is an hereditary friend

These friends should possess the following qualities:

They should tell the truth

They should not be changed by time

They should be favourable to your designs

They should be firm

They should be free from covetousness

They should not be capable of being gained over by others

They should not reveal your secrets

Charayana says that citizens form friendship with washermen, barbers, cowherds, florists, druggists, betel-leaf sellers, tavern keepers, beggars, Pithamardas, Vitas and Vidushekas, as also with the wives of all these people.

A messenger should possess the following qualities:

Skilfulness

Boldness

Knowledge of the intention of men by their outward signs

Absence of confusion, i.e. no shyness

Knowledge of the exact meaning of what others do or say

Good manners

Knowledge of appropriate times and places for doing different things

Ingenuity in business

Quick comprehension

Quick application of remedies, i.e. quick and ready resources

And this part ends with a verse:

'The man who is ingenious and wise, who is accompanied by a friend, and who knows the intentions of others, as also the proper time and place for doing everything, can gain over, very easily, even a woman who is very hard to be obtained.'

PART II

OF SEXUAL UNION

CHAPTER I

KINDS OF SEXUAL UNION ACCORDING TO DIMENSIONS, FORCE OF DESIRE OR PASSION, TIME

Kinds of Union

MAN is divided into three classes, viz. the hare man, the bull man, and the horse man, according to the size of his lingam.

Woman also, according to the depth of her yoni, is either a female deer, a mare, or a female elephant.

There are thus three equal unions between persons of corresponding dimensions, and there are six unequal unions, when the dimensions do not correspond, or nine in all, as the following table shows:

EQUAL		UNEQUAL	
MEN	WOMEN	MEN	WOMEN
Hare	Deer	Hare	Mare
Bull	Mare	Hare	Elephant
Horse	Elephant	Bull	Deer
		Bull	Elephant
		Horse	Deer
		Horse	Mare

In these unequal unions, when the male exceeds the female in point of size, his union with a woman who is immediately next to him in size is called high union, and is of two kinds; while his union with the woman most remote from his size is called the highest union, and is of one kind only. On the other hand, when the female exceeds the male in point of size, her union with a man immediately next to her in size is called low union, and is of two kinds; while her union with a man most remote from her in size is called the lowest union, and is of one kind only.

In other words, the horse and mare, the bull and deer, form the high union, while the horse and deer form the highest union. On the female side, the elephant and bull, the mare and hare, form low unions, while the elephant and the hare make the lowest unions.

There are, then, nine kinds of union according to dimensions. Amongst all these, equal unions are the best, those of a superlative degree, i.e. the highest and the lowest, are the worst, and the rest are middling, and with them the high[1] are better than the low.

There are also nine kinds of union according to the force of passion or carnal desire, as follows:

MEN	WOMEN	MEN	WOMEN
Small	Small	Small	Middling
Middling	Middling	Small	Intense
Intense	Intense	Middling	Small
		Middling	Intense
		Intense	Small
		Intense	Middling

A man is called a man of small passion whose desire at the time of sexual union is not great, whose semen is scanty, and who cannot bear the warm embraces of the female.

Those who differ from this temperament are called men

[1] High unions are said to be better than low ones, for in the former it is possible for the male to satisfy his own passion without injuring the female, while in the latter it is difficult for the female to be satisfied by any means.

of middling passion, while those of intense passion are full of desire.

In the same way, women are supposed to have the three degrees of feeling as specified above.

Lastly, according to time there are three kinds of men and women, the short-timed, the moderate-timed, and the long-timed; and of these, as in the previous statements, there are nine kinds of union.

But on this last head there is a difference of opinion about the female, which should be stated.

Auddalika says, 'Females do not emit as males do. The males simply remove their desire, while the females, from their consciousness of desire, feel a certain kind of pleasure, which gives them satisfaction, but it is impossible for them to tell you what kind of pleasure they feel. The fact from which this becomes evident is, that males, when engaged in coition, cease of themselves after emission, and are satisfied, but it is not so with females.'

This opinion is however objected to on the grounds that, if a male be a long-timed, the female loves him the more, but if he be short-timed, she is dissatisfied with him. And this circumstance, some say, would prove that the female emits also.

But this opinion does not hold good, for if it takes a long time to allay a woman's desire, and during this time she is enjoying great pleasure, it is quite natural then that she should wish for its continuation. And on this subject there is a verse as follows:

'By union with men the lust, desire, or passion of women is satisfied, and the pleasure derived from the consciousness of it is called their satisfaction.'

The followers of Babhravya, however, say that the semen of women continues to fall from the beginning of the sexual union to its end, and it is right that it should be so, for if they had no semen there would be no embryo.

To this there is an objection. In the beginning of coition the passion of the woman is middling, and she cannot bear the vigorous thrusts of her lover, but by degrees her passion increases until she ceases to think about her body, and then finally she wishes to stop from further coition.

This objection, however, does not hold good, for even in ordinary things that revolve with great force, such as a potter's wheel, or a top, we find that the motion at first is slow, but by degrees it becomes very rapid. In the same way the passion of the woman having gradually increased, she has a desire to discontinue coition, when all the semen has fallen away. And there is a verse with regard to this as follows:

'The fall of the semen of the man takes place only at the end of coition, while the semen of the woman falls continually, and after the semen of both has all fallen away then they wish for the discontinuance of coition.'[1]

Lastly, Vatsyayana is of opinion that the semen of the female falls in the same way as that of the male.

Now some may ask here: If men and women are beings of the same kind, and are engaged in bringing about the same results, why should they have different works to do?

Vatsya says that this is so, because the ways of working as well as the consciousness of pleasure in men and women are different. The difference in the ways of working, by which men are the actors, and women are the persons acted upon, is owing to the nature of the male and the female, otherwise the actor would be sometimes the person acted upon, and vice versa. And from this difference in the ways of working follows the difference in the consciousness of

[1] The strength of passion with women varies a great deal, some being easily satisfied, and others eager and willing to go on for a long time. To satisfy these last thoroughly a man must have recourse to art. It is certain that a fluid flows from the woman in larger or smaller quantities, but her satisfaction is not complete until she has experienced the 'spasme génêtique', as described in a French work recently published and called *Breviare de l'Amour Experimental par le Dr Jules Guyot*.

pleasure, for a man thinks, 'this woman is united with me', and a woman thinks, 'I am united with this man'.

It may be said that, if the ways of working in men and women are different, why should not there be a difference, even in the pleasure they feel, and which is the result of those ways.

But this objection is groundless, for, the person acting and the person acted upon being of different kinds, there is a reason for the difference in their ways of working; but there is no reason for any difference in the pleasure they feel, because they both naturally derive pleasure from the act they perform.[1]

On this again some may say that when different persons are engaged in doing the same work, we find that they accomplish the same end or purpose; while, on the contrary, in the case of men and women we find that each of them accomplishes his or her own end separately, and this is inconsistent. But this is a mistake, for we find that sometimes two things are done at the same time, as for instance in the fighting of rams, both the rams receive the shock at the same time on their heads. Again, in throwing one wood apple against another, and also in a fight or struggle of wrestlers. If it be said that in these cases the things employed are of the same kind, it is answered that even in the case of men and women, the nature of the two persons is the same. And as the difference in their ways of working arises from the difference of their conformation only, it follows that men experience the same kind of pleasure as women do.

[1] This is a long dissertation very common among Sanscrit authors, both when writing and talking socially. They start certain propositions, and then argue for and against them. What it is presumed the author means is that, though both men and women derive pleasure from the act of coition, the way it is produced is brought about by different means, each individual performing his own work in the matter, irrespective of the other, and each deriving individually their own consciousness of pleasure from the act they perform. There is a difference in the work that each does, and a difference in the consciousness of pleasure that each has, but no difference in the pleasure they feel, for each feels that pleasure to a greater or lesser degree.

There is also a verse on this subject as follows:

'Men and women, being of the same nature, feel the same kind of pleasure, and therefore a man should marry such a woman as will love him ever afterwards.'

The pleasure of men and women being thus proved to be of the same kind, it follows that, in regard to time, there are nine kinds of sexual intercourse, in the same way as there are nine kinds, according to the force of passion.

There being thus nine kinds of union with regard to dimensions, force of passion, and time, respectively, by making combinations of them, innumerable kinds of union would be produced. Therefore in each particular kind of sexual union, men should use such means as they may think suitable for the occasion.[1]

At the first time of sexual union the passion of the male is intense, and his time is short, but in subsequent unions on the same day the reverse of this is the case. With the female, however, it is the contrary, for at the first time her passion is weak, and then her time long, but on subsequent occasions on the same day, her passion is intense and her time short, until her passion is satisfied.

On the different Kinds of Love

Men learned in the humanities are of opinion that love is of four kinds:

Love acquired by continual habit
Love resulting from the imagination
Love resulting from belief
Love resulting from the perception of external objects

Love resulting from the constant and continual per-

[1] This paragraph should be particularly noted, for it specially applies to married men and their wives. So many men utterly ignore the feelings of the women, and never pay the slightest attention to the passion of the latter. To understand the subject thoroughly, it is absolutely necessary to study it, and then a person will know that, as dough is prepared for baking, so must a woman be prepared for sexual intercourse, if she is to derive satisfaction from it.

formance of some act is called love acquired by constant practice and habit, as for instance the love of sexual intercourse, the love of hunting, the love of drinking, the love of gambling, etc., etc.

Love which is felt for things to which we are not habituated, and which proceeds entirely from ideas, is called love resulting from imagination, as for instance that love which some men and women and eunuchs feel for the Auparishtaka or mouth congress, and that which is felt by all for such things as embracing, kissing, etc., etc.

The love which is mutual on both sides, and proved to be true, when each looks upon the other as his or her very own, such is called love resulting from belief by the learned.

The love resulting from the perception of external objects is quite evident and well known to the world. because the pleasure which it affords is superior to the pleasure of the other kinds of love, which exists only for its sake.

What has been said in this chapter upon the subject of sexual union is sufficient for the learned; but for the edification of the ignorant, the same will now be treated of at length and in detail.

CHAPTER II

OF THE EMBRACE

THIS part of the Kama Shastra, which treats of sexual union, is also called 'Sixty-four' (Chatushshashti). Some old authors say that it is called so, because it contains sixty-four chapters. Others are of opinion that the author of this part being a person named Panchala, and the person who recited the part of the Rig Veda called Dashatapa, which contains sixty-four verses, being also called Panchala, the name 'sixty-four' has been given to the part of the work in honour of the Rig Vedas. The followers of Babhravya say on the other hand that this part contains eight subjects, viz. the embrace, kissing, scratching with the nails or fingers, biting, lying down, making various sounds, playing the part of a man, and the Auparishtaka, or mouth congress. Each of these subjects being of eight kinds, and eight multiplied by eight being sixty-four, this part is therefore named 'sixty-four'. But Vatsyayana affirms that as this part contains also the following subjects, viz. striking, crying, the acts of a man during congress, the various kinds of congress, and other subjects, the name 'sixty-four' is given to it only accidentally. As, for instance, we say this tree is 'Saptaparna', or seven-leaved, this offering of rice is 'Panchavarna', or five-coloured, but the tree has not seven leaves, neither has the rice five colours.

However the part sixty-four is now treated of, and the embrace, being the first subject, will now be considered.

Now the embrace which indicates the mutual love of a man and woman who have come together is of four kinds:

Touching — Rubbing
Piercing — Pressing

The action in each case is denoted by the meaning of the word which stands for it.

When a man under some pretext or other goes in front or alongside of a woman and touches her body with his own, it is called the 'touching embrace'.

When a woman in a lonely place bends down, as if to pick up something, and pierces, as it were, a man sitting or standing, with her breasts, and the man in return takes hold of them, it is called a 'piercing embrace'.

The above two kinds of embrace take place only between persons who do not, as yet, speak freely with each other.

When two lovers are walking slowly together, either in the dark, or in a place of public resort, or in a lonely place, and rub their bodies against each other, it is called a 'rubbing embrace'.

When on the above occasion one of them presses the other's body forcibly against a wall or pillar, it is called a 'pressing embrace'.

These two last embraces are peculiar to those who know the intentions of each other.

At the time of the meeting the four following kinds of embrace are used:

Jataveshtitaka, or the twining of a creeper.

Vrikshadhirudhaka, or climbing a tree.

Tila-Tandulaka, or the mixture of sesamum seed with rice.

Kshiraniraka, or milk and water embrace.

When a woman, clinging to a man as a creeper twines round a tree, bends his head down to hers with the desire of kissing him and slightly makes the sound of sut sut, embraces him, and looks lovingly towards him, it is called an embrace like the 'twining of a creeper'.

When a woman, having placed one of her feet on the foot of her lover, and the other on one of his thighs, passes one of her arms round his back, and the other on his shoulders, makes slightly the sounds of singing and cooing, and wishes, as it were, to climb up him in order to have a kiss, it is called an embrace like the 'climbing of a tree'.

These two kinds of embrace take place when the lover is standing.

When lovers lie on a bed, and embrace each other so closely that the arms and thighs of the one are encircled by the arms and thighs of the other, and are, as it were, rubbing up against them, this is called an embrace like 'the mixture of sesamum seed with rice'.

When a man and a woman are very much in love with each other, and, not thinking of any pain or hurt, embrace each other as if they were entering into each other's bodies either while the woman is sitting on the lap of the man, or in front of him, or on a bed, then it is called an embrace like a 'mixture of milk and water'.

These two kinds of embrace take place at the time of sexual union.

Babhravya has thus related to us the above eight kinds of embraces.

Suvarnanabha moreover gives us four ways of embracing simple members of the body, which are:

The embrace of the thighs.

The embrace of the jaghana, i.e. the part of the body from the navel downwards to the thighs.

The embrace of the breasts.

The embrace of the forehead.

When one of two lovers presses forcibly one or both of the thighs of the other between his or her own, it is called the 'embrace of thighs'.

When a man presses the jaghana or middle part of the woman's body against his own, and mounts upon her to practise, either scratching with the nail or finger, or biting, or striking, or kissing, the hair of the woman being loose and flowing, it is called the 'embrace of the jaghana'.

When a man places his breast between the breasts of a

woman and presses her with it, it is called the 'embrace of the breasts'.

When either of the lovers touches the mouth, the eyes and the forehead of the other with his or her own, it is called the 'embrace of the forehead'.

Some say that even shampooing is a kind of embrace, because there is a touching of bodies in it. But Vatsyayana thinks that shampooing is performed at a different time, and for a different purpose, and it is also of a different character, it cannot be said to be included in the embrace.

There are also some verses on the subject as follows:

'The whole subject of embracing is of such a nature that men who ask questions about it, or who hear about it, or who talk about it, acquire thereby a desire for enjoyment. Even those embraces that are not mentioned in the Kama Shastra should be practised at the time of sexual enjoyment, if they are in any way conducive to the increase of love or passion. The rules of the Shastra apply so long as the passion of man is middling, but when the wheel of love is once set in motion, there is then no Shastra and no order.'

CHAPTER III

ON KISSING

IT is said by some that there is no fixed time or order between the embrace, the kiss, and the pressing or scratching with the nails or fingers, but that all these things should be done generally before sexual union takes place, while striking and making the various sounds generally takes place at the time of the union. Vatsyayana, however, thinks that anything may take place at any time, for love does not care for time or order.

On the occasion of the first congress, kissing and the other things mentioned above should be done moderately, they should not be continued for a long time, and should be done alternately. On subsequent occasions, however, the reverse of all this may take place, and moderation will not be necessary, they may continue for a long time, and, for the purpose of kindling love, they may be all done at the same time.

The following are the places for kissing: the forehead, the eyes, the cheeks, the throat, the bosom, the breasts, the lips, and the interior of the mouth. Moreover the people of the Lat country kiss also on the following places: the joints of the thighs, the arms and the navel. But Vatsyayana thinks that though kissing is practised by these people in the above places on account of the intensity of their love, and the customs of their country, it is not fit to be practised by all.

Now in a case of a young girl there are three sorts of kisses:

The nominal kiss
The throbbing kiss
The touching kiss

When a girl only touches the mouth of her lover with her own, but does not herself do anything, it is called the 'nominal kiss'.

When a girl, setting aside her bashfulness a little, wishes to touch the lip that is pressed into her mouth, and with that object moves her lower lip, but not the upper one, it is called the 'throbbing kiss'.

When a girl touches her lover's lip with her tongue, and having shut her eyes, places her hands on those of her lover, it is called the 'touching kiss'.

Other authors describe four other kinds of kisses:

The straight kiss
The bent kiss
The turned kiss
The pressed kiss

When the lips of two lovers are brought into direct contact with each other, it is called a 'straight kiss'.

When the heads of two lovers are bent towards each other, and when so bent, kissing takes place, it is called a 'bent kiss'.

When one of them turns up the face of the other by holding the head and chin, and then kissing, it is called a 'turned kiss'.

Lastly when the lower lip is pressed with much force, it is called a 'pressed kiss'.

There is also a fifth kind of kiss called the 'greatly pressed kiss', which is effected by taking hold of the lower lip between two fingers, and then, after touching it with the tongue, pressing it with great force with the lip.

As regards kissing, a wager may be laid as to which will get hold of the lips of the other first. If the woman loses, she should pretend to cry, should keep her lover off by shaking her hands, and turn away from him and dispute with him saying, 'let another wager be laid'. If she loses this a second time, she should appear doubly distressed, and when her lover is off his guard or asleep, she should get hold of his lower lip, and hold it in her teeth, so that it should not slip away, and then she should laugh, make a loud noise, deride him, dance about, and say whatever she likes in a joking way, moving her eyebrows and rolling her eyes. Such are the wagers and quarrels as far as kissing is concerned, but the same may be applied with regard to the pressing or scratching with the nails and fingers, biting and striking. All these however are only peculiar to men and women of intense passion.

When a man kisses the upper lip of a woman, while she in return kisses his lower lip, it is called the 'kiss of the upper lip'.

When one of them takes both the lips of the other between his or her own, it is called 'a clasping kiss'. A woman, however, only takes this kind of kiss from a man who has no moustache. And on the occasion of this kiss, if one of them touches the teeth, the tongue, and the palate of the other, with his or her tongue, it is called the 'fighting of the tongue'. In the same way, the pressing of the teeth of the one against the mouth of the other is to be practised.

Kissing is of four kinds: moderate, contracted, pressed, and soft, according to the different parts of the body which are kissed, for different kinds of kisses are appropriate for different parts of the body.

When a woman looks at the face of her lover while he is asleep and kisses it to show her intention or desire, it is called a 'kiss that kindles love'.

When a woman kisses her lover while he is engaged in business, or while he is quarrelling with her, or while he is looking at something else, so that his mind may be turned away, it is called a 'kiss that turns away'.

When a lover coming home late at night kisses his beloved, who is asleep on her bed, in order to show her his desire, it is called a 'kiss that awakens'. On such an occasion the woman may pretend to be asleep at the time of her lover's arrival, so that she may know his intention and obtain respect from him.

When a person kisses the reflection of the person he loves in a mirror, in water, or on a wall, it is called a 'kiss showing the intention'.

When a person kisses a child sitting on his lap, or a picture, or an image, or figure, in the presence of the person beloved by him, it is called a 'transferred kiss'.

When at night at a theatre, or in an assembly of caste men, a man coming up to a woman kisses a finger of her hand if she be standing, or a toe of her foot if she be sitting, or when a woman is shampooing her lover's body, places her face on his thigh (as if she was sleepy) so as to inflame his passion, and kisses his thigh or great toe, it is called a 'demonstrative kiss'.

There is also a verse on this subject as follows:

'Whatever things may be done by one of the lovers to the other, the same should be returned by the other, i.e. if the woman kisses him he should kiss her in return, if she strikes him he should also strike her in return.'

CHAPTER IV

ON PRESSING, OR MARKING, OR SCRATCHING WITH THE NAILS

WHEN love becomes intense, pressing with the nails or scratching the body with them is practised, and it is done on the following occasions: on the first visit; at the time of setting out on a journey; on the return from a journey; at the time when an angry lover is reconciled; and lastly when the woman is intoxicated.

But pressing with the nails is not a usual thing except with those who are intensely passionate, i.e. full of passion. It is employed, together with biting, by those to whom the practice is agreeable.

Pressing with the nails is of the eight following kinds, according to the forms of the marks which are produced:

Sounding
Half moon
A circle
A line
A tiger's nail or claw
A peacock's foot
The jump of a hare
The leaf of a blue lotus

The places that are to be pressed with the nails are as follows: the arm pit, the throat, the breasts, the lips, the jaghana, or middle parts of the body, and the thighs. But Suvarnanabha is of opinion that when the impetuosity of passion is excessive, the places need not be considered.

The qualities of good nails are that they should be bright,

well set, clean, entire, convex, soft, and glossy in appearance. Nails are of three kinds according to their size:

Small
Middling
Large

Large nails, which give grace to the hands, and attract the hearts of women from their appearance, are possessed by the Bengalees.

Small nails, which can be used in various ways, and are to be applied only with the object of giving pleasure, are possessed by the people of the southern districts.

Middling nails, which contain the properties of both the above kinds, belong to the people of the Maharashtra.

When a person presses the chin, the breasts, the lower lip, or the jaghana of another so softly that no scratch or mark is left, but only the hair on the body becomes erect from the touch of the nails, and the nails themselves make a sound, it is called a 'sounding or pressing with the nails'.

This pressing is used in the case of a young girl when her lover shampoos her, scratches her head, and wants to trouble or frighten her.

The curved mark with the nails, which is impressed on the neck and the breasts, is called the 'half moon'.

When the half moons are impressed opposite to each other, it is called a 'circle'. This mark with the nails is generally made on the navel, the small cavities about the buttocks, and on the joints of the thigh.

A mark in the form of a small line, and which can be made on any part of the body, is called a 'line'.

This same line, when it is curved, and made on the breast, is called a 'tiger's nail'.

When a curved mark is made on the breast by means of the five nails, it is called a 'peacock's foot'. This mark is made with the object of being praised, for it requires a great deal of skill to make it properly.

When five marks with the nails are made close to one another near the nipple of the breast, it is called 'the jump of a hare'.

A mark made on the breast or on the hips in the form of a leaf of the blue lotus is called the 'leaf of a blue lotus'.

When a person is going on a journey, and makes a mark on the thighs, or on the breast, it is called a 'token of remembrance'. On such an occasion three or four lines are impressed close to one another with the nails.

Here ends the marking with the nails. Marks of other kinds than the above may also be made with the nails, for the ancient authors say that, as there are innumerable degrees of skill among men (the practice of this art being known to all), so there are innumerable ways of making these marks. And as pressing or marking with the nails is independent of love, no one can say with certainty how many different kinds of marks with the nails do actually exist. The reason of this is, Vatsyayana says, that as variety is necessary in love, so love is to be produced by means of variety. It is on this account that courtesans, who are well acquainted with various ways and means, become so desirable, for if variety is sought in all the arts and amusements, such as archery and others, how much more should it be sought after in the present case.

The marks of the nails should not be made on married women, but particular kinds of marks may be made on their private parts for the remembrance and increase of love.

There are also some verses on the subject, as follows:

'The love of a woman who sees the marks of nails on the private parts of her body, even though they are old and almost worn out, becomes again fresh and new. If there be no marks of nails to remind a person of the passages of love, then love is lessened in the same way as when no union takes place for a long time.'

Even when a stranger sees at a distance a young woman

with the marks of nails on her breast,[1] he is filled with love and respect for her.

A man, also, who carries the marks of nails and teeth on some parts of his body, influences the mind of a woman, even though it be ever so firm. In short, nothing tends to increase love so much as the effects of marking with the nails, and biting.

[1] From this it would appear that in ancient times the breasts of women were not covered, and this is seen in the paintings of the Ajunta and other caves, where we find that the breasts of even royal ladies and others are exposed.

CHAPTER V

ON BITING, AND THE MEANS TO BE EMPLOYED WITH REGARD TO WOMEN OF DIFFERENT COUNTRIES

ALL the places that can be kissed are also the places that can be bitten, except the upper lip, the interior of the mouth, and the eyes.

The qualities of good teeth are as follows: They should be equal, possessed of a pleasing brightness, capable of being coloured, of proper proportions, unbroken, and with sharp ends.

The defects of teeth on the other hand are that they are blunt, protruding from the gums, rough, soft, large, and loosely set.

The following are the different kinds of biting:

The hidden bite
The swollen bite
The point
The line of points
The coral and the jewel
The line of jewels
The broken cloud
The biting of the boar

The biting, which is shown only by the excessive redness of the skin that is bitten, is called the 'hidden bite'.

When the skin is pressed down on both sides, it is called the 'swollen bite'.

When a small portion of the skin is bitten with two teeth only, it is called the 'point'.

When such small portions of the skin are bitten with all the teeth, it is called the 'line of points'.

The biting, which is done by bringing together the teeth

and the lips, is called the 'coral and the jewel'. The lip is the coral, and the teeth the jewel.

When biting is done with all the teeth, it is called the 'line of jewels'.

The biting, which consists of unequal risings in a circle, and which comes from the space between the teeth, is called the 'broken cloud'. This is impressed on the breasts.

The biting, which consists of many broad rows of marks near to one another, and with red intervals, is called the 'biting of a boar'. This is impressed on the breasts and the shoulders; and these two last modes of biting are peculiar to persons of intense passion.

The lower lip is the place on which the 'hidden bite', the 'swollen bite', and the 'point' are made; again the 'swollen bite' and the 'coral and the jewel' bite are done on the cheek. Kissing, pressing with the nails, and biting are the ornaments of the left cheek, and when the word cheek is used it is to be understood as the left cheek.

Both the 'line of points' and the 'line of jewels' are to be impressed on the throat, the arm pit, and the joints of the thighs; but the 'line of points' alone is to be impressed on the forehead and the thighs.

The marking with the nails, and the biting of the following things—an ornament of the forehead, an ear ornament, a bunch of flowers, a betel leaf, or a tamala leaf, which are worn by, or belong to the woman that is beloved—are signs of the desire of enjoyment.

Here end the different kinds of biting.

In the affairs of love a man should do such things as are agreeable to the women of different countries.

The women of the central countries (i.e. between the Ganges and the Jumna) are noble in their character, not accustomed to disgraceful practices, and dislike pressing the nails and biting.

The women of the Balhika country are gained over by striking.

The women of Avantika are fond of foul pleasures, and have not good manners.

The women of the Maharashtra are fond of practising the sixty-four arts, they utter low and harsh words, and like to be spoken to in the same way, and have an impetuous desire of enjoyment.

The women of Pataliputra (i.e. the modern Patna) are of the same nature as the women of the Maharashtra, but show their likings only in secret.

The women of the Dravida country, though they are rubbed and pressed about at the time of sexual enjoyment, have a slow fall of semen, that is they are very slow in the act of coition.

The women of Vanavasi are moderately passionate, they go through every kind of enjoyment, cover their bodies, and abuse those who utter low, mean and harsh words.

The women of Avanti hate kissing, marking with the nails, and biting, but they have a fondness for various kinds of sexual union.

The women of Malwa like embracing and kissing, but not wounding, and they are gained over by striking.

The women of Abhira, and those of the country about the Indus and five rivers (i.e. the Punjab), are gained over by the Auparishtaka or mouth congress.

The women of Aparatika are full of passion, and make slowly the sound 'Sit'.

The women of the Lat country have even more impetuous desire, and also make the sound 'Sit'.

The women of the Stri Rajya, and of Koshola (Oude), are full of impetuous desire, their semen falls in large quantities and they are fond of taking medicine to make it do so.

The women of the Andhra country have tender bodies, they are fond of enjoyment, and have a liking for voluptuous pleasures.

The women of Ganda have tender bodies, and speak sweetly.

Now Suvarnanabha is of opinion that that which is agreeable to the nature of a particular person, is of more consequence than that which is agreeable to a whole nation, and that therefore the peculiarities of the country should not be observed in such cases. The various pleasures, the dress, and the sports of one country are in time borrowed by another, and in such a case these things must be considered as belonging originally to that country.

Among the things mentioned above, viz. embracing, kissing, etc., those which increase passion should be done first, and those which are only for amusement or variety should be done afterwards.

There are also some verses on this subject as follows:

'When a man bites a woman forcibly, she should angrily do the same to him with double force. Thus a "point" should be returned with a "line of points", and a "line of points" with a "broken cloud", and if she be excessively chafed, she should at once begin a love quarrel with him. At such a time she should take hold of her lover by the hair, and bend his head down, and kiss his lower lip, and then, being intoxicated with love, she should shut her eyes and bite him in various places. Even by day, and in a place of public resort, when her lover shows her any mark that she may have inflicted on his body, she should smile at the sight of it, and turning her face as if she were going to chide him, she should show him with an angry look the marks on her own body that have been made by him. Thus if men and women act according to each other's liking, their love for each other will not be lessened even in one hundred years.'

CHAPTER VI

OF THE DIFFERENT WAYS OF LYING DOWN, AND VARIOUS KINDS OF CONGRESS

ON the occasion of a 'high congress' the Mrigi (Deer) woman should lie down in such a way as to widen her yoni, while in a 'low congress' the Hastini (Elephant) woman should lie down so as to contract hers. But in an 'equal congress' they should lie down in the natural position. What is said above concerning the Mrigi and the Hastini applies also to the Vadawa (Mare) woman. In a 'low congress' the woman should particularly make use of medicine, to cause her desires to be satisfied quickly.

The Deer-woman has the following three ways of lying down:

The widely opened position
The yawning position
The position of the wife of Indra

When she lowers her head and raises her middle parts, it is called the 'widely opened position'. At such a time the man should apply some unguent, so as to make the entrance easy.

When she raises her thighs and keeps them wide apart and engages in congress, it is called the 'yawning position'.

When she places her thighs with her legs doubled on them upon her sides, and thus engages in congress, it is called the position of Indrani and this is learnt only by practice. The position is also useful in the case of the 'highest congress'.

The 'clasping position' is used in 'low congress', and in the 'lowest congress', together with the 'pressing position', the 'twining position', and the 'mare's position'.

When the legs of both the male and the female are stretched straight out over each other, it is called the 'clasping position'. It is of two kinds, the side position and the supine position, according to the way in which they lie down. In the side position the male should invariably lie on his left side, and cause the woman to lie on her right side, and this rule is to be observed in lying down with all kinds of women.

When, after congress has begun in the clasping position, the woman presses her lover with her thighs, it is called the 'pressing position'.

When the woman places one of her thighs across the thigh of her lover it is called the 'twining position'.

When a woman forcibly holds in her yoni the lingam after it is in, it is called the 'mare's position'. This is learnt by practice only, and is chiefly found among the women of the Andhra country.

The above are the different ways of lying down, mentioned by Babhravya. Suvarnanabha, however, gives the following in addition:

When the female raises both of her thighs straight up, it is called the 'rising position'.

When she raises both of her legs, and places them on her lover's shoulders, it is called the 'yawning position'.

When the legs are contracted, and thus held by the lover before his bosom, it is called the 'pressed position'.

When only one of her legs is stretched out, it is called the 'half pressed position'.

When the woman places one of her legs on her lover's shoulder, and stretches the other out, and then places the latter on his shoulder, and stretches out the other, and continues to do so alternately, it is called the 'splitting of a bamboo'.

When one of her legs is placed on the head, and the other is stretched out, it is called the 'fixing of a nail'. This is learnt by practice only.

When both the legs of the woman are contracted, and placed on her stomach, it is called the 'crab's position'.

When the thighs are raised and placed one upon the other, it is called the 'packed position'.

When the shanks are placed one upon the other, it is called the 'lotus-like position'.

When a man, during congress, turns round, and enjoys the woman without leaving her, while she embraces him round the back all the time, it is called the 'turning position', and is learnt only by practice.

Thus, says Suvarnanabha, these different ways of lying down, sitting, and standing should be practised in water, because it is easy to do so therein. But Vatsyayana is of opinion that congress in water is improper, because it is prohibited by the religious law.

When a man and a woman support themselves on each other's bodies, or on a wall, or pillar, and thus while standing engage in congress, it is called the 'supported congress'.

When a man supports himself against a wall, and the woman, sitting on his hands joined together and held underneath her, throws her arms round his neck, and putting her thighs alongside his waist, moves herself by her feet, which are touching the wall against which the man is leaning, it is called the 'suspended congress'.

When a woman stands on her hands and feet like a quadruped, and her lover mounts her like a bull, it is called the 'congress of a cow'. At this time everything that is ordinarily done on the bosom should be done on the back.

In the same way can be carried on the congress of a dog, the congress of a goat, the congress of a deer, the forcible mounting of an ass, the congress of a cat, the jump of a tiger, the pressing of an elephant, the rubbing of a boar, and the mounting of a horse. And in all these cases the characteristics of these different animals should be manifested by acting like them.

When a man enjoys two women at the same time, both of whom love him equally, it is called the 'united congress'.

When a man enjoys many women altogether, it is called the 'congress of a herd of cows'.

The following kinds of congress—sporting in water, or the congress of an elephant with many female elephants which is said to take place only in the water, the congress of a collection of goats, the congress of a collection of deer—take place in imitation of these animals.

In Gramaneri many young men enjoy a woman that may be married to one of them, either one after the other, or at the same time. Thus one of them holds her, another enjoys her, a third uses her mouth, a fourth holds her middle part, and in this way they go on enjoying her several parts alternately.

The same things can be done when several men are sitting in company with one courtesan, or when one courtesan is alone with many men. In the same way this can be done by the women of the king's harem when they accidentally get hold of a man.

The people in the Southern countries have also a congress in the anus, that is called the 'lower congress'.

Thus ends the various kinds of congress. There are also two verses on the subject as follows:

'An ingenious person should multiply the kinds of congress after the fashion of the different kinds of beasts and of birds. For these different kinds of congress, performed according to the usage of each country, and the liking of each individual, generate love, friendship, and respect in the hearts of women.'

CHAPTER VII

OF THE VARIOUS MODES OF STRIKING, AND OF THE SOUNDS APPROPRIATE TO THEM

SEXUAL intercourse can be compared to a quarrel, on account of the contrarieties of love and its tendency to dispute. The place of striking with passion is the body, and on the body the special places are :

The shoulders
The head
The space between the breasts
The back
The jaghana, or middle part of the body
The sides

Striking is of four kinds:

Striking with the back of the hand
Striking with the fingers a little contracted
Striking with the fist
Striking with the open palm of the hand

On account of its causing pain, striking gives rise to the hissing sound, which is of various kinds, and to the eight kinds of crying:

The sound Hin
The thundering sound
The cooing sound
The weeping sound
The sound Phut
The sound Phât
The sound Sût
The sound Plât

Besides these, there are also words having a meaning, such as 'mother', and those that are expressive of prohibition, sufficiency, desire of liberation, pain or praise, and to which may be added sounds like those of the dove, the cuckoo, the green pigeon, the parrot, the bee, the sparrow, the flamingo, the duck, and the quail, which are all occasionally made use of.

Blows with the fist should be given on the back of the woman while she is sitting on the lap of the man, and she should give blows in return, abusing the man as if she were angry, and making the cooing and the weeping sounds. While the woman is engaged in congress the space between the breasts should be struck with the back of the hand, slowly at first, and then proportionately to the increasing excitement, until the end.

At this time the sounds Hin and others may be made, alternately or optionally, according to habit. When the man, making the sound Phât, strikes the woman on the head, with the fingers of his hand a little contracted, it is called Prasritaka, which means striking with the fingers of the hand a little contracted. In this case the appropriate sounds are the cooing sound, the sound Phât and the sound Phut in the interior of the mouth, and at the end of congress the sighing and weeping sounds. The sound Phât is an imitation of the sound of a bamboo being split, while the sound Phut is like the sound made by something falling into water. At all times when kissing and such like things are begun, the woman should give a reply with a hissing sound. During the excitement when the woman is not accustomed to striking, she continually utters words expressive of prohibition, sufficiently, or desire of liberation, as well as the words 'father', 'mother', intermingled with the sighing, weeping and thundering sounds.[1] Towards the con-

[1] Men who are well acquainted with the art of love are well aware how often one woman differs from another in her sighs and sounds during the time of congress. Some women like to be talked to in the most loving way, others in the most lustful way, others in the most abusive way, and so on. Some women enjoy themselves with closed eyes in silence, others make a great noise over it, and some almost faint away. The great art is to ascertain what gives them the greatest pleasure, and what specialities they like best.

clusion of the congress, the breasts, the jaghana, and the sides of the woman should be pressed with the open palms of the hand, with some force, until the end of it, and then sounds like those of the quail or the goose should be made.

There are two verses on the subject as follows:

'The characteristics of manhood are said to consist of roughness and impetuosity, while weakness, tenderness, sensibility, and an inclination to turn away from unpleasant things are the distinguishing marks of womanhood. The excitement of passion, and peculiarities of habit may sometimes cause contrary results to appear, but these do not last long, and in the end the natural state is resumed.'

The wedge on the bosom, the scissors on the head, the piercing instrument on the cheeks, and the pinchers on the breasts and sides, may also be taken into consideration with the other four modes of striking, and thus give eight ways altogether. But these four ways of striking with instruments are peculiar to the people of the southern countries, and the marks caused by them are seen on the breasts of their women. They are local peculiarities, but Vatsyayana is of opinion that the practice of them is painful, barbarous, and base, and quite unworthy of imitation.

In the same way anything that is a local peculiarity should not always be adopted elsewhere, and even in the place where the practice is prevalent, excess of it should always be avoided. Instances of the dangerous use of them may be given as follows. The king of the Panchalas killed the courtesan Madhavasena by means of the wedge during congress. King Satakarni Satavahana of the Kuntalas deprived his great Queen Malayavati of her life by a pair of scissors, and Naradeva, whose hand was deformed, blinded a dancing girl by directing a piercing instrument in a wrong way.

There are also two verses on the subject as follows:

'About these things there cannot be either enumeration

or any definite rule. Congress having once commenced, passion alone gives birth to all the acts of the parties.'

'Such passionate actions and amorous gesticulations or movements, which arise on the spur of the moment, and during sexual intercourse, cannot be defined, and are as irregular as dreams. A horse having once attained the fifth degree of motion goes on with blind speed, regardless of pits, ditches, and posts in his way; and in the same manner a loving pair become blind with passion in the heat of congress, and go on with great impetuosity, paying not the least regard to excess. For this reason one who is well acquainted with the science of love, and knowing his own strength, as also the tenderness, impetuosity, and strength of the young women, should act accordingly. The various modes of enjoyment are not for all times or for all persons, but they should only be used at the proper time. and in the proper countries and places.'

CHAPTER VIII

ABOUT WOMEN ACTING THE PART OF A MAN; AND OF THE WORK OF A MAN

WHEN a woman sees that her lover is fatigued by constant congress, without having his desire satisfied, she should, with his permission, lay him down upon his back, and give him assistance by acting his part. She may also do this to satisfy the curiosity of her lover, or her own desire of novelty.

There are two ways of doing this, the first is when during congress she turns round, and gets on the top of her lover, in such a manner as to continue the congress, without obstructing the pleasure of it; and the other is when she acts the man's part from the beginning. At such a time, with flowers in her hair hanging loose, and her smiles broken by hard breathings, she should press upon her lover's bosom with her own breasts, and lowering her head frequently, should do in return the same actions which he used to do before, returning his blows and chaffing him, should say, 'I was laid down by you, and fatigued with hard congress, I shall now therefore lay you down in return.' She should then again manifest her own bashfulness, her fatigue, and her desire of stopping the congress. In this way she should do the work of a man, which we shall presently relate.

Whatever is done by a man for giving pleasure to a woman is called the work of a man, and is as follows:

While the woman is lying on his bed, and is as it were abstracted by his conversation, he should loosen the knot of her undergarments, and when she begins to dispute with him, he should overwhelm her with kisses. Then when his lingam is erect he should touch her with his hands in various places, and gently manipulate various parts of the body. If the woman is bashful, and if it is the first time that they have come together, the man should place his hands between her thighs, which she would probably keep close together, and if she is a very young girl, he should first get his hands upon her breasts, which she would probably cover with her own hands, and under her armpits and on her neck. If however she is a seasoned woman, he should do whatever is agreeable either to him or to her, and whatever is fitting for the occasion. After this he should take hold of her hair, and hold her chin in his fingers for the purpose of kissing her. On this, if she is a young girl, she will become bashful and close her eyes. Anyhow he should gather from the action of the woman what things would be pleasing to her during congress.

Here Suvarnanabha says that while a man is doing to the woman what he likes best during congress, he should always make a point of pressing those parts of her body on which she turns her eyes.

The signs of the enjoyment and satisfaction of the woman are as follows: her body relaxes, she closes her eyes, she puts aside all bashfulness, and shows increased willingness to unite the two organs as closely together as possible. On the other hand, the signs of her want of enjoyment and of failing to be satisfied are as follows: she shakes her hands, she does not let the man get up, feels dejected, bites the man, kicks him, and continues to go on moving after the man has finished. In such cases the man should rub the yoni of the woman with his hand and fingers (as the elephant rubs anything with his trunk) before engaging in congress, until it is softened, and after that is done he should proceed to put his lingam into her.

The acts to be done by the man are:

Moving forward
Friction or churning
Piercing

Rubbing
Pressing
Giving a blow
The blow of a boar
The blow of a bull
The sporting of a sparrow

When the organs are brought together properly and directly it is called 'moving the organ forward'.

When the lingam is held with the hand, and turned all round in the yoni, it is called 'churning'.

When the yoni is lowered, and the upper part of it is struck with the lingam, it is called 'piercing'.

When the same thing is done on the lower part of the yoni, it is called 'rubbing'.

When the yoni is pressed by the lingam for a long time, it is called 'pressing'.

When the lingam is removed to some distance from the yoni, and then forcibly strikes it, it is called 'giving a blow'.

When only one part of the yoni is rubbed with the lingam, it is called the 'blow of a boar'.

When both sides of the yoni are rubbed in this way, it is called the 'blow of a bull'.

When the lingam is in the yoni, and moved up and down frequently, and without being taken out, it is called the 'sporting of a sparrow'. This takes place at the end of congress.

When a woman acts the part of a man, she has the following things to do in addition to the nine given above:

The pair of tongs
The top
The swing

When the woman holds the lingam in her yoni, draws it in, presses it, and keeps it thus in her for a long time, it is called the 'pair of tongs'.

When, while engaged in congress, she turns round like a wheel, it is called the 'top'. This is learnt by practice only.

When, on such an occasion, the man lifts up the middle part of his body, and the woman turns round her middle part, it is called the 'swing'.

When the woman is tired, she should place her forehead on that of her lover, and should thus take rest without disturbing the union of the organs, and when the woman has rested herself the man should turn round and begin the congress again.

There are also some verses on the subject as follows:

'Though a woman is reserved, and keeps her feelings concealed, yet when she gets on the top of a man, she then shows all her love and desire. A man should gather from the actions of the woman of what disposition she is, and in what way she likes to be enjoyed. A woman during her monthly courses, a woman who has been lately confined, and a fat woman should not be made to act the part of a man.'

CHAPTER IX

OF THE AUPARISHTAKA OR MOUTH CONGRESS

THERE are two kinds of eunuchs, those that are disguised as males, and those that are disguised as females. Eunuchs disguised as females imitate their dress, speech, gestures, tenderness, timidity, simplicity, softness and bashfulness. The acts that are done on the jaghana or middle parts of women, are done in the mouths of these eunuchs, and this is called Auparishtaka.[1] These eunuchs derive their imaginable pleasure, and their livelihood from this kind of congress, and they lead the life of courtesans. So much concerning eunuchs disguised as females.

Eunuchs disguised as males keep their desires secret, and when they wish to do anything they lead the life of shampooers. Under the pretence of shampooing, a eunuch of this kind embraces and draws towards himself the thighs of the man whom he is shampooing, and after this he touches the joints of his thighs and his jaghana, or central portions of his body. Then, if he finds the lingam of the man erect, he presses it with his hands and chaffs him for getting into that state. If after this, and after knowing his intention, the man does not tell the eunuch to proceed, then the latter does it of his own accord and begins the

[1] This practice appears to have been prevalent in some parts of India from a very ancient time. The *Shustruta*, a work on medicine some two thousand years old, describes the wounding of the lingam with the teeth as one of the causes of a disease treated upon in that work. Traces of the practice are found as far back as the eighth century, for various kinds of the Auparishtaka are represented in the sculptures of many Shaiva temples at Bhuvaneshwara, near Cuttack, in Orissa, and which were built about that period. From these sculptures being found in such places, it would seem that this practice was popular in that part of the country at that time. It does not seem to be so prevalent now in Hindustan, its place perhaps is filled up by the practice of sodomy, introduced since the Mahomedan period.

congress. If however he is ordered by the man to do it, then he disputes with him, and only consents at last with difficulty.

The following eight things are then done by the eunuch one after the other:

The nominal congress
Biting the sides
Pressing outside
Pressing inside
Kissing
Rubbing
Sucking a mango fruit
Swallowing up

At the end of each of these, the eunuch expresses his wish to stop, but when one of them is finished, the man desires him to do another, and after that is done, then the one that follows it, and so on.

When, holding the man's lingam with his hand, and placing it between his lips, the eunuch moves about his mouth, it is called the 'nominal congress'.

When, covering the end of the lingam with his fingers collected together like the bud of a plant or flower, the eunuch presses the sides of it with his lips, using his teeth also, it is called 'biting the sides'.

When, being desired to proceed, the eunuch presses the end of the lingam with his lips closed together, and kisses it as if he were drawing it out, it is called the 'outside pressing'.

When, being asked to go on, he puts the lingam further into his mouth, and presses it with his lips and then takes it out, it is called the 'inside pressing'.

When, holding the lingam in his hand, the eunuch kisses it as if he were kissing the lower lip, it is called 'kissing'.

When, after kissing it, he touches it with his tongue everywhere, and passes the tongue over the end of it, it is called 'rubbing'.

When, in the same way, he puts the half of it into his

mouth, and forcibly kisses and sucks it, this is called 'sucking a mango fruit'.

And lastly, when, with the consent of the man, the eunuch puts the whole lingam into his mouth, and presses it to the very end, as if he were going to swallow it up, it is called 'swallowing up'.

Striking, scratching, and other things may also be done during this kind of congress.

The Auparishtaka is practised also by unchaste and wanton women, female attendants and serving maids, i.e. those who are not married to anybody, but who live by shampooing.

The Acharyas (i.e. ancient and venerable authors) are of opinion that this Auparishtaka is the work of a dog and not of a man, because it is a low practice, and opposed to the orders of the Holy Writ, and because the man himself suffers by bringing his lingam into contact with the mouths of eunuchs and women. But Vatsyayana says that the orders of the Holy Writ do not affect those who resort to courtesans, and the law prohibits the practice of the Auparishtaka with married women only. As regards the injury to the male, that can be easily remedied.

The people of Eastern India do not resort to women who practise the Auparishtaka.

The people of Ahichhatra resort to such women, but do nothing with them, so far as the mouth is concerned.

The people of Saketa do with these women every kind of mouth congress, while the people of Nagara do not practise this, but do every other thing.

The people of the Shurasena country, on the southern bank of the Jumna, do everything without any hesitation, for they say that women being naturally unclean, no one can be certain about their character, their purity, their conduct, their practices, their confidences, or their speech. They are not however on this account to be abandoned, because religious law, on the authority of which they are reckoned pure, lays down that the udder of a cow is clean at the time of milking, though the mouth of a cow, and also the mouth of her calf, are considered unclean by the Hindoos. Again a dog is clean when he seizes a deer in hunting, though food touched by a dog is otherwise considered very unclean. A bird is clean when it causes a fruit to fall from a tree by pecking at it, though things eaten by crows and other birds are considered unclean. And the mouth of a woman is clean for kissing and such like things at the time of sexual intercourse. Vatsyayana moreover thinks that in all these things connected with love, everybody should act according to the custom of his country, and his own inclination.

There are also the following verses on the subject:

'The male servants of some men carry on the mouth congress with their masters. It is also practised by some citizens, who know each other well, among themselves. Some women of the harem, when they are amorous, do the acts of the mouth on the yonis of one another, and some men do the same thing with women. The way of doing this (i.e. of kissing the yoni) should be known from kissing the mouth. When a man and woman lie down in an inverted order, i.e. with the head of the one towards the feet of the other and carry on this congress, it is called the "congress of a crow".'

For the sake of such things courtesans abandon men possessed of good qualities, liberal and clever, and become attached to low persons, such as slaves and elephant drivers. The Auparishtaka, or mouth congress, should never be done by a learned Brahman, by a minister that carries on the business of a state, or by a man of good reputation, because though the practice is allowed by the Shastras, there is no reason why it should be carried on, and need only be practised in particular cases. As for instance, the taste, and the strength, and the digestive qualities of the flesh of dogs are mentioned in works on medicine, but it does not therefore follow that it should be eaten by the wise. In the same way there are some men, some places and some times, with respect to which these practices can be made use of. A man should therefore pay regard to the place, to the time, and to the practice which is to be carried out, as also as to whether it is agreeable to his nature and to himself, and then he may or may not practise these things according to circumstances. But after all, these things being done secretly, and the mind of the man being fickle, how can it be known what any person will do at any particular time and for any particular purpose.

CHAPTER X

OF THE WAY HOW TO BEGIN AND HOW TO END THE CONGRESS. DIFFERENT KINDS OF CONGRESS AND LOVE QUARRELS

In the pleasure-room, decorated with flowers, and fragrant with perfumes, attended by his friends and servants, the citizen should receive the woman, who will come bathed and dressed, and will invite her to take refreshment and to drink freely. He should then seat her on his left side, and holding her hair, and touching also the end and knot of her garment, he should gently embrace her with his right arm. They should then carry on an amusing conversation on various subjects, and may also talk suggestively of things which would be considered as coarse, or not to be mentioned generally in society. They may then sing, either with or without gesticulations, and play on musical instruments, talk about the arts, and persuade each other to drink. At last when the woman is overcome with love and desire, the citizen should dismiss the people that may be with him, giving them flowers, ointments, and betel leaves, and then when the two are left alone, they should proceed as has been already described in the previous chapters.

Such is the beginning of sexual union. At the end of the congress, the lovers with modesty, and not looking at each other, should go separately to the washing-room. After this, sitting in their own places, they should eat some betel leaves, and the citizen should apply with his own hand to the body of the woman some pure sandal wood ointment, or ointment of some other kind. He should then embrace her with his left arm, and with agreeable words should cause her to drink from a cup held in his own hand, or he may give her water to drink. They can then eat sweetmeats, or anything else, according to their likings and may drink fresh juice,[1] soup, gruel, extracts of meat, sherbet, the juice of mango fruits, the extract of the juice of the citron tree mixed with sugar, or anything that may be liked in different countries, and known to be sweet, soft, and pure. The lovers may also sit on the terrace of the palace or house, and enjoy the moonlight, and carry on an agreeable conversation. At this time, too, while the woman lies in his lap, with her face towards the moon, the citizen should show her the different planets, the morning star, the polar star, and the seven Rishis, or Great Bear.

This is the end of sexual union.

Congress is of the following kinds:

Loving congress
Congress of subsequent love
Congress of artificial love
Congress of transferred love
Congress like that of eunuchs
Deceitful congress
Congress of spontaneous love

When a man and a woman, who have been in love with each other for some time, come together with great difficulty, or when one of the two returns from a journey, or is reconciled after having been separated on account of a quarrel, then congress is called the 'loving congress'. It is carried on according to the liking of the lovers, and as long as they choose.

When two persons come together, while their love for each other is still in its infancy, their congress is called the 'congress of subsequent love'.

When a man carries on the congress by exciting him-

[1] The fresh juice of the cocoa nut tree, the date tree, and other kinds of palm trees are drunk in India. It will keep fresh very long, but ferments rapidly, and is then distilled into liquor.

self by means of the sixty-four ways, such as kissing, etc., etc., or when a man and a woman come together, though in reality they are both attached to different persons, their congress is then called 'congress of artificial love'. At this time all the ways and means mentioned in the Kama Shastra should be used.

When a man, from the beginning to the end of the congress, though having connection with the woman, thinks all the time that he is enjoying another one whom he loves, it is called the 'congress of transferred love'.

Congress between a man and a female water carrier, or a female servant of a caste lower than his own, lasting only until the desire is satisfied, is called 'congress like that of eunuchs'. Here external touches, kisses, and manipulation are not to be employed.

The congress between a courtesan and a rustic, and that between citizens and the women of villages, and bordering countries, is called 'deceitful congress'.

The congress that takes place between two persons who are attached to one another, and which is done according to their own liking is called 'spontaneous congress'.

Thus end the kinds of congress.

We shall now speak of love quarrels.

A woman who is very much in love with a man cannot bear to hear the name of her rival mentioned, or to have any conversation regarding her, or to be addressed by her name through mistake. If such takes place, a great quarrel arises, and the woman cries, becomes angry, tosses her hair about, strikes her lover, falls from her bed or seat, and, casting aside her garlands and ornaments, throws herself down on the ground.

At this time, the lover should attempt to reconcile her with conciliatory words, and should take her up carefully and place her on her bed. But she, not replying to his questions, and with increased anger, should bend down his head by pulling his hair, and having kicked him once, twice, or thrice on his arms, head, bosom or back, should then proceed to the door of the room. Dattaka says that she should then sit angrily near the door and shed tears, but should not go out, because she would be found fault with for going away. After a time, when she thinks that the conciliatory words and actions of her lover have reached their utmost, she should then embrace him, talking to him with harsh and reproachful words, but at the same time showing a loving desire for congress.

When the woman is in her own house, and has quarrelled with her lover, she should go to him and show how angry she is, and leave him. Afterwards the citizen having sent the Vita, the Vidushaka or the Pithamarda[1] to pacify her, she should accompany them back to the house, and spend the night with her lover.

Thus end the love quarrels.

In conclusion.

A man, employing the sixty-four means mentioned by Babhravya, obtains his object, and enjoys the woman of the first quality. Though he may speak well on other subjects, if he does not know the sixty-four divisions, no great respect is paid to him in the assembly of the learned. A man, devoid of other knowledge, but well acquainted with the sixty-four divisions, becomes a leader in any society of men and women. What man will not respect the sixty-four arts,[2] considering they are respected by the learned, by the cunning, and by the courtesans. As the sixty-four arts are respected, are charming, and add to the talent of women, they are called by the Acharyas dear to women. A man skilled in the sixty-four arts is looked upon with love by his own wife, by the wives of others, and by courtesans.

[1] The characteristics of these three individuals have been given in Part I, page 117.

[2] A definition of the sixty-four arts is given in Part I, Chapter III, pages 107-111.

PART III

ABOUT THE ACQUISITION OF A WIFE

CHAPTER I

ON MARRIAGE

When a girl of the same caste, and a virgin, is married in accordance with the precepts of Holy Writ, the results of such a union are the acquisition of Dharma and Artha, offspring, affinity, increase of friends, and untarnished love. For this reason a man should fix his affections upon a girl who is of good family, whose parents are alive, and who is three years or more younger than himself. She should be born of a highly respectable family, possessed of wealth, well connected, and with many relations and friends. She should also be beautiful, of a good disposition, with lucky marks on her body, and with good hair, nails, teeth, ears, eyes and breasts, neither more nor less than they ought to be, and no one of them entirely wanting, and not troubled with a sickly body. The man should, of course, also possess these qualities himself. But at all events, says Ghotakamukha, a girl who has been already joined with others (i.e. no longer a maiden) should never be loved, for it would be reproachable to do such a thing.

Now in order to bring about a marriage with such a girl as described above, the parents and relations of the man should exert themselves, as also such friends on both sides as may be desired to assist in the matter. These friends should bring to the notice of the girl's parents, the faults, both present and future, of all the other men that may wish to marry her, and should at the same time extol even to exaggeration all the excellencies, ancestral, and paternal, of their friend, so as to endear him to them, and particularly to those that may be liked by the girl's mother. One of the friends should also disguise himself as an astrologer, and declare the future good fortune and wealth of his friend by showing the existence of all the lucky omens[1] and signs,[2] the good influence of planets, the auspicious entrance of the sun into a sign of the Zodiac, propitious stars and fortunate marks on his body. Others again should rouse the jealousy of the girl's mother by telling her that their friend has a chance of getting from some other quarter even a better girl than hers.

A girl should be taken as a wife, as also given in marriage, when fortune, signs, omens, and the words[3] of others are favourable, for, says Ghotakamukha, a man should not marry at any time he likes. A girl who is asleep, crying, or gone out of the house when sought in marriage, or who is betrothed to another, should not be married. The following also should be avoided:

One who is kept concealed
One who has an ill-sounding name
One who has her nose depressed
One who has her nostril turned up
One who is formed like a male
One who is bent down
One who has crooked thighs
One who has a projecting forehead
One who has a bald head
One who does not like purity
One who has been polluted by another
One who is affected with the Gulma[4]
One who is disfigured in any way
One who has fully arrived at puberty
One who is a friend

[1] The flight of a blue jay on a person's left side is considered a lucky omen when one starts on any business; the appearance of a cat before anyone at such a time is looked on as a bad omen. There are many omens of the same kind.

[2] Such as the throbbing of the right eye of men and the left eye of women, etc.

[3] Before anything is begun it is a custom to go early in the morning to a neighbour's house, and overhear the first words that may be spoken in his family, and according as the words heard are of good or bad import, to draw an inference as to the success or failure of the undertaking.

[4] A disease consisting of any glandular enlargement in any part of the body.

One who is a younger sister
One who is a Varshakari[1]

In the same way a girl who is called by the name of one of the twenty-seven stars, or by the name of a tree, or of a river, is considered worthless, as also a girl whose name ends in 'r' or 'l'. But some authors say that prosperity is gained only by marrying that girl to whom one becomes attached, and that therefore no other girl but the one who is loved should be married by anyone.

When a girl becomes marriageable her parents should dress her smartly, and should place her where she can be easily seen by all. Every afternoon, having dressed her and decorated her in a becoming manner, they should send her with her female companions to sports, sacrifices, and marriage ceremonies, and thus show her to advantage in society, because she is a kind of merchandise. They should also receive with kind words and signs of friendliness those of an auspicious appearance who may come accompanied by their friends and relations for the purpose of marrying their daughter, and under some pretext or other having first dressed her becomingly, should then present her to them. After this they should await the pleasure of fortune, and with this object should appoint a future day on which a determination could be come to with regard to their daughter's marriage. On this occasion when the persons have come, the parents of the girl should ask them to bathe and dine, and should say, 'Everything will take place at the proper time', and should not then comply with the request, but should settle the matter later.

When a girl is thus acquired, either according to the custom of the country, or according to his own desire, the man should marry her in accordance with the precepts of the Holy Writ, according to one of the four kinds of marriage.

[1] **A woman, the palms of whose hands and the soles of whose feet are always perspiring.**

Thus ends marriage.

There are also some verses on the subject as follows:

'Amusement in society, such as completing verses begun by others, marriages, and auspicious ceremonies should be carried on neither with superiors, nor inferiors, but with our equals. That should be known as a high connection when a man, after marrying a girl, has to serve her and her relations afterwards like a servant, and such a connection is censured by the good. On the other hand, that reproachable connection, where a man, together with his relations, lords it over his wife, is called a low connection by the wise. But when both the man and the woman afford mutual pleasure to each other, and when the relatives on both sides pay respect to one another, such is called a connection in the proper sense of the word. Therefore a man should contract neither a high connection by which he is obliged to bow down afterwards to his kinsmen, nor a low connection, which is universally reprehended by all.'

CHAPTER II

OF CREATING CONFIDENCE IN THE GIRL

FOR the first three days after marriage, the girl and her husband should sleep on the floor, abstain from sexual pleasures, and eat their food without seasoning it either with alkali or salt. For the next seven days they should bathe amidst the sounds of auspicious musical instruments, should decorate themselves, dine together, and pay attention to their relations as well as to those who may have come to witness their marriage. This is applicable to persons of all castes. On the night of the tenth day the man should begin in a lonely place with soft words, and thus create confidence in the girl. Some authors say that for the purpose of winning her over he should not speak to her for three days, but the followers of Babhravya are of opinion that if the man does not speak with her for three days, the girl may be discouraged by seeing him spiritless like a pillar, and, becoming dejected, she may begin to despise him as a eunuch. Vatsyayana says that the man should begin to win her over, and to create confidence in her, but should abstain at first from sexual pleasures. Women, being of a tender nature, want tender beginnings, and when they are forcibly approached by men with whom they are but slightly acquainted, they sometimes suddenly become haters of sexual connection, and sometimes even haters of the male sex. The man should therefore approach the girl according to her liking, and should make use of those devices by which he may be able to establish himself more and more into her confidence. These devices are as follows:

He should embrace her first of all in a way she likes most, because it does not last for a long time.

He should embrace her with the upper part of his body because that is easier and simpler. If the girl is grown up, or if the man has known her for some time, he may embrace her by the light of a lamp, but if he is not well acquainted with her, or if she is a young girl, he should then embrace her in darkness.

When the girl accepts the embrace, the man should put a tambula or screw of betel nut and betel leaves in her mouth, and if she will not take it, he should induce her to do so by conciliatory words, entreaties, oaths, and kneeling at her feet, for it is a universal rule that however bashful or angry a woman may be she never disregards a man's kneeling at her feet. At the time of giving this tambula he should kiss her mouth softly and gracefully without making any sound. When she is gained over in this respect he should then make her talk, and so that she may be induced to talk he should ask her questions about things of which he knows or pretends to know nothing, and which can be answered in a few words. If she does not speak to him, he should not frighten her, but should ask her the same thing again and again in a conciliatory manner. If she does not then speak he should urge her to give a reply because, as Ghotakamukha says, 'all girls hear everything said to them by men, but do not themselves sometimes say a single word'. When she is thus importuned, the girl should give replies by shakes of the head, but if she has quarrelled with the man she should not even do that. When she is asked by the man whether she wishes for him, and whether she likes him, she should remain silent for a long time, and when at last importuned to reply, should give him a favourable answer by a nod of her head. If the man is previously acquainted with the girl he should converse with her by means of a female friend, who may be favourable to him, and in the confidence of both, and carry on the conversation on both sides. On such an occasion the girl should smile with her head bent down, and if the female friend say more on her part than she was desired to do, she should chide her and dispute with her. The female friend should say in jest even what she is not desired to say by the girl, and add, 'she says so', on which the girl should say indistinctly and prettily, 'O no! I did not say so', and she should then smile and throw an occasional glance towards the man.

If the girl is familiar with the man, she should place near him, without saying anything, the tambula, the ointment, or the garland that he may have asked for, or she may tie them up in his upper garment. While she is engaged in this, the man should touch her young breasts in the sounding way of pressing with the nails, and if she prevents him doing this he should say to her, ' I will not do it again if you will embrace me', and should in this way cause her to embrace him. While he is being embraced by her he should pass his hand repeatedly over and about her body. By and by he should place her in his lap, and try more and more to gain her consent, and if she will not yield to him he should frighten her by saying 'I shall impress marks of my teeth and nails on your lips and breasts, and then make similar marks on my own body, and shall tell my friends that you did them. What will you say then?' In this and other ways, as fear and confidence are created in the minds of children, so should the man gain her over to his wishes.

On the second and third nights, after her confidence has increased still more, he should feel the whole of her body with his hands, and kiss her all over; he should also place his hands upon her thighs and shampoo them, and if he succeed in this he should then shampoo the joints of her thighs. If she tries to prevent him doing this he should say to her, 'What harm is there in doing it?' and should persuade her to let him do it. After gaining this point he should touch her private parts, should loosen her girdle and the knot of her dress, and turning up her lower garment should shampoo the joints of her naked thighs. Under various pretences he should do all these things, but he should not at that time begin actual congress. After this he should teach her the sixty-four arts, should tell her how much he loves her, and describe to her the hopes which he formerly entertained regarding her. He should also promise to be faithful to her in future, and should dispel all her fears with respect to rival women, and, at last, after having overcome her bashfulness, he should begin to enjoy her in a way so as not to frighten her. So much about creating confidence in the girl; and there are, moreover, some verses on the subject as follows:

'A man acting according to the inclinations of a girl should try to gain her over so that she may love him and place her confidence in him. A man does not succeed either by implicitly following the inclination of a girl, or by wholly opposing her, and he should therefore adopt a middle course. He who knows how to make himself beloved by women, as well as to increase their honour and create confidence in them, this man becomes an object of their love. But he who neglects a girl, thinking she is too bashful, is despised by her as a beast ignorant of the working of the female mind. Moreover, a girl forcibly enjoyed by one who does not understand the hearts of girls becomes nervous, uneasy, and dejected, and suddenly begins to hate the man who has taken advantage of her; and then, when her love is not understood or returned, she sinks into despondency, and becomes either a hater of mankind altogether, or, hating her own man, she has recourse to other men.'[1]

[1] These last few lines have been exemplified in many ways in many novels of this century.

CHAPTER III

ON COURTSHIP, AND THE MANIFESTATION OF THE FEELINGS BY OUTWARD SIGNS AND DEEDS

A POOR man possessed of good qualities, a man born of a low family possessed of mediocre qualities, a neighbour possessed of wealth, and one under the control of his father, mother or brothers, should not marry without endeavouring to gain over the girl from her childhood to love and esteem him. Thus a boy separated from his parents, and living in the house of his uncle, should try to gain over the daughter of his uncle, or some other girl, even though she be previously betrothed to another. And this way of gaining over a girl, says Ghotakamukha, is unexceptional, because Dharma can be accomplished by means of it as well as by any other way of marriage.

When a boy has thus begun to woo the girl he loves, he should spend his time with her and amuse her with various games and diversions fitted for their age and acquaintanceship, such as picking and collecting flowers, making garlands of flowers, playing the parts of members of a fictitious family, cooking food, playing with dice, playing with cards, the game of odd and even, the game of finding out the middle finger, the game of six pebbles, and such other games as may be prevalent in the country, and agreeable to the disposition of the girl. In addition to this, he should carry on various amusing games played by several persons together, such as hide and seek, playing with seeds, hiding things in several small heaps of wheat and looking for them, blind-man's buff, gymnastic exercises, and other games of the same sort, in company with the girl, her friends and female attendants. The man should also show great kindness to any woman whom the girl thinks fit to be trusted, and should also make new acquaintances, but above all he should attach to himself by kindness and little services the daughter of the girl's nurse, for if she be gained over, even though she comes to know of his design, she does not cause any obstruction, but is sometimes even able to effect a union between him and the girl. And though she knows the true character of the man, she always talks of his many excellent qualities to the parents and relations of the girl, even though she may not be desired to do so by him.

In this way the man should do whatever the girl takes most delight in, and he should get for her whatever she may have a desire to possess. Thus he should procure for her such playthings as may be hardly known to other girls. He may also show her a ball dyed with various colours, and other curiosities of the same sort; and should give her dolls made of cloth, wood, buffalo-horn, wax, flour, or earth; also utensils for cooking food, and figures in wood, such as a man and woman standing, a pair of rams, or goats, or sheep; also temples made of earth, bamboo, or wood, dedicated to various goddesses; and cages for parrots, cuckoos, starlings, quails, cocks, and partridges; water-vessels of different sorts and of elegant forms, machines for throwing water about, guitars, stands for putting images upon, stools, lac, red arsenic, yellow ointment, vermilion and collyrium, as well as sandal-wood, saffron, betel nut and betel leaves. Such things should be given at different times whenever he gets a good opportunity of meeting her, and some of them should be given in private, and some in public, according to circumstances. In short, he should try in every way to make her look upon him as one who would do for her everything that she wanted to be done.

In the next place he should get her to meet him in some place privately, and should then tell her that the reason of his giving presents to her in secret was the fear that the parents of both of them might be displeased, and then he may add that the things which he had given her had been much desired by other people. When her love begins to show signs of increasing he should relate to her agreeable stories if she expresses a wish to hear such narratives. Or if she takes delight in legerdemain, he should amaze her by performing various tricks of jugglery; or if she feels a great curiosity to see a performance of the various arts, he should show his own skill in them. When she is delighted with singing he should entertain her with music, and on certain days, and at the time of going together to moonlight fairs and festivals, and at the time of her return after being absent from home, he should present her with bouquets of flowers, and with chaplets for the head, and with ear ornaments and rings, for these are the proper occasions on which such things should be presented.

He should also teach the daughter of the girl's nurse all the sixty-four means of pleasure practised by men, and under this pretext should also inform her of his great skill in the art of sexual enjoyment. All this time he should wear a fine dress, and make as good an appearance as possible, for young women love men who live with them, and who are handsome, good looking and well dressed. As for the sayings that though women may fall in love, they still make no effort themselves to gain over the object of their affections, that is only a matter of idle talk.

Now a girl always shows her love by outward signs and actions, such as the following:

She never looks the man in the face, and becomes abashed when she is looked at by him; under some pretext or other she shows her limbs to him; she looks secretly at him though he has gone away from her side, hangs down her head when she is asked some question by him, and answers in indistinct words and unfinished sentences, delights to be in his company for a long time, speaks to her attendants in a peculiar tone with the hope of attracting his attention towards her when she is at a distance from him, does not wish to go from the place where he is, under some pretext or other she makes him look at different things, narrates to him tales and stories very slowly so that she may continue conversing with him for a long time, kisses and embraces before him a child sitting in her lap, draws ornamental marks on the foreheads of her female servants, performs sportive and graceful movements when her attendants speak jestingly to her in the presence of her lover, confides in her lover's friends, and respects and obeys them, shows kindness to his servants, converses with them, and engages them to do her work as if she were their mistress, and listens attentively to them when they tell stories about her lover to somebody else, enters his house when induced to do so by the daughter of her nurse, and by her assistance manages to converse and play with him, avoids being seen by her lover when she is not dressed and decorated, gives him by the hand of her female friend her ear ornament, ring, or garland of flowers that he may have asked to see, always wears anything that he may have presented to her, becomes dejected when any other bridegroom is mentioned by her parents, and does not mix with those who may be of his party, or who may support his claims.

There are also some verses on the subject as follows:

'A man, who has seen and perceived the feelings of the girl towards him, and who has noticed the outward signs and movements by which those feelings are expressed, should do everything in his power to effect a union with her. He should gain over a young girl by childlike sports, a damsel come of age by his skill in the arts, and a girl that loves him by having recourse to persons in whom she confides.'

CHAPTER IV

ABOUT THINGS TO BE DONE ONLY BY THE MAN, AND THE ACQUISITION OF THE GIRL THEREBY. ALSO WHAT IS TO BE DONE BY A GIRL TO GAIN OVER A MAN, AND SUBJECT HIM TO HER

Now when the girl begins to show her love by outward signs and motions, as described in the last chapter, the lover should try to gain her over entirely by various ways and means, such as the following:

When engaged with her in any game or sport he should intentionally hold her hand. He should practise upon her the various kinds of embraces, such as the touching embrace, and others already described in a preceding chapter (Part II, Chapter II). He should show her a pair of human beings cut out of the leaf of a tree, and such like things, at intervals. When engaged in water sports, he should dive at a distance from her, and come up close to her. He should show an increased liking for the new foliage of trees and such like things. He should describe to her the pangs he suffers on her account. He should relate to her the beautiful dream that he has had with reference to other women. At parties and assemblies of his caste he should sit near her, and touch her under some pretence or other, and having placed his foot upon hers, he should slowly touch each of her toes, and press the ends of the nails; if successful in this, he should get hold of her foot with his hand and repeat the same thing. He should also press a finger of her hand between his toes when she happens to be washing his feet; and whenever he gives anything to her or takes anything from her, he should show her by his manner and look how much he loves her.

He should sprinkle upon her the water brought for rinsing his mouth; and when alone with her in a lonely place, or in darkness, he should make love to her, and tell her the true state of his mind without distressing her in any way.

Whenever he sits with her on the same seat or bed he should say to her, 'I have something to tell you in private', and then, when she comes to hear it in a quiet place, he should express his love to her more by manner and signs than by words. When he comes to know the state of her feelings towards him he should pretend to be ill, and should make her come to his house to speak to him. There he should intentionally hold her hand and place it on his eyes and forehead, and under the pretence of preparing some medicine for him he should ask her to do the work for his sake in the following words: 'This work must be done by you, and by nobody else.' When she wants to go away he should let her go, with an earnest request to come and see him again. This device of illness should be continued for three days and three nights. After this, when she begins coming to see him frequently, he should carry on long conversations with her, for, says Ghotakamukha, 'though a man loves a girl ever so much, he never succeeds in winning her without a great deal of talking'. At last, when the man finds the girl completely gained over, he may then begin to enjoy her. As for the saying that women grow less timid than usual during the evening, and in darkness, and are desirous of congress at those times, and do not oppose men then, and should only be enjoyed at these hours, it is a matter of talk only.

When it is impossible for the man to carry on his endeavours alone, he should, by means of the daughter of her nurse, or of a female friend in whom she confides, cause the girl to be brought to him without making known to her his design, and he should then proceed with her in the manner above described. Or he should in the beginning send his own female servant to live with the girl as her friend, and should then gain her over by her means.

At last, when he knows the state of her feelings by her outward manner and conduct towards him at religious ceremonies, marriage ceremonies, fairs, festivals, theatres, public assemblies, and such like occasions, he should begin to enjoy her when she is alone, for Vatsyayana lays it down, that women, when resorted to at proper times and in proper places, do not turn away from their lovers.

When a girl, possessed of good qualities and well-bred, though born in a humble family, or destitute of wealth, and not therefore desired by her equals, or an orphan girl, or one deprived of her parents, but observing the rules of her family and caste, should wish to bring about her own marriage when she comes of age, such a girl should endeavour to gain over a strong and good looking young man, or a person whom she thinks would marry her on account of the weakness of his mind, and even without the consent of his parents. She should do this by such means as would endear her to the said person, as well as by frequently seeing and meeting him. Her mother also should constantly cause them to meet by means of her female friends, and the daughter of her nurse. The girl herself should try to get alone with her beloved in some quiet place, and at odd times should give him flowers, betel nut, betel leaves and perfumes. She should also show her skill in the practice of the arts, in shampooing, in scratching and in pressing with the nails. She should also talk to him on the subjects he likes best, and discuss with him the ways and means of gaining over and winning the affections of a girl.

But old authors say that although the girl loves the man ever so much, she should not offer herself, or make the first overtures, for a girl who does this loses her dignity, and is liable to be scorned and rejected. But when the man shows his wish to enjoy her, she should be favourable to him and should show no change in her demeanour when he embraces her, and should receive all the manifestations of his love as if she were ignorant of the state of his mind. But when he tries to kiss her she should oppose him; when he begs to be allowed to have sexual intercourse with her she should let him touch her private parts only and with considerable difficulty; and though importuned by him, she should not yield herself up to him as if of her own accord, but should resist his attempts to have her. It is only, moreover, when she is certain that she is truly loved, and that her over is indeed devoted to her, and will not change his mind, that she should then give herself up to him, and persuade him to marry her quickly. After losing her virginity she should tell her confidential friends about it.

Here end the efforts of a girl to gain over a man.

There are also some verses on the subject as follows:

'A girl who is much sought after should marry the man that she likes, and whom she thinks would be obedient to her, and capable of giving her pleasure. But when from the desire of wealth a girl is married by her parents to a rich man without taking into consideration the character or looks of the bridegroom, or when given to a man who has several wives, she never becomes attached to the man, even though he be endowed with good qualities, obedient to her will, active, strong, and healthy, and anxious to please her in every way.[1] A husband who is obedient but yet master of himself, though he be poor and not good looking, is better than one who is common to many women, even though he be handsome and attractive. The wives of rich men, where there are many wives, are not generally attached to their husbands, and are not confi-

[1] There is a good deal of truth in the last few observations. Woman is a monogamous animal, and loves but one, and likes to feel herself alone in the affections of one man, and cannot bear rivals. It may also be taken as a general rule that women either married to, or kept by, rich men love them for their wealth but not for themselves.

dential with them, and even though they possess all the external enjoyments of life, still have recourse to other men. A man who is of a low mind, who has fallen from his social position, and who is much given to travelling, does not deserve to be married; neither does one who has many wives and children, or one who is devoted to sport and gambling, and who comes to his wife only when he likes. Of all the lovers of a girl he only is her true husband who possesses the qualities that are liked by her, and such a husband only enjoys real superiority over her, because he is the husband of love.'

CHAPTER V

ON CERTAIN FORMS OF MARRIAGE[1]

WHEN a girl cannot meet her lover frequently in private, she should send the daughter of her nurse to him, it being understood that she has confidence in her, and had previously gained her over to her interests. On seeing the man, the daughter of the nurse should, in the course of conversation, describe to him the noble birth, the good disposition, the beauty, talent, skill, knowledge of human nature and affection of the girl in such a way as not to let him suppose that she had been sent by the girl, and should thus create affection for the girl in the heart of the man. To the girl also she should speak about the excellent qualities of the man, especially of those qualities which she knows are pleasing to the girl. She should, moreover, speak with disparagement of the other lovers of the girl, and talk about the avarice and indiscretion of their parents, and the fickleness of their relations. She should also quote samples of many girls of ancient times, such as Sakoontala and others, who, having united themselves with lovers of their own caste and their own choice, were ever happy afterwards in their society. And she should also tell of other girls who married into great families, and being troubled by rival wives, became wretched and miserable, and were finally abandoned. She should further speak of the good fortune, the continual happiness, the chastity, obedience, and affection of the man, and if the girl gets amorous about him, she should endeavour to allay her shame[2] and

[1] These forms of marriage differ from the four kinds of marriage mentioned in Chapter I, and are only to be made use of when the girl is gained over in the way mentioned in Chapters III and IV.

[2] About this, see a story on the fatal effects of love at page 114 of *Early Ideas; a Group of Hindoo Stories*, collected and collated by Anaryan, W. H. Allen and Co., London, 1881.

her fear as well as her suspicions about any disaster that might result from her marriage. In a word, she should act the whole part of a female messenger by telling the girl all about the man's affection for her, the places he frequented, and the endeavours he made to meet her, and by frequently repeating, 'It will be all right if the man will take you away forcibly and unexpectedly.'

The Forms of Marriage

When the girl is gained over, and acts openly with the man as his wife, he should cause fire to be brought from the house of a Brahman, and having spread the Kusha grass upon the ground, and offered an oblation to the fire, he should marry her according to the precepts of the religious law. After this he should inform his parents of the fact, because it is the opinion of ancient authors that a marriage solemnly contracted in the presence of fire cannot afterwards be set aside.

After the consummation of the marriage, the relations of the man should gradually be made acquainted with the affair, and the relations of the girl should also be apprised of it in such a way that they may consent to the marriage, and overlook the manner in which it was brought about, and when this is done they should afterwards be reconciled by affectionate presents and favourable conduct. In this manner the man should marry the girl according to the Gandharva form of marriage.

When the girl cannot make up her mind, or will not express her readiness to marry, the man should obtain her in any one of the following ways:

On a fitting occasion, and under some excuse, he should, by means of a female friend with whom he is well acquainted, and whom he can trust, and who also is well known to the girl's family, get the girl brought unexpectedly to his house, and he should then bring fire from the house of a Brahman, and proceed as before described.

When the marriage of the girl with some other person draws near, the man should disparage the future husband to the utmost in the mind of the mother of the girl, and then having got the girl to come with her mother's consent to a neighbouring house, he should bring fire from the house of a Brahman, and proceed as above.

The man should become a great friend of the brother of the girl, the said brother being of the same age as himself, and addicted to courtesans, and to intrigues with the wives of other people, and should give him assistance in such matters, and also give him occasional presents. He should then tell him about his great love for his sister, as young men will sacrifice even their lives for the sake of those who may be of the same age, habits, and dispositions as themselves. After this the man should get the girl brought by means of her brother to some secure place, and having brought fire from the house of a Brahman should proceed as before.

The man should on the occasion of festivals get the daughter of the nurse to give the girl some intoxicating substance, and then cause her to be brought to some secure place under the pretence of some business, and there having enjoyed her before she recovers from her intoxication, should bring fire from the house of a Brahman, and proceed as before.

The man should, with the connivance of the daughter of the nurse, carry off the girl from her house while she is asleep, and then, having enjoyed her before she recovers from her sleep, should bring fire from the house of a Brahman, and proceed as before.

When the girl goes to a garden, or to some village in the neighbourhood, the man should, with his friends, fall on her guards, and having killed them, or frightened them away, forcibly carry her off, and proceed as before.

There are verses on this subject as follows:

'In all the forms of marriage given in this chapter of this

work, the one that precedes is better than the one that follows it on account of its being more in accordance with the commands of religion, and therefore it is only when it is impossible to carry the former into practice that the latter should be resorted to, As the fruit of all good marriages is love, the Gandharva[1] form of marriage is respected, even though it is formed under unfavourable circumstances, because it fulfils the object sought for. Another cause of the respect accorded to the Gandharva form of marriage is that it brings forth happiness, causes less trouble in its performance than the other forms of marriage, and is above all the result of previous love.'

[1] About the Gandharvavivaha form of marriage, see note to page 28 of Captain R. F. Burton's *Vickram and the Vampire; or Tales of Hindu Devilry*, Longmans, Green and Co., London 1870. This form of matrimony was recognised by the ancient Hindoos, and is frequent in books. It is a kind of Scotch Wedding —ultra-Caledonian—taking place by mutual consent without any form or ceremony. The Gandharvas are heavenly minstrels of Indra's court, who are supposed to be witnesses.

PART IV

ABOUT A WIFE

CHAPTER I

ON THE MANNER OF LIVING OF A VIRTUOUS WOMAN, AND OF HER BEHAVIOUR DURING THE ABSENCE OF HER HUSBAND

A VIRTUOUS woman, who has affection for her husband, should act in conformity with his wishes as if he were a divine being, and with his consent should take upon herself the whole care of his family. She should keep the whole house well cleaned, and arrange flowers of various kinds in different parts of it, and make the floor smooth and polished so as to give the whole a neat and becoming appearance. She should surround the house with a garden, and place ready in it all the materials required for the morning, noon and evening sacrifices. Moreover she should herself revere the sanctuary of the Household Gods, for, says Gonardiya, 'nothing so much attracts the heart of a householder to his wife as a careful observance of the things mentioned above'.

Towards the parents, relations, friends, sisters, and servants of her husband she should behave as they deserve. In the garden she should plant beds of green vegetables, bunches of the sugar cane, and clumps of the fig tree, the mustard plant, the parsley plant, the fennel plant, and the xanthochymus pictorius. Clusters of various flowers such as the trapa bispinosa, the jasmine, the jasminum grandiflorum, the yellow amaranth, the wild jasmine, the tabernamontana coronaria, the nadyaworta, the china rose and others, should likewise be planted, together with the fragrant grass andropogon schaenanthus, and the fragrant root of the plant andropogon miricatus. She should also have seats and arbours made in the garden, in the middle of which a well, tank, or pool should be dug.

The wife should always avoid the company of female beggars, female Buddhist mendicants, unchaste and roguish women, female fortune tellers and witches. As regards meals she should always consider what her husband likes and dislikes and what things are good for him, and what are injurious to him. When she hears the sounds of his footsteps coming home she should at once get up and be ready to do whatever he may command her, and either order her female servant to wash his feet, or wash them herself. When going anywhere with her husband, she should put on her ornaments, and without his consent she should not either give or accept invitations, or attend marriages and sacrifices, or sit in the company of female friends, or visit the temples of the Gods. And if she wants to engage in any kind of games or sports, she should not do it against his will. In the same way she should always sit down after him, and get up before him, and should never awaken him when he is asleep. The kitchen should be situated in a quiet and retired place, so as not to be accessible to strangers, and should always look clean.

In the event of any misconduct on the part of her husband, she should not blame him excessively, though she be a little displeased. She should not use abusive language towards him, but rebuke him with conciliatory words, whether he be in the company of friends or alone. Moreover, she should not be a scold, for, says Gonardiya, 'there is no cause of dislike on the part of a husband so great as this characteristic in a wife'. Lastly she should avoid bad expressions, sulky looks, speaking aside, standing in the doorway, and looking at passers-by, conversing in the pleasure groves, and remaining in a lonely place for a long time; and finally she should always keep her body, her teeth, her hair and everything belonging to her tidy, sweet, and clean.

When the wife wants to approach her husband in private her dress should consist of many ornaments, various kinds of flowers, and a cloth decorated with different colours, and some sweet-smelling ointments or unguents. But her every-day dress should be composed of a thin, close-textured cloth, a few ornaments and flowers, and a little scent, not too much. She should also observe the fasts and vows of her husband, and when he tries to prevent her doing this, she should persuade him to let her do it.

At appropriate times of the year, and when they happen to be cheap, she should buy earth, bamboos, firewood, skins, and iron pots, as also salt and oil. Fragrant substances, vessels made of the fruit of the plant wrightea antidysenterica, or oval leaved wrightea, medicines, and other things which are always wanted, should be obtained when required and kept in a secret place of the house. The seeds of the radish, the potato, the common beet, the Indian wormwood, the mango, the cucumber, the egg plant, the kushmanda, the pumpkin gourd, the surana, the bignonia indica, the sandal wood, the premna spinosa, the garlic plant, the onion, and other vegetables, should be bought and sown at the proper seasons.

The wife, moreover, should not tell to strangers the amount of her wealth, nor the secrets which her husband has confided to her. She should surpass all the women of her own rank in life in her cleverness, her appearance, her knowledge of cookery, her pride, and her manner of serving her husband. The expenditure of the year should be regulated by the profits. The milk that remains after the meals should be turned into ghee or clarified butter. Oil and sugar should be prepared at home; spinning and weaving should also be done there; and a store of ropes and cords, and barks of trees for twisting into ropes should be kept. She should also attend to the pounding and cleaning of rice, using its small grain and chaff in some way or other. She should pay the salaries of the servants, look after the tilling of the fields, and keeping of the flocks and herds, superintend the making of vehicles, and take care of the rams, cocks, quails, parrots, starlings, cuckoos, peacocks, monkeys, and deer; and finally adjust the income and expenditure of the day. The worn-out clothes should be given to those servants who have done good work, in order to show them that their services have been appreciated, or they may be applied to some other use. The vessels in which wine is prepared, as well as those in which it is kept, should be carefully looked after, and put away at the proper time. All sales and purchases should also be well attended to. The friends of her husband she should welcome by presenting them with flowers, ointment, incense, betel leaves, and betel nut. Her father-in-law and mother-in-law she should treat as they deserve, always remaining dependent on their will, never contradicting them, speaking to them in few and not harsh words, not laughing loudly in their presence, and acting with their friends and enemies as with her own. In addition to the above she should not be vain, or too much taken up with her enjoyments. She should be liberal towards her servants, and reward them on holidays and festivals; and not give away anything without first making it known to her husband.

Thus ends the manner of living of a virtuous woman.

During the absence of her husband on a journey the virtuous woman should wear only her auspicious ornaments, and observe the fasts in honour of the Gods. While anxious to hear the news of her husband, she should still look after her household affairs. She should sleep near the elder women of the house, and make herself agreeable to them. She should look after and keep in repair the things that are liked by her husband, and continue the works that have been begun by him. To the abode of her relations she should not go except on occasions of joy and sorrow, and then she should go in her usual travelling dress, accompanied by her husband's servants, and not remain there for a long time. The fasts and feasts should be observed with the consent of the elders of the house. The resources should be increased by making purchases and sales according to the practice of the merchants and by means of honest servants, superintended by herself. The income should be increased, and the expenditure diminished as much as possible. And when her husband returns from his journey, she should receive him at first in her ordinary clothes, so that he may know in what way she has lived during his absence, and should bring to him some presents, as also materials for the worship of the Deity.

Thus ends the part relating to the behaviour of a wife during the absence of her husband on a journey.

There are also some verses on the subject as follows:

'The wife, whether she be a woman of noble family, or a virgin widow[1] remarried, or a concubine, should lead a chaste life, devoted to her husband, and doing everything for his welfare. Women acting thus acquire Dharma, Artha, and Kama, obtain a high position, and generally keep their husbands devoted to them.'

[1] This probably refers to a girl married in her infancy, or when very young and whose husband had died before she arrived at the age of puberty. Infant marriages are still the common custom of the Hindoos.

CHAPTER II

ON THE CONDUCT OF THE ELDER WIFE TOWARDS THE OTHER WIVES OF HER HUSBAND, AND ON THAT OF A YOUNGER WIFE TOWARDS THE ELDER ONES. ALSO ON THE CONDUCT OF A VIRGIN WIDOW RE-MARRIED; OF A WIFE DISLIKED BY HER HUSBAND; OF THE WOMEN IN THE KING'S HAREM; AND LASTLY ON THE CONDUCT OF A HUSBAND TOWARDS MANY WIVES

THE causes of re-marrying during the lifetime of the wife are as follows:

The folly or ill-temper of the wife
Her husband's dislike to her
The want of offspring
The continual birth of daughters
The incontinence of the husband

From the very beginning, a wife should endeavour to attract the heart of her husband, by showing to him continually her devotion, her good temper, and her wisdom. If however she bears him no children, she should herself tell her husband to marry another woman. And when the second wife is married, and brought to the house, the first wife should give her a position superior to her own, and look upon her as a sister. In the morning the elder wife should forcibly make the younger one decorate herself in the presence of their husband, and should not mind all the husband's favour being given to her. If the younger wife does anything to displease her husband the elder one should not neglect her, but should always be ready to give her most careful advice, and should teach her to do various things in the presence of her husband. Her children she should treat as her own, her attendants she should look upon with more regard, even than on her own servants, her friends she should cherish with love and kindness, and her relations with great honour.

When there are many other wives besides herself, the elder wife should associate with the one who is immediately next to her in rank and age, and should instigate the wife who has recently enjoyed her husband's favour to quarrel with the present favourite. After this she should sympathize with the former, and having collected all the other wives together, should get them to denounce the favourite as a scheming and wicked woman, without however committing herself in any way. If the favourite wife happens to quarrel with the husband, then the elder wife should take her part and give her false encouragement, and thus cause the quarrel to be increased. If there be only a little quarrel between the two, the elder wife should do all she can to work it up into a large quarrel. But if after all this she finds the husband still continues to love his favourite wife she should then change her tactics, and endeavour to bring about a conciliation between them, so as to avoid her husband's displeasure.

Thus ends the conduct of the elder wife.

The younger wife should regard the elder wife of her husband as her mother, and should not give anything away, even to her own relations, without her knowledge. She should tell her everything about herself, and not approach her husband without her permission. Whatever is told to her by the elder wife she should not reveal to others, and she should take care of the children of the senior even more than of her own. When alone with her husband she should serve him well, but should not tell him of the pain she suffers from the existence of a rival wife. She may also obtain secretly from her husband some marks of his particular regard for her, and may tell him that she lives only for him, and for the regard that he has for her. She should never reveal her love for her husband, nor her husband's love for her to any person, either in pride or in anger, for a wife that reveals the secrets of her husband is despised by him. As for seeking to obtain the regard of her husband, Gonardiya says, that it should always be done in private, for fear of the elder wife. If the elder wife be disliked by her husband, or be childless, she should sympathize with her, and should ask her husband to do the same, but should surpass her in leading the life of a chaste woman.

Thus ends the conduct of the younger wife towards the elder.

A widow in poor circumstances, or of a weak nature, and who allies herself again to a man, is called a widow re-married.

The followers of Babhravya say that a virgin widow should not marry a person whom she may be obliged to leave on account of his bad character, or of his being destitute of the excellent qualities of a man, she thus being obliged to have recourse to another person. Gonardiya is of opinion that as the cause of a widow's marrying again is her desire for happiness, and as happiness is secured by the possession of excellent qualities in her husband, joined to love of enjoyment, it is better therefore to secure a person endowed with such qualities in the first instance. Vatsyayana however thinks that a widow may marry any person that she likes, and that she thinks will suit her.

At the time of her marriage the widow should obtain from her husband the money to pay the cost of drinking parties, and picnics with her relations, and of giving them and her friends kindly gifts and presents; or she may do these things at her own cost if she likes. In the same way she may wear either her husband's ornaments or her own. As to the presents of affection mutually exchanged between the husband and herself there is no fixed rule about them. If she leaves her husband after marriage of her own accord, she should restore to him whatever he may have given her, with the exception of the mutual presents. If however she is driven out of the house by her husband she should not return anything to him.

After her marriage she should live in the house of her husband like one of the chief members of the family, but should treat the other ladies of the family with kindness, the servants with generosity, and all the friends of the house with familiarity and good temper. She should show that she is better acquainted with the sixty-four arts than the other ladies of the house, and in any quarrels with her husband she should not rebuke him severely but in private do everything that he wishes, and make use of the sixty-four ways of enjoyment. She should be obliging to the other wives of her husband, and to their children she should give presents, behave as their mistress, and make ornaments and playthings for their use. In the friends and servants of her husband she should confide more than in his other wives, and finally she should have a liking for drinking parties, going to picnics, attending fairs and festivals, and for carrying out all kinds of games and amusements.

Thus ends the conduct of a virgin widow re-married.

A woman who is disliked by her husband, and annoyed and distressed by his other wives, should associate with the wife who is liked most by her husband, and who serves him more than the others, and should teach her all the arts with which she is acquainted. She should act as the nurse to her husband's children, and having gained over his friends to her side, should through them make him acquainted of her devotion to him. In religious ceremonies she should be a leader, as also in vows and fasts, and should not hold too good an opinion of herself. When her husband is lying on his bed she should only go near him when it is agreeable to him, and should never rebuke him, or show obstinacy in any way. If her husband happens to quarrel with any of his other wives, she should reconcile them to each other, and if he desires to see any woman secretly, she should manage to bring about the meeting between them. She should moreover make herself acquainted with the weak points of her husband's character, but always keep them secret, and on the whole behave herself in such a way as may lead him to look upon her as a good and devoted wife.

Here ends the conduct of a wife disliked by her husband.

The above sections will show how all the women of the king's seraglio are to behave, and therefore we shall now speak separately only about the king.

The female attendants in the harem (called severally Kanchukiyas,[1] Mahallarikas,[2] and Mahallikas[3]) should bring flowers, ointments and clothes from the king's wives to the king, and he having received these things should give them as presents to the servants, along with the things worn by him the previous day. In the afternoon the king, having dressed and put on his ornaments, should interview the women of the harem, who should also be dressed and decorated with jewels. Then having given to each of them such a place and such respect as may suit the occasion and as they may deserve, he should carry on with them a cheerful conversation. After that he should see such of his

[1] A name given to the maid servants of the zenana of the kings in ancient times, on account of their always keeping their breasts covered with a cloth called Kanchuki. It was customary in the olden time for the maid servants to cover their breasts with a cloth, while the queens kept their breasts uncovered. This custom is distinctly to be seen in the Ajunta cave paintings.

[2] The meaning of this word is a superior woman, so it would seem that a Mahallarika must be a person in authority over the maid servants of the house.

[3] This was also appertaining to the rank of women employed in the harem. In latter times this place was given to eunuchs.

wives as may be virgin widows re-married, and after them the concubines and dancing girls. All of these should be visited in their own private rooms.

When the king rises from his noonday sleep, the woman whose duty it is to inform the king regarding the wife who is to spend the night with him should come to him accompanied by the female attendants of that wife whose turn may have arrived in the regular course, and of her who may have been accidentally passed over as her turn arrived, and of her who may have been unwell at the time of her turn. These attendants should place before the king the ointments and unguents sent by each of these wives, marked with the seal of her ring, and their names and their reasons for sending the ointments should be told to the king. After this the king accepts the ointment of one of them, who then is informed that her ointment has been accepted, and that her day has been settled.[1]

At festivals, singing parties and exhibitions, all the wives of the king should be treated with respect and served with drinks.

But the women of the harem should not be allowed to go out alone, neither should any women outside the harem be allowed to enter it except those whose character is well known. And lastly the work which the king's wives have to do should not be too fatiguing.

Thus ends the conduct of the king towards the women of the harem, and of their own conduct.

A man marrying many wives should act fairly towards them all. He should neither disregard nor pass over their faults, and should not reveal to one wife the love, passion,

[1] As kings generally had many wives, it was usual for them to enjoy their wives by turns. But as it happened sometimes that some of them lost their turns owing to the king's absence, or to their being unwell, then in such cases the women whose turns had been passed over, and those whose turns had come, used to have a sort of lottery, and the ointments of all the claimants were sent to the king, who accepted the ointment of one of them, and thus settled the question.

bodily blemishes and confidential reproaches of the other. No opportunity should be given to any one of them of speaking to him about their rivals, and if one of them should begin to speak ill of another, he should chide her and tell her that she has exactly the same blemishes in her character. One of them he should please by secret confidence, another by secret respect, and another by secret flattery, and he should please them all by going to gardens, by amusements, by presents, by honouring their relations, by telling them secrets, and lastly by loving unions. A young woman who is of a good temper, and who conducts herself according to the precepts of the Holy Writ, wins her husband's attachments, and obtains a superiority over her rivals.

Thus ends the conduct of a husband towards many wives.

PART V

ABOUT THE WIVES OF OTHER MEN

CHAPTER I

OF THE CHARACTERISTICS OF MEN AND WOMEN. THE REASONS WHY WOMEN REJECT THE ADDRESSES OF MEN. ABOUT MEN WHO HAVE SUCCESS WITH WOMEN, AND ABOUT WOMEN WHO ARE EASILY GAINED OVER

THE wives of other people may be resorted to on the occasions already described in Part I, Chapter V, of this work, but the possibility of their acquisition, their fitness for cohabitation, the danger to oneself in uniting with them, and the future effect of these unions, should first of all be examined. A man may resort to the wife of another, for the purpose of saving his own life, when he perceives that his love for her proceeds from one degree of intensity to another. These degrees are ten in number, and are distinguished by the following marks:

Love of the eye
Attachment of the mind
Constant reflection
Destruction of sleep
Emaciation of the body
Turning away from objects of enjoyment
Removal of shame
Madness
Fainting
Death

Ancient authors say that a man should know the disposition, truthfulness, purity, and will of a young woman, as also the intensity, or weakness of her passions, from the form of her body, and from her characteristic marks and signs. But Vatsyayana is of opinion that the forms of bodies, and the characteristic marks or signs are but erring tests of character, and that women should be judged by their conduct, by the outward expression of their thoughts, and by the movements of their bodies.

Now as a general rule Gonikaputra says that a woman falls in love with every handsome man she sees, and so does every man at the sight of a beautiful woman, but frequently they do not take any further steps, owing to various considerations. In love the following circumstances are peculiar to the woman. She loves without regard to right or wrong,[1] and does not try to gain over a man simply for the attainment of some particular purpose. Moreover, when a man first makes up to her she naturally shrinks from him, even though she may be willing to unite herself with him. But when the attempts to gain her are repeated and renewed, she at last consents. But with a man, even though he may have begun to love, he conquers his feelings from a regard for morality and wisdom, and although his thoughts are often on the woman, he does not yield, even though an attempt be made to gain him over. He sometimes makes an attempt or effort to win the object of his affections, and having failed, he leaves her alone for the future. In the same way, when a woman is once gained, he often becomes indifferent about her. As for the saying that a man does not care for what is easily gained, and only desires a thing which cannot be obtained without difficulty, it is only a matter of talk.

The causes of a woman rejecting the addresses of a man are as follows:

Affection for her husband
Desire of lawful progeny
Want of opportunity
Anger at being addressed by the man too familiarly
Difference in rank of life

[1] On peut tout attendre et tout supposer d'une femme amoureuse.—Balzac.

Want of certainty on account of the man being devoted to travelling

Thinking that the man may be attached to some other person

Fear of the man's not keeping his intentions secret

Thinking that the man is too devoted to his friends, and has too great a regard for them

The apprehension that he is not in earnest

Bashfulness on account of his being an illustrious man

Fear on account of his being powerful, or possessed of too impetuous passion, in the case of the deer woman

Bashfulness on account of his being too clever

The thought of having once lived with him on friendly terms only

Contempt of his want of knowledge of the world

Distrust of his low character

Disgust at his want of perception of her love for him

In the case of an elephant woman, the thought that he is a hare man, or a man of weak passion

Compassion lest anything should befall him on account of his passion

Despair at her own imperfections

Fear of discovery

Disillusion at seeing his grey hair or shabby appearance

Fear that he may be employed by her husband to test her chastity

The thought that he has too much regard for morality

Whichever of the above causes a man may detect, he should endeavour to remove it from the very beginning. Thus, the bashfulness that may arise from his greatness or his ability, he should remove by showing his great love and affection for her. The difficulty of the want of opportunity, or of his inaccessibility, he should remove by showing her some easy way of access. The excessive respect entertained by the woman for him should be removed by making himself very familiar. The difficulties that arise from his being thought a low character he should remove by showing his valour and his wisdom; those that come from neglect by extra attention; and those that arise from fear by giving her proper encouragement.

The following are the men who generally obtain success with women:

Men well versed in the science of love
Men skilled in telling stories
Men acquainted with women from their childhood
Men who have secured their confidence
Men who send presents to them
Men who talk well
Men who do things that they like
Men who have not loved other women previously
Men who act as messengers
Men who know their weak points
Men who are desired by good women
Men who are united with their female friends
Men who are good looking
Men who have been brought up with them
Men who are their neighbours
Men who are devoted to sexual pleasures, even though these be with their own servants
The lovers of the daughters of their nurse
Men who have been lately married
Men who like picnics and pleasure parties
Men who are liberal
Men who are celebrated for being very strong (Bull men)
Enterprising and brave men
Men who surpass their husbands in learning and good looks, in good qualities, and in liberality
Men whose dress and manner of living are magnificent

The following are the women who are easily gained over:

Women who stand at the doors of their houses

Women who are always looking out on the street

Women who sit conversing in their neighbour's house

A woman who is always staring at you

A female messenger

A woman who looks sideways at you

A woman whose husband has taken another wife without any just cause

A woman who hates her husband, or who is hated by him

A woman who has nobody to look after her, or keep her in check

A woman who has not had any children

A woman whose family or caste is not well known

A woman whose children are dead

A woman who is very fond of society

A woman who is apparently very affectionate with her husband

The wife of an actor

A widow

A poor woman

A woman fond of enjoyments

The wife of a man with many younger brothers

A vain woman

A woman whose husband is inferior to her in rank or abilities

A woman who is proud of her skill in the arts

A woman disturbed in mind by the folly of her husband

A woman who has been married in her infancy to a rich man, and not liking him when she grows up, desires a man possessing a disposition, talents, and wisdom suitable to her own tastes

A woman who is slighted by her husband without any cause

A woman who is not respected by other women of the same rank or beauty as herself

A woman whose husband is devoted to travelling

The wife of a jeweller

A jealous woman
A covetous woman
An immoral woman
A barren woman
A lazy woman
A cowardly woman
A humpbacked woman
A dwarfish woman
A deformed woman
A vulgar woman
An ill-smelling woman
A sick woman
An old woman

There are also two verses on the subject as follows:

'Desire, which springs from nature, and which is increased by art, and from which all danger is taken away by wisdom, becomes firm and secure. A clever man, depending on his own ability, and observing carefully the ideas and thoughts of women, and removing the causes of their turning away from men, is generally successful with them.'

CHAPTER II

ABOUT MAKING ACQUAINTANCE WITH THE WOMAN, AND OF THE EFFORTS TO GAIN HER OVER

ANCIENT authors are of opinion that girls are not so easily seduced by employing female messengers as by the efforts of the man himself, but that the wives of others are more easily got at by the aid of female messengers than by the personal efforts of the man. But Vatsyayana lays it down that whenever it is possible a man should always act himself in these matters, and it is only when such is impracticable, or impossible, that female messengers should be employed. As for the saying that women who act and talk boldly and freely are to be won by the personal efforts of the man, and that women who do not possess those qualities are to be got at by female messengers, it is only a matter of talk.

Now when a man acts himself in the matter he should first of all make the acquaintance of the woman he loves in the following manner:

He should arrange to be seen by the woman either on a natural or special opportunity. A natural opportunity is when one of them goes to the house of the other, and a special opportunity is when they meet either at the house of a friend, or a caste-fellow, or a minister, or a physician, as also on the occasion of marriage ceremonies, sacrifices, festivals, funerals, and garden parties.

When they do meet, the man should be careful to look at her in such a way as to cause the state of his mind to be made known to her; he should pull about his moustache, make a sound with his nails, cause his own ornaments to tinkle, bite his lower lip, and make various other signs of that description. When she is looking at him he should speak to his friends about her and other women, and should show to her his liberality and his appreciation of enjoyments. When sitting by the side of a female friend he should yawn and twist his body, contract his eyebrows, speak very slowly as if he was weary, and listen to her indifferently. A conversation having two meanings should also be carried on with a child or some other person, apparently having regard to a third person, but really having reference to the woman he loves, and in this way his love should be made manifest under the pretext of referring to others rather than to herself. He should make marks that have reference to her, on the earth with his nails, or with a stick, and should embrace and kiss a child in her presence, and give it the mixture of betel nut and betel leaves with his tongue, and press its chin with his fingers in a caressing way. All these things should be done at the proper time and in proper places.

The man should fondle a child that may be sitting on her lap, and give it something to play with, and also take the same back again. Conversation with respect to the child may also be held with her, and in this manner he should gradually become well acquainted with her, and he should also make himself agreeable to her relations. Afterwards, this acquaintance should be made a pretext for visiting her house frequently, and on such occasions he should converse on the subject of love in her absence but within her hearing. As his intimacy with her increases he should place in her charge some kind of deposit or trust, and take away from it a small portion at a time; or he may give her some fragrant substances, or betel nuts to be kept for him by her. After this he should endeavour to make her well acquainted with his own wife, and get them to carry on confidential conversations, and to sit together in lonely places. In order to see her frequently he should arrange so that the same goldsmith, the same jeweller, the same basket maker, the same dyer, and the same washerman should be employed by the two families. And he should also pay her long visits openly under the pretence of being engaged with her on business, and one business should lead to another, so as to keep up the intercourse between them. Whenever she wants anything, or is in need of money, or wishes to acquire skill in one of the arts, he should cause her to understand that he is willing and able to do anything that she wants, to give her money, or teach her one of the arts, all these things being quite within his ability and power. In the same way he should hold discussions with her in company with other people, and they should talk of the doings and sayings of other persons, and examine different things, like jewellery, precious stones, etc. On such occasions he should show her certain things with the values of which she may be unacquainted, and if she begins to dispute with him about the things or their value, he should not contradict her, but point out that he agrees with her in every way.

Thus end the ways of making the acquaintance of the woman desired.

Now after a girl has become acquainted with the man as above described, and has manifested her love to him by the various outward signs and by the motions of her body, the man should make every effort to gain her over. But as girls are not acquainted with sexual union, they should be treated with the greatest delicacy, and the man should proceed with considerable caution, though in the case of other women, accustomed to sexual intercourse, this is not necessary. When the intentions of the girl are known, and her bashfulness put aside, the man should begin to make use of her money, and an interchange of clothes, rings, and flowers should be made. In this the man should take particular care that the things given by him are handsome and valuable. He should moreover receive from her a mixture of betel nut and betel leaves, and when he is going to a party he should ask for the flower in her hair, or for the flower in her hand. If he himself gives her a flower it should be a sweet smelling one, and marked with marks made by his nails or teeth. With increasing assiduity he should dispel her fears, and by degrees get her to go with him to some lonely place, and there he should embrace and kiss her. And finally at the time of giving her some betel nut, or of receiving the same from her, or at the time of making an exchange of flowers, he should touch and press her private parts, thus bringing his efforts to a satisfactory conclusion.

When a man is endeavouring to seduce one woman, he should not attempt to seduce any other at the same time. But after he has succeeded with the first, and enjoyed her for a considerable time, he can keep her affections by giving her presents that she likes, and then commence making up to another woman. When a man sees the husband of a woman going to some place near his house, he should not enjoy the woman then, even though she may be easily gained over at that time. A wise man having a regard for his reputation should not think of seducing a woman who is apprehensive, timid, not to be trusted, well guarded, or possessed of a father-in-law, or mother-in-law.

CHAPTER III

EXAMINATION OF THE STATE OF A WOMAN'S MIND

WHEN a man is trying to gain over a woman he should examine the state of her mind, and act as follows:

If she listens to him, but does not manifest to him in any way her own intentions, he should then try to gain her over by means of a go-between.

If she meets him once, and again comes to meet him better dressed than before, or comes to him in some lonely place, he should be certain that she is capable of being enjoyed by the use of a little force. A woman who lets a man make up to her, but does not give herself up, even after a long time, should be considered as a trifler in love, but owing to the fickleness of the human mind, even such a woman can be conquered by always keeping up a close acquaintance with her.

When a woman avoids the attentions of a man, and on account of respect for him, and pride in herself, will not meet him or approach him, she can be gained over with difficulty, either by endeavouring to keep on familiar terms with her, or else by an exceedingly clever go-between.

When a man makes up to a woman, and she reproaches him with harsh words, she should be abandoned at once.

When a woman reproaches a man, but at the same time acts affectionately towards him, she should be made love to in every way.

A woman, who meets a man in lonely places, and puts up with the touch of his foot, but pretends, on account of the indecision of her mind, not to be aware of it, should be conquered by patience, and by continued efforts as follows:

If she happens to go to sleep in his vicinity he should put

his left arm round her, and see when she awakes whether she repulses him in reality, or only repulses him in such a way as if she was desirous of the same thing being done to her again. And what is done by the arm can also be done by the foot. If the man succeeds in this point he should embrace her more closely, and if she will not stand the embrace and gets up, but behaves with him as usual the next day, he should consider then that she is not unwilling to be enjoyed by him. If however she does not appear again, the man should try to get over her by means of a go-between; and if, after having disappeared for some time, she again appears, and behaves with him as usual, the man should then consider that she would not object to be united with him.

When a woman gives a man an opportunity, and makes her own love manifest to him, he should proceed to enjoy her. And the signs of a woman manifesting her love are these:

She calls out to a man without being addressed by him in the first instance.

She shows herself to him in secret places.

She speaks to him tremblingly and inarticulately.

She has the fingers of her hand, and the toes of her feet moistened with perspiration, and her face blooming with delight.

She occupies herself with shampooing his body and pressing his head.

When shampooing him she works with one hand only, and with the other she touches and embraces parts of his body.

She remains with both hands placed on his body motionless as if she had been surprised by something, or was overcome by fatigue.

She sometimes bends down her face upon his thighs and, when asked to shampoo them does not manifest any unwillingness to do so.

She places one of her hands quite motionless on his body, and even though the man should press it between two members of his body, she does not remove it for a long time.

Lastly, when she has resisted all the efforts of the man to gain her over, she returns to him next day to shampoo his body as before.

When a woman neither gives encouragement to a man, nor avoids him, but hides herself and remains in some lonely place, she must be got at by means of the female servant who may be near her. If when called by the man she acts in the same way, then she should be gained over by means of a skilful go-between. But if she will have nothing to say to the man, he should consider well about her before he begins any further attempts to gain her over.

Thus ends the examination of the state of a woman's mind.

A man should first get himself introduced to a woman, and then carry on a conversation with her. He should give her hints of his love for her, and if he finds from her replies that she receives these hints favourably, he should then set to work to gain her over without any fear. A woman who shows her love by outward signs to the man at his first interview should be gained over very easily. In the same way a lascivious woman, who when addressed in loving words replies openly in words expressive of her love, should be considered to have been gained over at that very moment. With regard to all women, whether they be wise, simple, or confiding, this rule is laid down that those who make an open manifestation of their love are easily gained over.

CHAPTER IV

ABOUT THE BUSINESS OF A GO-BETWEEN

If a woman has manifested her love or desire, either by signs or by motions of the body, and is afterwards rarely or never seen anywhere, or if a woman is met for the first time, the man should get a go-between to approach her.

Now the go-between, having wheedled herself into the confidence of the woman by acting according to her disposition, should try to make her hate or despise her husband by holding artful conversations with her, by telling her about medicines for getting children, by talking to her about other people, by tales of various kinds, by stories about the wives of other men, and by praising her beauty, wisdom, generosity and good nature, and then saying to her: 'It is indeed a pity that you, who are so excellent a woman in every way, should be possessed of a husband of this kind. Beautiful lady, he is not fit even to serve you.' The go-between should further talk to the woman about the weakness of the passion of her husband, his jealousy, his roguery, his ingratitude, his aversion to enjoyments, his dullness, his meanness, and all the other faults that he may have, and with which she may be acquainted. She should particularly harp upon that fault or that failing by which the wife may appear to be the most affected. If the wife be a deer woman, and the husband a hare man, then there would be no fault in that direction, but in the event of his being a hare man, and she a mare woman or elephant woman, then this fault should be pointed out to her.

Gonikaputra is of opinion that when it is the first affair of the woman, or when her love has only been very secretly shown, the man should then secure and send to her a go-between, with whom she may be already acquainted, and in whom she confides.

But to return to our subject. The go-between should tell the woman about the obedience and love of the man, and as her confidence and affection increase, she should then explain to her the thing to be accomplished in the following way. 'Hear this, Oh beautiful lady, that this man, born of a good family, having seen you, has gone mad on your account. The poor young man, who is tender by nature, has never been distressed in such a way before, and it is highly probable that he will succumb under his present affliction, and experience the pains of death.' If the woman listens with a favourable ear, then on the following day the go-between, having observed marks of good spirits in her face, in her eyes, and in her manner of conversation, should again converse with her on the subject of the man, and should tell her the stories of Ahalya[1] and Indra, of Sakoontala[2] and Dushyanti, and such others as may be fitted for the occasion. She should also describe to her the strength of the man, his talents, his skill in the sixty-four sorts of enjoyments mentioned by Babhravya, his good looks, and his liaison with some praiseworthy woman, no matter whether this last ever took place or not.

In addition to this, the go-between should carefully note the behaviour of the woman, which if favourable would be as follows: She would address her with a smiling look, would seat herself close beside her, and ask her, 'Where have you been? What have you been doing? Where did you dine? Where did you sleep? Where have you been sitting?' Moreover, the woman would meet the go-between in lonely places and tell her stories there, would

[1] The wife of the sage Gautama, she was seduced by Indra the king of the Gods.

[2] The heroine of one of the best, if not the best, of Hindoo plays, and the best known in Sanscrit dramatic literature. It was first brought to notice by Sir William Jones, and has been well and poetically translated by Dr Monier Williams under the title of Sakoontala, or the lost ring, an Indian drama, translated into English prose and verse from the Sanscrit of Kalidasa.

yawn contemplatively, draw long sighs, give her presents, remember her on occasions of festivals, dismiss her with a wish to see her again, and say to her jestingly, 'Oh, well-speaking woman, why do you speak these bad words to me?', would discourse on the sin of her union with the man, would not tell her about any previous visits or conversations that she may have had with him, but wish to be asked about these, and lastly would laugh at the man's desire, but would not reproach him in any way.

Thus ends the behaviour of the woman with the go-between.

When the woman manifests her love in the manner above described, the go-between should increase it by bringing to her love tokens from the man. But if the woman be not acquainted with the man personally, the go-between should win her over by extolling and praising his good qualities, and by telling stories about his love for her. Here Auddalaka says that when a man or woman are not personally acquainted with each other, and have not shown each other any signs of affection, the employment of a go-between is useless.

The followers of Babhravya on the other hand affirm that even though they be personally unacquainted, but have shown each other signs of affection there is an occasion for the employment of a go-between. Gonikaputra asserts that a go-between should be employed, provided they are acquainted with each other, even though no signs of affection may have passed b etween them. Vatsyayana however lays it down that even though they may not be personally acquainted with each other, and may not have shown each other any signs of affection, still they are both capable of placing confidence in a go-between.

Now the go-between should show the woman the presents, such as the betel nut and betel leaves, the perfumes, the flowers, and the rings which the man may have given to her for the sake of the woman, and on these presents should be impressed the marks of the man's teeth, and nails, and other signs. On the cloth that he may send he should draw with saffron both his hands joined together as if in earnest entreaty.

The go-between should also show to the woman ornamental figures of various kinds cut in leaves, together with ear ornaments, and chaplets made of flowers containing love letters expressive of the desire of the man,[1] and she should cause her to send affectionate presents to the man in return. After they have mutually accepted each other's presents, then a meeting should be arranged between them on the faith of the go-between.

The followers of Babhravya say that this meeting should take place at the time of going to the temple of a Deity, or on occasions of fairs, garden parties, theatrical performances, marriages, sacrifices, festivals and funerals, as also at the time of going to the river to bathe, or at times of natural calamities,[2] fear of robbers or hostile invasions of the country.

Gonikaputra is of opinion however that these meetings had better be brought about in the abodes of female friends, mendicants, astrologers, and ascetics. But Vatsyayana decides that that place is only well suited for the purpose which has proper means of ingress and egress, and where arrangements have been made to prevent any accidental

[1] It is presumed that something like the following French verses are intended:

> Quand on a juré le plus profond hommage,
> Voulez vous qu'infidèle on change de langage;
> Vous seul captivez mon esprit et mon coeur
> Que je puisse dans vos bras seuls goûter le bonheur;
> Je voudrais, mais en vain, que mon coeur en délire
> Couche où ce papier n'oserait vous dire.
> Avec soin, de ces vers lisez leurs premiers mots,
> Vous verrez quel remède il faut à tous mes maux.

Or these:

> Quand on vous voit, on vous aime;
> Quand on vous aime, où vous voit on?

[2] It is supposed that storms, earthquakes, famines and pestilent diseases are here alluded to.

occurrence, and when a man who has once entered the house can also leave it at the proper time without any disagreeable encounter.

Now go-betweens or female messengers are of the following different kinds:

A go-between who takes upon herself the whole burden of the business

A go-between who does only a limited part of the business

A go-between who is the bearer of a letter only

A go-between acting on her own account

The go-between of an innocent young woman

A wife serving as a go-between

A mute go-between

A go-between who acts the part of the wind

A woman who, having observed the mutual passion of a man and woman, brings them together and arranges it by the power of her own intellect, such a one is called a go-between who takes upon herself the whole burden of the business. This kind of go-between is chiefly employed when the man and the woman are already acquainted with each other, and have conversed together, and in such cases she is sent not only by the man (as is always done in all other cases) but by the woman also. The above name is also given to a go-between who, perceiving that the man and the woman are suited to each other, tries to bring about a union between them, even though they be not acquainted with each other.

A go-between who, perceiving that some part of the affair is already done, or that the advances on the part of the man are already made, completes the rest of the business, is called a go-between who performs only a limited part of the business.

A go-between who simply carries messages between a man and a woman, who love each other, but who cannot frequently meet, is called the bearer of a letter or message.

This name is also given to one who is sent by either of the lovers to acquaint either the one or the other with the time and place of their meeting.

A woman who goes herself to a man, and tells him of her having enjoyed sexual union with him in a dream, and expresses her anger at his wife having rebuked him for calling her by the name of her rival instead of by her own name, and gives him something bearing the marks of her teeth and nails and informs him that she knew she was formerly desired by him, and asks him privately whether she or his wife is the best looking, such a person is called a woman who is a go-between for herself. Now such a woman should be met and interviewed by the man in private and secretly.

The above name is also given to a woman who having made an agreement with some other woman to act as her go-between, gains over the man to herself, by the means of making him personally acquainted with herself, and thus causes the other woman to fail. The same applies to a man who, acting as a go-between for another, and having no previous connection with the woman, gains her over for himself, and thus causes the failure of the other man.

A woman who has gained the confidence of the innocent young wife of any man, and who has learned her secrets without exercising any pressure on her mind, and found out from her how her husband behaves to her, if this woman then teaches her the art of securing his favour, and decorates her so as to show her love, and instructs her how and when to be angry, or to pretend to be so, and then, having herself made marks of the nails and teeth on the body of the wife, gets the latter to send for her husband to show these marks to him, and thus excite him for enjoyment, such is called the go-between of an innocent young woman. In such cases the man should send replies to his wife through the same woman.

When a man gets his wife to gain the confidence of a

woman whom he wants to enjoy, and to call on her and talk to her about the wisdom and ability of her husband, that wife is called a wife serving as a go-between. In this case the feelings of the woman with regard to the man should also be made known through the wife.

When any man sends a girl or a female servant to any woman under some pretext or other, and places a letter in her bouquet of flowers, or in her ear ornaments, or marks something about her with his teeth or nails, that girl or female servant is called a mute go-between. In this case the man should expect an answer from the woman through the same person.

A person, who carries a message to a woman, which has a double meaning, or which relates to some past transactions, or which is unintelligible to other people, is called a go-between who acts the part of the wind. In this case the reply should be asked for through the same woman.

Thus end the different kinds of go-betweens.

A female astrologer, a female servant, a female beggar, or a female artist are well acquainted with the business of a go-between, and very soon gain the confidence of other women. Any one of them can raise enmity between any two persons if she wishes to do so, or extol the loveliness of any woman that she wishes to praise, or describe the arts practised by other women in sexual union. They can also speak highly of the love of a man, of his skill in sexual enjoyment, and of the desire of other women, more beautiful even than the woman they are addressing, for him, and explain the restraint under which he may be at home.

Lastly a go-between can, by the artfulness of her conversation, unite a woman with a man even though he may not have been thought of by her, or may have been considered beyond her aspirations. She can also bring back a man to a woman, who, owing to some cause or other, has separated himself from her.

CHAPTER V

ABOUT THE LOVE OF PERSONS IN AUTHORITY FOR THE WIVES OF OTHER MEN

KINGS and their ministers have no access to the abodes of others, and moreover their mode of living is constantly watched and observed and imitated by the people at large, just as the animal world, seeing the sun rise, get up after him, and when he sits in the evening, lie down again in the same way. Persons in authority should not therefore do any improper act in public, as such are impossible from their position, and would be deserving of censure. But if they find that such an act is necessary to be done, they should make use of the proper means as described in the following paragraphs.

The head man of the village, the king's officer employed there, and the man[1] whose business it is to glean corn, can gain over female villagers simply by asking them. It is on this account that this class of woman are called unchaste women by voluptuaries.

The union of the above mentioned men with this class of woman takes place on the occasions of unpaid labour, of filling the granaries in their houses, of taking things in and out of the house, of cleaning the houses, of working in the fields, and of purchasing cotton, wool, flax, hemp, and thread, and at the season of the purchase, sale, and exchange of various other articles, as well as at the time of doing various other works. In the same way the superintendents of cow pens enjoy the women in the cow pens; and the officers, who have the superintendence of widows, of the women who are

[1] This is a phrase used for a man who does the work of everybody, and who is fed by the whole village.

without supporters, and of women who have left their husbands, have sexual intercourse with these women. The intelligent accomplish their object by wandering at night in the village, and while villagers also unite with the wives of their sons, being much alone with them. Lastly the superintendents of markets have a great deal to do with the female villagers at the time of their making purchases in the market.

During the festival of the eighth moon, i.e. during the bright half of the month of Nargashirsha, as also during the moon-light festival of the month of Kartika, and the spring festival of Chaitra, the women of cities and towns generally visit the women of the king's harem in the royal palace. These visitors go to the several apartments of the women of the harem, as they are acquainted with them, and pass the night in conversation, and in proper sports, and amusement, and go away in the morning. On such occasions a female attendant of the king (previously acquainted with the woman whom the king desires) should loiter about, and accost this woman when she sets out to go home, and induce her to come and see the amusing things in the palace. Previous to these festivals even, she should have caused it to be intimated to this woman that on the occasion of this festival she would show her all the interesting things in the royal palace. Accordingly she should show her the bower of the coral creeper, the garden house with its floor inlaid with precious stones, the bower of grapes, the building on the water, the secret passages in the walls of the palace, the pictures, the sporting animals, the machines, the birds, and the cages of the lions and the tigers. After this, when alone with her, she should tell her about the love of the king for her, and should describe to her the good fortune which would attend upon her union with the king, giving her at the time a strict promise of secrecy. If the woman does not accept the offer, she should conciliate and please her with handsome presents befitting the position of the king, and having accompanied her for some distance should dismiss her with great affection.

Or, having made the acquaintance of the husband of the woman whom the king desires, the wives of the king should get the wife to pay them a visit in the harem, and on this occasion a female attendant of the king, having been sent thither, should act as above described.

Or, one of the king's wives should get acquainted with the woman that the king desires, by sending one of the female attendants to her, who should, on their becoming more intimate, induce her to come and see the royal abode. Afterwards when she has visited the harem, and acquired confidence, a female confidante of the king, sent thither, should act as before described.

Or, the king's wife should invite the woman, whom the king desires, to come to the royal palace, so that she might see the practice of the art in which the king's wife may be skilled, and after she has come to the harem, a female attendant of the king, sent thither, should act as before described.

Or, a female beggar, in league with the king's wife, should say to the woman desired by the king, and whose husband may have lost his wealth, or may have some cause of fear from the king: 'This wife of the king has influence over him, and she is, moreover, naturally kind-hearted, we must therefore go to her in this matter. I shall arrange for your entrance into the harem, and she will do away with all cause of danger and fear from the king.' If the woman accepts this offer, the female beggar should take her two or three times to the harem, and the king's wife there should give her a promise of protection. After this, when the woman, delighted with her reception and promise of protection, again goes to the harem, then a female attendant of the king, sent thither, should act as directed.

What has been said above regarding the wife of one

who has some cause of fear from the king applies also to the wives of those who seek service under the king, or who are oppressed by the king's ministers, or who are poor, or who are not satisfied with their position, or who are desirous of gaining the king's favour, or who wish to become famous among the people, or who are oppressed by the members of their own caste, or who want to injure their caste fellows, or who are spies of the king, or who have any other object to attain.

Lastly, if the woman desired by the king be living with some person who is not her husband, then the king should cause her to be arrested, and having made her a slave, on account of her crime, should place her in the harem. Or the king should cause his ambassador to quarrel with the husband of the woman desired by him, and should then imprison her as the wife of an enemy of the king, and by this means should place her in the harem.

Thus end the means of gaining over the wives of others secretly.

The above mentioned ways of gaining over the wives of other men are chiefly practised in the palaces of kings. But a king should never enter the abode of another person, for Abhira,[1] the king of the Kottas, was killed by a washerman while in the house of another, and in the same way Jayasana, the king of the Kashis, was slain by the commandant of his cavalry.

But according to the customs of some countries there are facilities for kings to make love to the wives of other men. Thus in the country of the Andhras[2] the newly married daughters of the people thereof enter the king's harem with some presents on the tenth day of their marriage, and having been enjoyed by the king are then dismissed. In the country of the Vatsagulmas[3] the wives of the chief

[1] The exact date of the reign of these kings is not known. It is supposed to have been about the beginning of the Christian era.

[2] The modern country of Tailangam which is to the South of Rajamundry.

[3] Supposed to be a tract of the country to the south of Malwa.

ministers approach the king at night to serve him. In the country of the Vaidarbhas[1] the beautiful wives of the inhabitants pass a month in the king's harem under the pretence of affection for the king. In the country of the Aparatakas[2] the people gave their beautiful wives as presents to the ministers and the kings. And lastly in the country of the Saurashtras[3] the women of the city and the country enter the royal harem for the king's pleasure either together or separately.

There are also two verses on the subject as follows:

'The above and other ways are the means employed in different countries by kings with regard to the wives of other persons. But a king, who has the welfare of his people at heart, should not on any account put them into practice.'

'A king, who has conquered the six[4] enemies of mankind, becomes the master of the whole earth.'

[1] Now known by the name of Berar. Its capital was Kundinpura, which has been identified with the modern Oomravati.

[2] Also called Aparantakas, being the northern and southern Concan.

[3] The modern provinces of Katteeawar. Its capital was called Girinaguda, or the modern Junagurh.

[4] These are Lust, Anger, Avarice, Spiritual Ignorance, Pride, and Envy.

CHAPTER VI

ABOUT THE WOMEN OF THE ROYAL HAREM; AND OF THE KEEPING OF ONE'S OWN WIFE

THE women of the royal harem cannot see or meet any men on account of their being strictly guarded, neither do they have their desires satisfied, because their only husband is common to many wives. For this reason among themselves they give pleasure to each other in various ways as now described.

Having dressed the daughters of their nurses, or their female friends, or their female attendants, like men, they accomplish their object by means of bulbs, roots, and fruits having the form of the lingam, or they lie down upon the statue of a male figure, in which the lingam is visible and erect.

Some kings, who are compassionate, take or apply certain medicines to enable them to enjoy many wives in one night, simply for the purpose of satisfying the desire of their women, though they perhaps have no desire of their own. Others enjoy with great affection only those wives that they particularly like, while others only take them, according as the turn of each wife arrives in due course. Such are the ways of enjoyment prevalent in Eastern countries, and what is said about the means of enjoyment of the female is also applicable to the male.

By means of their female attendants the ladies of the royal harem generally get men into their apartments in the disguise or dress of women. Their female attendants, and the daughters of their nurses, who are acquainted with their secrets, should exert themselves to get men to come to the harem in this way by telling them of the good fortune attending it, and by describing the facilities of entering and leaving the palace, the large size of the premises, the carelessness of the sentinels, and the irregularities of the attendants about the persons of the royal wives. But these women should never induce a man to enter the harem by telling him falsehoods, for that would probably lead to his destruction.

As for the man himself he had better not enter a royal harem, even though it may be easily accessible, on account of the numerous disasters to which he may be exposed there. If however he wants to enter it, he should first ascertain whether there is an easy way to get out, whether it is closely surrounded by the pleasure garden, whether it has separate enclosures belonging to it, whether the sentinels are careless, whether the king has gone abroad, and then, when he is called by the women of the harem, he should carefully observe the localities, and enter by the way pointed out by them. If he is able to manage it, he should hang about the harem every day, and under some pretext or other, make friends with the sentinels, and show himself attached to the female attendants of the harem, who may have become acquainted with his design, and to whom he should express his regret at not being able to obtain the object of his desire. Lastly he should cause the whole business of a go-between to be done by the woman who may have access to the harem, and he should be careful to be able to recognize the emissaries of the king.

When a go-between has no access to the harem, then the man should stand in some place where the lady, whom he loves and whom he is anxious to enjoy, can be seen.

If that place is occupied by the king's sentinels, he should then disguise himself as a female attendant of the lady who comes to the place, or passes by it. When she looks at him he should let her know his feelings by outward signs and gestures, and should show her pictures, things with double meanings, chaplets of flowers, and rings. He should carefully mark the answer she gives, whether by word or by sign, or by gesture, and should then try and get into the harem. If he is certain of her coming to some particular place he should conceal himself there, and at the appointed time should enter along with her as one of the guards. He may also go in and out, concealed in a folded bed, or bed covering, or with his body made invisible,[1] by means of external applications, a receipt for one of which is as follows:

The heart of an ichneumon, the fruit of the long gourd (tumbi), and the eyes of a serpent should all be burnt without letting out the smoke. The ashes should then be ground and mixed in equal quantities with water. By putting this mixture upon the eyes a man can go about unseen.

Other means of invisibility are prescribed by Duyana Brahmans and Jogashiras.

Again the man may enter the harem during the festival of the eighth moon in the month of Nargashirsha, and during the moonlight festivals when the female attendants of the harem are all busily occupied, or in confusion.

The following principles are laid down on this subject.

The entrance of young men into harems, and their exit from them, generally take place when things are being brought into the palace, or when things are being taken out of it, or when drinking festivals are going on, or when the female attendants are in a hurry, or when the residence of some of the royal ladies is being changed, or when the king's wives go to gardens, or to fairs, or when they enter the palace on their return from them, or lastly, when the king is absent on a long pilgrimage. The women of the royal harem know each other's secrets, and having but one object to attain, they give assistance to each other. A young man, who enjoys all of them, and who is common to them all,

[1] The way to make oneself invisible, the knowledge of the art of transmigration, or changing ourselves or others into any shape or form by the use of charms and spells, the power of being in two places at once, and other occult sciences are frequently referred to in all Oriental literature.

can continue enjoying his union with them so long as it is kept quiet, and is not known abroad.

Now in the country of the Aparatakas the royal ladies are not well protected, and consequently many young men are passed into the harem by the women who have access to the royal palace. The wives of the king of the Ahira country accomplish their objects with those sentinels in the harem who bear the name of Kashtriyas. The royal ladies in the country of the Vatsagulmas cause such men as are suitable to enter into the harem along with their female messengers. In the country of the Vaidarbhas the sons of the royal ladies enter the royal harem when they please and enjoy the women, with the exception of their own mothers. In the Stri-rajya the wives of the king are enjoyed by his caste fellows and relations. In the Ganda country the royal wives are enjoyed by Brahmans, friends, servants and slaves. In the Samdhava country servants, foster children, and other persons like them enjoy the women of the harem. In the country of the Haimavatas adventurous citizens bribe the sentinels and enter the harem. In the country of the Vanyas and the Kalmyas, Brahmans, with the knowledge of the king, enter the harem under the pretence of giving flowers to the ladies, and speak with them from behind a curtain, and from such conversation union afterwards takes place. Lastly the women in the harem of the king of the Prachyas conceal one young man in the harem for every batch of nine or ten of the women.

Thus act the wives of others.

For these reasons a man should guard his own wife. Old authors say that a king should select for sentinels in his harem such men as have their freedom from carnal desires well tested. But such men, though free themselves from carnal desire, by reason of their fear or avarice, may cause other persons to enter the harem, and therefore Gonikaputra says that kings should place such men in the harem as may have had their freedom from carnal desires, their fears, and their avarice well tested. Lastly Vatsyayana says that under the influence of Dharma[1] people might be admitted, and therefore men should be selected who are free from carnal desires, fear, avarice, and Dharma.[2]

The followers of Babhravya say that a man should cause his wife to associate with a young woman who would tell him the secrets of other people, and thus find out from her about his wife's chastity. But Vatsyayana says that, as wicked persons are always successful with women, a man should not cause his innocent wife to be corrupted by bringing her into the company of a deceitful woman.

The following are the causes of the destruction of a woman's chastity:

Always going into society, and sitting in company
Absence of restraint
The loose habits of her husband
Want of caution in her relations with other men
Continued and long absence of her husband
Living in a foreign country
Destruction of her love and feelings by her husband
The company of loose women
The jealousy of her husband

There are also the following verses on the subject:

'A clever man, learning from the Shastras the ways of winning over the wives of other people, is never deceived in the case of his own wives. No one, however, should make use of these ways for seducing the wives of others, because they do not always succeed, and, moreover, often cause disasters, and the destruction of Dharma and Artha. This book, which is intended for the good of the people, and to teach them the ways of guarding their own wives, should not be made use of merely for gaining over the wives of others.'

[1] This may be considered as meaning religious influence, and alludes to persons who may be gained over by that means.

[2] It will be noted from the above remarks that eunuchs do not appear to have been employed in the king's harem in those days, though they seem to have been employed for other purposes. See Part II, Chapter XI.

PART VI

ABOUT COURTESANS

INTRODUCTORY REMARKS

THIS Part VI, about courtesans, was prepared by Vatsyayana from a treatise on the subject that was written by Dattaka, for the women of Pataliputra (the modern Patna), some two thousand years ago. Dattaka's work does not appear to be extant now, but this abridgement of it is very clever, and quite equal to any of the productions of Emile Zola, and other writers of the realistic school of today.

Although a great deal has been written on the subject of the courtesan, nowhere will be found a better description of her, of her belongings, of her ideas, and of the working of her mind, than is contained in the following pages.

The details of the domestic and social life of the early Hindoos would not be complete without mention of the courtesan, and Part VI is entirely devoted to this subject. The Hindoos have ever had the good sense to recognise courtesans as a part and portion of human society, and so long as they behaved themselves with decency and propriety they were regarded with a certain respect. Anyhow, they have never been treated in the East with that brutality and contempt so common in the West, while their education has always been of a superior kind to that bestowed upon the rest of womankind in Oriental countries.

In the earlier days the well-educated Hindoo dancing girl and courtesan doubtless resembled the Hetera of the Greeks, and, being educated and amusing, were far more acceptable as companions than the generality of the married or unmarried women of that period. At all times and in all countries, there has ever been a little rivalry between the chaste and the unchaste. But while some women are born courtesans, and follow the instincts of their nature in every class of society, it has been truly said by some authors that every woman has got an inkling of the profession in her nature, and does her best, as a general rule, to make herself agreeable to the male sex.

The subtlety of women, their wonderful perceptive powers, their knowledge, and their intuitive appreciation of men and things are all shown in the following pages, which may be looked upon as a concentrated essence that has been since worked up into detail by many writers in every quarter of the globe.

CHAPTER I

OF THE CAUSES OF A COURTESAN RESORTING TO MEN; OF THE MEANS OF ATTACHING TO HERSELF THE MAN DESIRED; AND OF THE KIND OF MAN THAT IT IS DESIRABLE TO BE ACQUAINTED WITH

By having intercourse with men courtesans obtain sexual pleasure, as well as their own maintenance. Now when a courtesan takes up with a man from love, the action is natural; but when she resorts to him for the purpose of getting money, her action is artificial or forced. Even in the latter case, however, she should conduct herself as if her love were indeed natural, because men repose their confidence on those women who apparently love them. In making known her love to the man, she should show an entire freedom from avarice, and for the sake of her future credit she should abstain from acquiring money from him by unlawful means.

A courtesan, well dressed and wearing her ornaments, should sit or stand at the door of her house, and, without exposing herself too much, should look on the public road so as to be seen by the passers by, she being like an object on view for sale.[1] She should form friendships with such persons as would enable her to separate men from other women, and attach them to herself, to repair her own misfortunes, to acquire wealth, and to protect her from being bullied, or set upon by persons with whom she may have dealings of some kind or another.

[1] In England the lower classes of courtesans walk the streets; in India and other places in the East, they sit at the windows, or at the doors of their houses.

These persons are:
The guards of the town, or the police
The officers of the courts of justice
Astrologers
Powerful men, or men with interest
Learned men
Teachers of the sixty-four arts
Pithamardas or confidants
Vitas or parasites
Vidushakas or jesters
Flower sellers
Perfumers
Vendors of spirits
Washermen
Barbers
Beggars
And such other persons as may be found necessary for the particular object to be acquired.

The following kinds of men may be taken up with, simply for the purpose of getting their money:
Men of independent income
Young men
Men who are free from any ties
Men who hold places of authority under the king
Men who have secured their means of livelihood without difficulty
Men possessed of unfailing sources of income
Men who consider themselves handsome
Men who are always praising themselves
One who is a eunuch, but wishes to be thought a man
One who hates his equals
One who is naturally liberal
One who has influence with the king or his ministers
One who is always fortunate
One who is proud of his wealth

One who disobeys the orders of his elders
One upon whom the members of his caste keep an eye
An only son whose father is wealthy
An ascetic who is internally troubled with desire
A brave man
A physician of the king
Previous acquaintances

On the other hand, those who are possessed of excellent qualities are to be resorted to for the sake of love, and fame. Such men are as follows:

Men of high birth, learned, with a good knowledge of the world, and doing the proper things at the proper times, poets, good story tellers, eloquent men, energetic men, skilled in various arts, far-seeing into the future, possessed of great minds, full of perseverance, of a firm devotion, free from anger, liberal, affectionate to their parents, and with a liking for all social gatherings, skilled in completing verses begun by others and in various other sports, free from all disease, possessed of a perfect body, strong, and not addicted to drinking, powerful in sexual enjoyment, sociable, showing love towards women and attracting their hearts to himself, but not entirely devoted to them, possessed of independent means of livelihood, free from envy, and last of all, free from suspicion.

Such are the good qualities of a man.

The woman also should have the following characteristics:

She should be possessed of beauty, and amiability, with auspicious body marks. She should have a liking for good qualities in other people, as also a liking for wealth. She should take delight in sexual unions, resulting from love, and should be of a firm mind, and of the same class as the man with regard to sexual enjoyment.

She should always be anxious to acquire and obtain experience and knowledge, be free from avarice, and always have a liking for social gatherings, and for the arts.

The following are the ordinary qualities of all women: To be possessed of intelligence, good disposition, and good manners; to be straightforward in behaviour, and to be grateful; to consider well the future before doing anything; to possess activity, to be of consistent behaviour, and to have a knowledge of the proper times and places for doing things; to speak always without meanness, loud laughter, malignity, anger, avarice, dullness, or stupidity; to have a knowledge of the Kama Sutra, and to be skilled in all the arts connected with it.

The faults of women are to be known by the absence of any of the above mentioned good qualities.

The following kinds of men are not fit to be resorted to by courtesans:

One who is consumptive; one who is sickly; one whose mouth contains worms; one whose breath smells like human excrement; one whose wife is dear to him; one who speaks harshly; one who is always suspicious; one who is avaricious; one who is pitiless; one who is a thief; one who is self-conceited; one who has a liking for sorcery; one who does not care for respect or disrespect; one who can be gained over even by his enemies by means of money; and lastly, one who is extremely bashful.

Ancient authors are of opinion that the causes of a courtesan resorting to men are love, fear, money, pleasure, returning some act of enmity, curiosity, sorrow, constant intercourse, Dharma, celebrity, compassion, the desire of having a friend, shame, the likeness of the man to some beloved person, the search after good fortune, the getting rid of the love of somebody else, the being of the same class as the man with respect to sexual union, living in the same place, constancy, and poverty. But Vatsyayana decides that desire of wealth, freedom from misfortune, and love are the only causes that affect the union of courtesans with men.

Now a courtesan should not sacrifice money to her love, because money is the chief thing to be attended to. But in cases of fear, etc., she should pay regard to strength and other qualities. Moreover, even though she be invited by any man to join him, she should not at once consent to a union, because men are apt to despise things which are easily acquired. On such occasions she should first send the shampooers, and the singers, and the jesters, who may be in her service, or, in their absence the Pithamardas, or confidants, and others, to find out the state of his feelings, and the condition of his mind. By means of these persons she should ascertain whether the man is pure or impure, affected, or the reverse, capable of attachment, or indifferent, liberal or niggardly; and if she finds him to her liking, she should then employ the Vita and others to attach his mind to her.

Accordingly, the Pithamarda should bring the man to her house, under the pretence of seeing the fights of quails, cocks, and rams, of hearing the maina (a kind of starling) talk, or of seeing some other spectacle, or the practice of some art; or he may take the woman to the abode of the man. After this, when the man comes to her house the woman should give him something capable of producing curiosity, and love in his heart, such as an affectionate present, telling him that it was specially designed for his use. She should also amuse him for a long time by telling him such stories, and doing such things as he may take most delight in. When he goes away she should frequently send to him a female attendant, skilled in carrying on a jesting conversation, and also a small present at the same time. She should also sometimes go to him herself under the pretence of some business, and accompanied by the Pithamarda.

Thus end the means of attaching to herself the man desired.

There are also some verses on the subject as follows:

'When a lover comes to her abode, a courtesan should give him a mixture of betel leaves and betel nut, garlands of flowers, and perfumed ointments, and, showing her skill in arts, should entertain him with a long conversation. She should also give him some loving presents, and make an exchange of her own things with his, and at the same time should show him her skill in sexual enjoyment. When a courtesan is thus united with her lover she should always delight him by affectionate gifts, by conversation, and by the application of tender means of enjoyment.'

CHAPTER II

OF LIVING LIKE A WIFE

WHEN a courtesan is living as a wife with her lover, she should behave like a chaste woman, and do everything to his satisfaction. Her duty in this respect, in short, is, that she should give him pleasure, but should not become attached to him, though behaving as if she were really attached.

Now the following is the manner in which she is to conduct herself, so as to accomplish the above mentioned purpose. She should have a mother dependent on her, one who should be represented as very harsh, and who looked upon money as her chief object in life. In the event of there being no mother, then an old and confidential nurse should play the same role. The mother or nurse, on their part, should appear to be displeased with the lover, and forcibly take her away from him. The woman herself should always show pretended anger, dejection, fear, and shame on this account, but should not disobey the mother or nurse at any time.

She should make out to the mother or nurse that the man is suffering from bad health, and making this a pretext for going to see him, she should go on that account. She is, moreover, to do the following things for the purpose of gaining the man's favour:

Sending her female attendant to bring the flowers used by him on the previous day, in order that she may use them herself as a mark of affection, also asking for the mixture of betel nut and leaves that have remained uneaten by him; expressing wonder at his knowledge of sexual intercourse, and the several means of enjoyment used by him; learning from him the sixty-four kinds of pleasure mentioned by Babhravya; continually practising the ways of enjoyment as taught by him, and according to his liking; keeping his secrets; telling him her own desires and secrets; concealing her anger; never neglecting him on the bed when he turns his face towards her; touching any parts of his body according to his wish; kissing and embracing him when he is asleep; looking at him with apparent anxiety when he is wrapt in thought, or thinking of some other subject than herself; showing neither complete shamelessness, nor excessive bashfulness when he meets her, or sees her standing on the terrace of her house from the public road; hating his enemies; loving those who are dear to him; showing a liking for that which he likes; being in high or low spirits according to the state that he is in himself; expressing a curiosity to see his wives; not continuing her anger for a long time; suspecting even the marks and wounds made by herself with her nails and teeth on his body to have been made by some other woman; keeping her love for him unexpressed by words, but showing it by deeds, and signs, and hints; remaining silent when he is asleep, intoxicated, or sick; being very attentive when he describes his good actions, and reciting them afterwards to his praise and benefit; giving witty replies to him if he be sufficiently attached to her; listening to all his stories, except those that relate to her rivals; expressing feelings of dejection and sorrow if he sighs, yawns, or falls down; pronouncing the words 'live long' when he sneezes; pretending to be ill, or to have the desire of pregnancy, when she feels dejected; abstaining from praising the good qualities of anybody else, and from censuring those who possess the same faults as her own man; wearing anything that may have been given to her by him; abstaining from putting on her ornaments, and from taking food when he is in pain, sick, low-spirited, or suffering from misfortune, and condoling and lamenting with him over the same; wishing to accompany him if he happens to leave the country himself or if he be banished from it by the king; expressing a desire not to live after him; telling him that the whole object and desire of her life was to be united with him; offering previously promised sacrifices to the Deity when he acquires wealth, or has some desire fulfilled, or when he has recovered from some illness or disease; putting on ornaments every day; not acting too freely with him; reciting his name and the name of his family in her songs; placing his hand on her loins, bosom and forehead, and falling asleep after feeling the pleasure of his touch; sitting on his lap and falling asleep there; wishing to have a child by him; desiring not to live longer than he does; abstaining from revealing his secrets to others; dissuading him from vows and fasts by saying 'let the sin fall upon me'; keeping vows and fasts along with him when it is impossible to change his mind on the subject; telling him that vows and fasts are difficult to be observed, even by herself, when she has any dispute with him about them; looking on her own wealth and his without any distinction; abstaining from going to public assemblies without him, and accompanying him when he desires her to do so; taking delight in using things previously used by him, and in eating food that he has left uneaten; venerating his family, his disposition, his skill in the arts, his learning, his caste, his complexion, his native country, his friends, his good qualities, his age, and his sweet temper; asking him to sing, and to do other such like things, if able to do them; going to him without paying any regard to fear, to cold, to heat, or to rain; saying with regard to the next world that he should be her lover even there; adapting her tastes, disposition and actions to his liking; abstaining from sorcery; disputing continually with her mother on the subject of going to him, and, when forcibly taken by her mother to some other place, expressing her desire to die by taking poison, by starving herself to death, by stabbing herself with some weapon, or by hanging herself; and lastly assuring the man of her constancy and love by means of her agents, and receiving money herself, but abstaining from any dispute with her mother with regard to pecuniary matters.

When the man sets out on a journey, she should make him swear that he will return quickly, and in his absence should put aside her vows of worshipping the Deity, and should wear no ornaments except those that are lucky. If the time fixed for his return has passed, she should endeavour to ascertain the real time of his return from omens, from the reports of the people, and from the positions of the planets, the moon and the stars. On occasions of amusement, and of auspicious dreams, she should say 'Let me be soon united to him.' If, moreover, she feels melancholy, or sees any inauspicious omen, she should perform some rite to appease the Deity.

When the man does return home she should worship the God Kama[1], and offer oblations to other Deities, and having caused a pot filled with water to be brought by her friends, she should perform the worship in honour of the crow who eats the offerings which we make to the manes of deceased relations. After the first visit is over she should ask her lover also to perform certain rites, and this he will do if he is sufficiently attached to her.

Now a man is said to be sufficiently attached to a woman when his love is disinterested; when he has the same object in view as his beloved one; when he is quite free from any suspicions on her account; and when he is indifferent to money with regard to her.

Such is the manner of a courtesan living with a man like a wife, and set forth here for the sake of guidance from the rules of Dattaka. What is not laid down here should be practised according to the custom of the people, and the nature of each individual man.

There are also two verses on the subject as follows:

'The extent of the love of women is not known, even to

[1] Kama, i.e. the Indian Cupid.

those who are the objects of their affection, on account of its subtlety, and on account of the avarice, and natural intelligence of womankind.'

'Women are hardly ever known in their true light, though they may love men, or become indifferent towards them, may give them delight, or abandon them, or may extract from them all the wealth that they may possess.'

CHAPTER III

OF THE MEANS OF GETTING MONEY, OF THE SIGNS OF THE CHANGE OF A LOVER'S FEELINGS, AND OF THE WAY TO GET RID OF HIM

MONEY is got out of a lover in two ways:

By natural or lawful means, and by artifices. Old authors are of opinion that when a courtesan can get as much money as she wants from her lover, she should not make use of artifice. But Vatsyayana lays down that though she may get some money from him by natural means, yet when she makes use of artifice he gives her doubly more, and therefore artifice should be resorted to for the purpose of extorting money from him at all events.

Now the artifices to be used for getting money from her lover are as follows:

Taking money from him on different occasions, for the purpose of purchasing various articles, such as ornaments, food, drink, flowers, perfumes and clothes, and either not buying them, or getting from him more than their cost.

Praising his intelligence to his face.

Pretending to be obliged to make gifts on occasion of festivals connected with vows, trees, gardens, temples, or tanks.[1]

Pretending that at the time of going to his house, her jewels have been stolen either by the king's guards, or by robbers.

Alleging that her property has been destroyed by fire, by the

[1] On the completion of a vow a festival takes place. Some trees, such as the Peepul and Banyan trees, are invested with sacred threads like the Brahman's, and on the occasion of this ceremony a festival is given. In the same way when gardens are made, and tanks or temples built, then also festivals are observed.

falling of her house, or by the carelessness of her servants.

Pretending to have lost the ornaments of her lover along with her own.

Causing him to hear through other people of the expenses incurred by her in coming to see him.

Contracting debts for the sake of her lover.

Disputing with her mother on account of some expense incurred by her for her lover, and which was not approved of by her mother.

Not going to parties and festivities in the houses of her friends for the want of presents to make to them, she having previously informed her lover of the valuable presents given to her by these very friends.

Not performing certain festive rites under the pretence that she has no money to perform them with.

Engaging artists to do something for her lover.

Entertaining physicians and ministers for the purpose of attaining some object.

Assisting friends and benefactors both on festive occasions, and in misfortune.

Performing household rites.

Having to pay the expenses of the ceremony of marriage of the son of a female friend.

Having to satisfy curious wishes during her state of pregnancy.

Pretending to be ill, and charging her cost of treatment.

Having to remove the troubles of a friend.

Selling some of her ornaments, so as to give her lover a present.

Pretending to sell some of her ornaments, furniture, or cooking utensils to a trader, who has been already tutored how to behave in the matter.

Having to buy cooking utensils of greater value than those of other people, so that they might be more easily distinguished, and not changed for others of an inferior description.

Remembering the former favours of her lover, and causing them always to be spoken of by her friends and followers.

Informing her lover of the great gains of other courtesans.

Describing before them, and in the presence of her lover, her own great gains, and making them out to be greater even than theirs, though such may not have been really the case.

Openly opposing her mother when she endeavours to persuade her to take up with men with whom she has been formerly acquainted, on account of the great gains to be got from them.

Lastly, pointing out to her lover the liberality of his rivals.

Thus end the ways and means of getting money.

A woman should always know the state of the mind, of the feelings, and of the disposition of her lover towards her from the changes of his temper, his manner, and the colour of his face.

The behaviour of a waning lover is as follows:

He gives the woman either less than is wanted, or something else than that which is asked for.

He keeps her in hopes by promises.

He pretends to do one thing, and does something else.

He does not fulfil her desires.

He forgets his promises, or does something else than that which he has promised.

He speaks with his own servants in a mysterious way.

He sleeps in some other house under the pretence of having to do something for a friend.

Lastly, he speaks in private with the attendants of a woman with whom he was formerly acquainted.

Now when a courtesan finds that her lover's disposition

towards her is changing, she should get possession of all his best things before he becomes aware of her intentions, and allow a supposed creditor to take them away forcibly from her in satisfaction of some pretended debt. After this, if the lover is rich, and has always behaved well towards her, she should ever treat him with respect; but if he is poor and destitute, she should get rid of him as if she had never been acquainted with him in any way before.

The means of getting rid of a lover are as follows:

Describing the habits and vices of the lover as disagreeable and censurable, with the sneer of the lip, and the stamp of the foot.

Speaking on a subject with which he is not acquainted.

Showing no admiration for his learning, and passing a censure upon it.

Putting down his pride.

Seeking the company of men who are superior to him in learning and wisdom.

Showing a disregard for him on all occasions.

Censuring men possessed of the same faults as her lover.

Expressing dissatisfaction at the ways and means of enjoyment used by him.

Not giving him her mouth to kiss.

Refusing access to her jaghana, i.e. the part of the body between the navel and the thighs.

Showing a dislike for the wounds made by his nails and teeth.

Not pressing close up against him at the time when he embraces her.

Keeping her limbs without movement at the time of congress.

Desiring him to enjoy her when he is fatigued.

Laughing at his attachment to her.

Not responding to his embraces.

Turning away from him when be begins to embrace her.

Pretending to be sleepy.

Going out visiting, or into company, when she perceives his desire to enjoy her during the daytime.

Mis-constructing his words.

Laughing without any joke, or, at the time of any joke made by him, laughing under some pretence.

Looking with side glances at her own attendants, and clapping her hands when he says anything.

Interrupting him in the middle of his stories, and beginning to tell other stories herself.

Reciting his faults and his vices, and declaring them to be incurable.

Saying words to her female attendants calculated to cut the heart of her lover to the quick.

Taking care not to look at him when he comes to her.

Asking him what cannot be granted.

And, after all, finally dismissing him.

There are also two verses on this subject as follows:

'The duty of a courtesan consists in forming connections with suitable men after due and full consideration, and attaching the person with whom she is united to herself; in obtaining wealth from the person who is attached to her, and then dismissing him after she has taken away all his possessions.'

'A courtesan leading in this manner the life of a wife is not troubled with too many lovers, and yet obtains abundance of wealth.'

CHAPTER IV

ABOUT RE-UNION WITH A FORMER LOVER

WHEN a courtesan abandons her present lover after all his wealth is exhausted, she may then consider about her re-union with a former lover. But she should return to him only if he has acquired fresh wealth, or is still wealthy, and if he is still attached to her. And if this man be living at the time with some other woman she should consider well before she acts.

Now such a man can only be in one of the six following conditions:

He may have left the first woman of his own accord, and may even have left another woman since then.

He may have been driven away from both women.

He may have left the one woman of her own accord, and been driven away by the other.

He may have left the one woman of his own accord, and be living with another woman.

He may have been driven away from the one woman, and left the other of his own accord.

He may have been driven away by the one woman, and may be living with another.

Now if the man has left both women of his own accord, he should not be resorted to, on account of the fickleness of his mind, and his indifference to the excellences of both of them.

As regards the man who may have been driven away from both women, if he has been driven away from the last one because the woman could get more money from some other man, then he should be resorted to, for if attached to the first woman he would give her more money, through vanity and emulation to spite the other woman. But if he has been driven away by the woman on account of his poverty, or stinginess, he should not then be resorted to.

In the case of the man who may have left the one woman of his own accord, and been driven away by the other, if he agrees to return to the former and give her plenty of money beforehand, then he should be resorted to.

In the case of the man who may have left the one woman of his own accord, and be living with another woman, the former (wishing to take up with him again) should first ascertain if he left her in the first instance in the hope of finding some particular excellence in the other woman, and that not having found any such excellence, he was willing to come back to her, and to give her much money on account of his conduct, and on account of his affection still existing for her.

Or, whether, having discovered many faults in the other woman, he would now see even more excellences in herself than actually exist, and would be prepared to give her much money for these qualities.

Or, lastly, to consider whether he was a weak man, or a man fond of enjoying many women, or one who liked a poor woman, or one who never did anything for the woman that he was with. After maturely considering all these things, she should resort to him or not, according to circumstances.

As regards the man who may have been driven away from the one woman, and left the other of his own accord, the former woman (wishing to re-unite with him) should first ascertain whether he still has any affection for her, and would consequently spend much money upon her; or whether, being attached to her excellent qualities, he did not take delight in any other woman; or whether, being driven away from her formerly before completely satisfying his sexual desires, he wished to get back to her, so as to be revenged for the injury done to him; or whether he wished to create confidence in her mind, and then take back from her the wealth which she formerly took from him, and finally destroy her; or, lastly, whether he wished first to separate her from her present lover, and then to break away from her himself. If, after considering all these things, she is of opinion that his intentions are really pure and honest, she can re-unite herself with him. But if his mind be at all tainted with evil intentions, he should be avoided.

In the case of the man who may have been driven away by one woman, and be living with another, if the man makes overtures to return to the first one, the courtesan should consider well before she acts, and while the other woman is engaged in attracting him to herself, she should try in her turn (though keeping herself behind the scenes) to gain him over, on the grounds of any of the following considerations:

That he was driven away unjustly and for no proper reason, and now that he has gone to another woman, every effort must be used to bring him back to myself.

That if he were once to converse with me again, he would break away from the other woman.

That the pride of my present lover would be put down by means of the former one.

That he has become wealthy, has secured a higher position, and holds a place of authority under the king.

That he is separate from his wife.

That he is now independent.

That he lives apart from his father, or brother.

That by making peace with him, I shall be able to get hold of a very rich man, who is now prevented from coming to me by my present lover.

That as he is not respected by his wife, I shall now be able to separate him from her.

That the friend of this man loves my rival, who hates me cordially, I shall therefore by this means separate the friend from his mistress.

And lastly, I shall bring discredit upon him by bringing

him back to me, thus showing the fickleness of his mind.

When a courtesan is resolved to take up again with a former lover, her Pithamarda and other servants should tell him that his former expulsion from the woman's house was caused by the wickedness of her mother; that the woman loved him just as much as ever at that time, but could not help the occurrence on account of her deference to her mother's will; that she hated the union of her present lover, and disliked him excessively. In addition to this, they should create confidence in his mind by speaking to him of her former love for him, and should allude to the mark of that love that she has ever remembered. This mark of her love should be connected with some kind of pleasure that may have been practised by him, such as his way of kissing her, or manner of having connection with her.

Thus end the ways of bringing about a re-union with a former lover.

When a woman has to choose between two lovers, one of whom was formerly united with her, while the other is a stranger, the Acharyas (sages) are of opinion that the first one is preferable, because his disposition and character being already known by previous careful observation, he can be easily pleased and satisfied; but Vatsyayana thinks that a former lover, having already spent a great deal of his wealth, is not able or willing to give much money again, and is not therefore to be relied upon so much as a stranger. Particular cases may however arise differing from this general rule on account of the different natures of men.

There are also verses on the subject as follows:

'Re-union with a former lover may be desirable so as to separate some particular woman from some particular man, or some particular man from some particular woman, or to have a certain effect upon the present lover.'

'When a man is excessively attached to a woman, he is afraid of her coming into contact with other men; he does not then regard or notice her faults and he gives her much wealth through fear of her leaving him.'

'A courtesan should be agreeable to the man who is attached to her, and despise the man who does not care for her. If while she is living with one man, a messenger comes to her from some other man, she may either refuse to listen to any negotiations on his part, or appoint a fixed time for him to visit her, but she should not leave the man who may be living with her and who may be attached to her.'

'A wise woman should only renew her connection with a former lover, if she is satisfied that good fortune, gain, love, and friendship, are likely to be the result of such a reunion.'

CHAPTER V

OF DIFFERENT KINDS OF GAIN

WHEN a courtesan is able to realize much money every day, by reason of many customers, she should not confine herself to a single lover; under such circumstances, she should fix her rate for one night, after considering the place, the season, and the condition of the people, and having regard to her own good qualities and good looks, and after comparing her rates with those of other courtesans. She can inform her lovers, and friends, and acquaintances about these charges. If, however, she can obtain a great gain from a single lover, she may resort to him alone, and live with him like a wife.

Now the sages are of opinion that, when a courtesan has the chance of an equal gain from two lovers at the same time, a preference should be given to the one who would give her the kind of thing which she wants. But Vatsyayana says that the preference should be given to the one who gives her gold, because it cannot be taken back like some other things, it can be easily received, and is also the means of procuring anything that may be wished for. Of such things as gold, silver, copper, bell metal, iron, pots, furniture, beds, upper garments, under vestments, fragrant substances, vessels made of gourds, ghee, oil, corn, cattle, and other things of a like nature, the first—gold—is superior to all the others.

When the same labour is required to gain any two lovers, or when the same kind of thing is to be got from each of them, the choice should be made by the advice of a friend, or it may be made from their personal qualities, or from the signs of good or bad fortune that may be connected with them.

When there are two lovers, one of whom is attached to the courtesan, and the other is simply very generous, the sages say that the preference should be given to the generous lover, but Vatsyayana is of opinion that the one who is really attached to the courtesan should be preferred, because he can be made to be generous, even as a miser gives money if he becomes fond of a woman, but a man who is simply generous cannot be made to love with real attachment. But among those who are attached to her, if there is one who is poor, and one who is rich, the preference is of course to be given to the latter.

When there are two lovers, one of whom is generous, and the other ready to do any service for the courtesan, some sages say that the one who is ready to do the service should be preferred, but Vatsyayana is of opinion that a man who does a service thinks that he has gained his object when he has done something once, but a generous man does not care for what he has given before. Even here the choice should be guided by the likelihood of the future good to be derived from her union with either of them.

When one of the two lovers is grateful, and the other liberal, some sages say that the liberal one should be preferred, but Vatsyayana is of opinion that the former should be chosen, because liberal men are generally haughty, plain spoken, and wanting in consideration towards others. Even though these liberal men have been on friendly terms for a long time, yet if they see any fault in the courtesan, or are told lies about her by some other woman, they do not care for past services, but leave abruptly. On the other hand the grateful man does not at once break off from her, on account of a regard for the pains she may have taken to please him. In this case also the choice is to be guided with respect to what may happen in future.

When an occasion for complying with the request of a friend, and a chance of getting money come together, the sages say that the chance of getting money should be preferred. But Vatsyayana thinks that the money can be obtained tomorrow as well as today, but if the request of a friend be not at once complied with, he may become disaffected. Even here, in making the choice, regard must be paid to future good fortune.

On such an occasion, however, the courtesan might pacify her friend by pretending to have some work to do, and telling him that his request will be complied with next day, and in this way secure the chance of getting the money that has been offered her.

When the chance of getting money and the chance of avoiding some disaster come at the same time, the sages are of opinion that the chance of getting money should be preferred, but Vatsyayana says that money has only a limited importance, while a disaster that is once averted may never occur again. Here, however, the choice should be guided by the greatness or smallness of the disaster.

The gains of the wealthiest and best kind of courtesans are to be spent as follows:

Building temples, tanks, and gardens; giving a thousand cows to different Brahmans; carrying on the worship of the Gods, and celebrating festivals in their honour; and lastly, performing such vows as may be within their means.

The gains of other courtesans are to be spent as follows:

Having a white dress to wear every day; getting sufficient food and drink to satisfy hunger and thirst; eating daily a perfumed tambula, i.e. a mixture of betel nut and betel leaves; and wearing ornaments gilt with gold. The sages say that these represent the gains of all the middle and lower classes of courtesans, but Vatsyayana is of opinion that their gains cannot be calculated, or fixed in any way, as these depend on the influence of the place, the customs of the people, their own appearance, and many other things.

When a courtesan wants to keep some particular man from some other woman; or wishes to get him away from some woman to whom he may be attached or to deprive some woman of the gains realized by her from him; or if she thinks that she would raise her position or enjoy some great good fortune or become desirable to all men by uniting herself with this man; or if she wishes to get his assistance in averting some misfortune; or is really attached to him and loves him; or wishes to injure some body through his means; or has regard to some former favour conferred upon her by him; or wishes to be united with him merely from desire; for any of the above reasons, she should agree to take from him only a small sum of money in a friendly way.

When a courtesan intends to abandon a particular lover, and take up with another one; or when she has reason to believe that her lover will shortly leave her, and return to his wives; or that having squandered all his money, and become penniless, his guardian, or master, or father would come and take him away; or that her lover is about to lose his position or, lastly, that he is of a very fickle mind, she should, under any of these circumstances, endeavour to get as much money as she can from him as soon as possible.

On the other hand, when the courtesan thinks that her lover is about to receive valuable presents; or get a place of authority from the king; or be near the time of inheriting a fortune; or that his ship would soon arrive laden with merchandise; or that he has large stocks of corn and other commodities; or that if anything was done for him it would not be done in vain; or that he is always true to his word; then should she have regard to her future welfare, and live with the man like a wife.

There are also verses on the subject as follows:

'In considering her present gains, and her future welfare, a courtesan should avoid such persons as have gained their means of subsistence with very great difficulty, as also those who have become selfish and hard-hearted by becoming the favourites of kings.'

'She should make every endeavour to unite herself with

prosperous and well-to-do people, and with those whom it is dangerous to avoid, or to slight in any way. Even at some cost to herself she should become acquainted with energetic and liberal-minded men, who when pleased would give her a large sum of money, even for very little service, or for some small thing.'

CHAPTER VI

OF GAINS AND LOSSES; ATTENDANT GAINS AND LOSSES; AND DOUBTS; AS ALSO OF THE DIFFERENT KINDS OF COURTESANS

IT sometimes happens that while gains are being sought for, or expected to be realized, losses only are the result of our efforts. The causes of these losses are:

Weakness of intellect
Excessive love
Excessive pride
Excessive self conceit
Excessive simplicity
Excessive confidence
Excessive anger
Carelessness
Recklessness
Influence of evil genius
Accidental circumstances

The results of these losses are:

Expense incurred without any result
Destruction of future good fortune
Stoppage of gains about to be realized
Loss of what is already obtained
Acquisition of a sour temper
Becoming unamiable to every body
Injury to health
Loss of hair and other accidents

Now gain is of three kinds: gain of wealth, gain of religious merit, and gain of pleasure; and similarly loss is of three kinds: loss of wealth, loss of religious merit, and loss of pleasure. At the time when gains are sought for, if other gains come along with them, these are called attendant gains. When gain is uncertain, the doubt of its being a gain is called a simple doubt. When there is a doubt whether either of two things will happen or not, it is called a mixed doubt. If while one thing is being done two results take place, it is called a combination of two results, and if several results follow from the same action, it is called a combination of results on every side.

We shall now give examples of the above.

As already stated, gain is of three kinds, and loss, which is opposed to gain, is also of three kinds.

When by living with a great man a courtesan acquires present wealth, and in addition to this becomes acquainted with other people, and thus obtains a chance of future fortune, and an accession of wealth, and becomes desirable to all, this is called a gain of wealth attended by other gain.

When by living with a man a courtesan simply gets money, this is called a gain of wealth not attended by any other gain.

When a courtesan receives money from other people besides her lover, the results are the chance of the loss of future good from her present lover; the chance of disaffection of a man securely attached to her; the hatred of all; and the chance of a union with some low person, tending to destroy her future good. This gain is called a gain of wealth attended by losses.

When a courtesan, at her own expense, and without any results in the shape of gain, has connection with a great man, or an avaricious minister, for the sake of diverting some misfortune, or removing some cause that may be threatening the destruction of a great gain, this loss is said to be a loss of wealth attended by gains of the future good which it may bring about.

When a courtesan is kind, even at her own expense, to a man who is very stingy, or to a man proud of his looks, or to an ungrateful man skilled in gaining the hearts of others, without any good resulting from these connections to her in the end, this loss is called a loss of wealth not attended by any gain.

When a courtesan is kind to any such man as described above, but who in addition is a favourite of the king, and moreover cruel and powerful, without any good result in the end, and with a chance of her being turned away at any moment, this loss is called a loss of wealth attended by other losses.

In this way gains and losses, and attendant gains and losses in religious merit and pleasures may become known to the reader, and combinations of all of them may also be made.

Thus end the remarks on gains and losses, and attendant gains and losses.

In the next place we come to doubts, which are again of three kinds: doubts about wealth, doubts about religious merit, and doubts about pleasures.

The following are examples:

When a courtesan is not certain how much a man may give her, or spend upon her, this is called a doubt about wealth.

When a courtesan feels doubtful whether she is right in entirely abandoning a lover from whom she is unable to get money, she having taken all his wealth from him in the first instance, this doubt is called a doubt about religious merit.

When a courtesan is unable to get hold of a lover to her liking, and is uncertain whether she will derive any pleasure from a person surrounded by his family, or from a low person, this is called a doubt about pleasure.

When a courtesan is uncertain whether some powerful but low principled fellow would cause loss to her on account of her not being civil to him this is called a doubt about the loss of wealth.

When a courtesan feels doubtful whether she would lose religious merit by abandoning a man who is attached to her without giving him the slightest favour, and thereby causing him unhappiness in this world and the next,[1] this doubt is called a doubt about the loss of a religious merit.

When a courtesan is uncertain as to whether she might create disaffection by speaking out, and revealing her love and thus not get her desire satisfied, this is called a doubt about the loss of pleasure.

Thus end the remarks on doubts.

Mixed Doubts

The intercourse or connection with a stranger, whose disposition is unknown, and who may have been introduced by a lover, or by one who possessed authority, may be productive either of gain or loss, and therefore this is called a mixed doubt about the gain and loss of wealth.

When a courtesan is requested by a friend, or is impelled by pity to have intercourse with a learned Brahman, a religious student, a sacrificer, a devotee, or an ascetic who may have all fallen in love with her, and who may be consequently at the point of death, by doing this she might either gain or lose religious merit, and therefore this is called a mixed doubt about the gain and loss of religious merit.

If a courtesan relies solely upon the report of other people (i.e. hearsay) about a man, and goes to him without ascertaining herself whether he possesses good qualities or not, she may either gain or lose pleasure in proportion as he may be good or bad, and therefore this is called a mixed doubt about the gain and loss of pleasure.

Uddalika has described the gains and losses on both sides as follows:

If, when living with a lover, a courtesan gets both

[1] The souls of men who die with their desires unfulfilled are said to go to the world of the Manes, and not direct to the Supreme Spirit.

wealth and pleasure from him, it is called a gain on both sides.

When a courtesan lives with a lover at her own expense without getting any profit out of it, and the lover even takes back from her what he may have formerly given her, it is called a loss on both sides.

When a courtesan is uncertain whether a new acquaintance would become attached to her, and, moreover, if he became attached to her, whether he would give her anything, it is then called a doubt on both sides about gains.

When a courtesan is uncertain whether a former enemy, if made up by her at her own expense, would do her some injury on account of his grudge against her; or, if becoming attached to her, would take away angrily from her anything that he may have given to her, this is called a doubt on both sides about loss.

Babhravya has described the gains and losses on both sides as follows:

When a courtesan can get money from a man whom she may go to see, and also money from a man whom she may not go to see, this is called a gain on both sides.

When a courtesan has to incur further expense if she goes to see a man, and yet runs the risk of incurring an irremediable loss if she does not go to see him, this is called a loss on both sides.

When a courtesan is uncertain whether a particular man would give her anything on her going to see him, without incurring expense on her part or whether on her neglecting him another man would give her something, this is called a doubt on both sides about gain.

When a courtesan is uncertain whether, on going at her own expense to see an old enemy, he would take back from her what he may have given her, or whether by her not going to see him he would cause some disaster to fall upon her, this is called a doubt on both sides about loss.

By combining the above, the following six kinds of mixed results are produced:

Gain on one side, and loss on the other
Gain on one side, and doubt of gain on the other
Gain on one side, and doubt of loss on the other
Loss on one side, and doubt of gain on the other
Doubt of gain on one side, and doubt of loss on the other
Doubt of loss on one side, and loss on the other

A courtesan, having considered all the above things and taken counsel with her friends, should act so as to acquire gain, the chances of great gain, and the warding off of any great disaster. Religious merit and pleasure should also be formed into separate combinations like those of wealth, and then all should be combined with each other, so as to form new combinations.

When a courtesan consorts with men she should cause each of them to give her money as well as pleasure. At particular times, such as the Spring Festivals, etc., she should make her mother announce to the various men, that on a certain day her daughter would remain with the man who would gratify such and such a desire of hers.

When young men approach her with delight, she should think of what she may accomplish through them.

The combination of gains and losses on all sides are gain on one side, and loss on all others; loss on one side and gain on all others; gain on all sides, loss on all sides.

A courtesan should also consider doubts about gain and doubts about loss with reference both to wealth, religious merit, and pleasure.

Thus ends the consideration of gain, loss, attendant gains, attendant losses, and doubts.

The different kinds of courtesans are:

A bawd
A female attendant
An unchaste woman

A dancing girl
A female artisan
A woman who has left her family
A woman living on her beauty
And, finally, a regular courtesan

All the above kinds of courtesans are acquainted with various kinds of men, and should consider the ways of getting money from them, of pleasing them, of separating themselves from them, and of re-uniting with them. They should also take into consideration particular gains and losses, attendant gains and losses, and doubts in accordance with their several conditions.

Thus end the considerations of courtesans.

There are also two verses on the subject as follows:

'Men want pleasure, while women want money, and therefore this part, which treats of the means of gaining wealth, should be studied.'

'There are some women who seek for love, and there are others who seek for money; for the former the ways of love are told in previous portions of this work, while the ways of getting money, as practised by courtesans, are described in this part.'

PART VII

ABOUT THE MEANS OF ATTRACTING OTHERS TO YOURSELF

CHAPTER I

ON PERSONAL ADORNMENT; ON SUBJUGATING THE HEARTS OF OTHERS; AND ON TONIC MEDICINES

WHEN a person fails to obtain the object of his desires by any of the ways previously related, he should then have recourse to other ways of attracting others to himself.

Now good looks, good qualities, youth, and liberality are the chief and most natural means of making a person agreeable in the eyes of others. But in the absence of these a man or a woman must have resort to artificial means, or to art, and the following are some recipes that may be found useful.

An ointment made of the tabernamontana coronaria, the costus speciosus or arabicus, and the flacourtia cataphracta, can be used as an unguent of adornment.

If a fine powder is made of the above plants, and applied to the wick of a lamp, which is made to burn with the oil of blue vitrol, the black pigment or lamp black produced therefrom, when applied to the eye-lashes, has the effect of making a person look lovely.

The oil of the hogweed, the echites putescens, the sarina plant, the yellow amaranth, and the leaf of the nymphæ, if applied to the body, has the same effect.

A black pigment from the same plants produces a similar effect.

By eating the powder of the nelumbrium speciosum, the blue lotus, and the mesna roxburghii, with ghee and honey, a man becomes lovely in the eyes of others.

The above things, together with the tabernamontana coronaria, and the xanthochymus pictorius, if used as an ointment, produce the same results.

If the bone of a peacock or of a hyena be covered with gold, and tied on the right hand, it makes a man lovely in the eyes of other people.

In the same way, if a bead, made of the seed of the jujube, or of the conch shell, be enchanted by the incantations mentioned in the Atharvana Veda, or by the incantations of those well skilled in the science of magic, and tied on the hand, it produces the same result as described above.

When a female attendant arrives at the age of puberty, her master should keep her secluded, and when men ardently desire her on account of her seclusion, and on account of the difficulty of approaching her, he should then bestow her hand on such a person as may endow her with wealth and happiness.

This is a means of increasing the loveliness of a person in the eyes of others.

In the same way, when the daughter of a courtesan arrives at the age of puberty, the mother should get together a lot of young men of the same age, disposition, and knowledge as her daughter, and tell them that she would give her in marriage to the person who would give her presents of a particular kind.

After this the daughter should be kept in seclusion as far as possible, and the mother should give her in marriage to the man who may be ready to give her the presents agreed upon. If the mother is unable to get so much out of the man, she should show some of her own things as having been given to the daughter by the bridegroom.

Or the mother may allow her daughter to be married to the man privately, as if she was ignorant of the whole affair, and then pretending that it has come to her knowledge, she may give her consent to the union.

The daughter, too, should make herself attractive to the sons of wealthy citizens, unknown to her mother, and make them attached to her, and for this purpose should meet them at the time of learning to sing, and in places where music is played, and at the houses of other people, and then request her mother, through a female friend, or servant, to be allowed to unite herself to the man who is most agreeable to her.[1]

When the daughter of a courtesan is thus given to a man, the ties of marriage should be observed for one year, and after that she may do what she likes. But even after the end of the year, when otherwise engaged, if she should be now and then invited by her first husband to come and see him, she should put aside her present gain, and go to him for the night.

Such is the mode of temporary marriage among courtesans, and of increasing their loveliness, and their value in the eyes of others. What has been said about them should also be understood to apply to the daughters of dancing women, whose mothers should give them only to such persons as are likely to become useful to them in various ways.

Thus end the ways of making oneself lovely in the eyes of others.

If a man, after anointing his lingam with a mixture of the powders of the white thorn apple, the long pepper and, the black pepper, and honey, engages in sexual union with a woman, he makes her subject to his will.

The application of a mixture of the leaf of the plant vatodbhranta, of the flowers thrown on a human corpse when carried out to be burnt, and the powder of the bones of the peacock, and of the jiwanjiva bird produces the same effect.

The remains of a kite who has died a natural death, ground into powder, and mixed with cowach and honey, has also the same effect.

[1] It is a custom of the courtesans of Oriental countries to give their daughters temporarily in marriage when they come of age, and after they have received an education in the Kama Sutra and other arts. Full details are given of this at page 76 of *Early Ideas*, a group of Hindoo stories, collected and collated by Anaryan, W. H. Allen and Co., London, 1881.

Anointing oneself with an ointment made of the plant emblica myrabolans has the power of subjecting women to one's will.

If a man cuts into small pieces the sprouts of the vajnasunhi plant, and dips them into a mixture of red arsenic and sulphur, and then dries them seven times, and applies this powder mixed with honey to his lingam, he can subjugate a woman to his will directly that he has had sexual union with her, or if, by burning these very sprouts at night and looking at the smoke, he sees a golden moon behind, he will then be successful with any woman; or if he throws some of the powder of these same sprouts mixed with the excrement of a monkey upon a maiden, she will not be given in marriage to anybody else.

If pieces of the arris root are dressed with the oil of the mango, and placed for six months in a hole made in the trunk of the sisu tree, and are then taken out and made up into an ointment, and applied to the lingam, this is said to serve as the means of subjugating women.

If the bone of a camel is dipped into the juice of the plant eclipta prostata, and then burnt, and the black pigment produced from its ashes is placed in a box also made of the bone of a camel, and applied together with antimony to the eye lashes with a pencil also made of the bone of a camel, then that pigment is said to be very pure, and wholesome for the eyes, and serves as a means of subjugating others to the person who uses it. The same effect can be produced by black pigment made of the bones of hawks, vultures, and peacocks.

Thus end the ways of subjugating others to one's own will.

Now the means of increasing sexual vigour are as follows:

A man obtains sexual vigour by drinking milk mixed with sugar, the root of the uchchata plant, the piper chaba, and liquorice.

Drinking milk, mixed with sugar, and having the testicle of a ram or a goat boiled in it, is also productive of vigour.

The drinking of the juice of the hedysarum gangeticum, the kuili, and the kshirika plant mixed with milk, produces the same effect.

The seed of the long pepper along with the seeds of the sanseviera roxburghiana, and the hedysarum gangeticum plant, all pounded together, and mixed with milk, is productive of a similar result.

According to ancient authors, if a man pounds the seeds or roots of the trapa bispinosa, the kasurika, the tuscan jasmine, and liquorice, together with the kshirakapoli (a kind of onion), and puts the powder into milk mixed with sugar and ghee, and having boiled the whole mixture on a moderate fire, drinks the paste so formed, he will be able to enjoy innumerable women.

In the same way, if a man mixes rice with the eggs of the sparrow, and having boiled this in milk, adds to it ghee and honey, and drinks as much of it as necessary, this will produce the same effect.

If a man takes the outer covering of sesamum seeds, and soaks them with the eggs of sparrows, and then, having boiled them in milk, mixed with sugar and ghee, along with the fruits of the trapa bispinosa and the kasurika plant, and adding to it the flour of wheat and beans, and then drinks this composition, he is said to be able to enjoy many women.

If ghee, honey, sugar and liquorice in equal quantities, the juice of the fennel plant, and milk are mixed together, this nectar-like composition is said to be holy, and provocative of sexual vigour, a preservative of life, and sweet to the taste.

The drinking of a paste composed of the asparagus racemosus, the shvadaushtra plant, the guduchi plant, the long pepper, and liquorice, boiled in milk, honey, and ghee, in the spring, is said to have the same effect as the above.

Boiling the asparagus racemosus, and the shvadaushtra plant, along with the pounded fruits of the premna spinosa in water, and drinking the same, is said to act in the same way.

Drinking boiled ghee, or clarified butter, in the morning during the spring season, is said to be beneficial to health and strength and agreeable to the taste.

If the powder of the seed of the shvadaushtra plant and the flower of barley are mixed together in equal parts, and a portion of it, i.e. two palas in weight, is eaten every morning on getting up, it has the same effect as the preceding recipe.

There are also verses on the subject as follows:

'The means[1] of producing love and sexual vigour should be learnt from the science of medicine, from the Vedas, from those who are learned in the arts of magic, and from confidential relatives. No means should be tried which are doubtful in their effects, which are likely to cause injury to the body, which involve the death of animals, and which bring us in contact with impure things. Such means should only be used as are holy, acknowledged to be good, and approved of by Brahmans, and friends.'

[1] From the earliest times Oriental authors have occupied themselves about aphrodisiacs. The following note on the subject is taken from a translation of the *Hindoo Art of Love*, otherwise the *Anunga Runga*, alluded to in the preface of this work, Part I, pages 87 and 88. 'Most Eastern treatises divide aphrodisiacs into two different kinds; 1. the mechanical or natural, such as scarification, flagellation, etc; and 2. the medicinal or artificial. To the former belong the application of insects, as is practised by some savage races; and all orientalists will remember the tale of the old Brahman, whose young wife insisted upon his being again stung by a wasp.'

CHAPTER II

OF THE WAYS OF EXCITING DESIRE, AND MISCELLANEOUS EXPERIMENTS, AND RECIPES

If a man is unable to satisfy a Hastini, or Elephant woman, he should have recourse to various means to excite her passion. At the commencement he should rub her yoni with his hand or fingers, and not begin to have intercourse with her until she becomes excited, or experiences pleasure. This is one way of exciting a woman.

Or, he may make use of certain Apadravyas, or things which are put on or around the lingam to supplement its length or its thickness, so as to fit it to the yoni. In the opinion of Babhravya, these Apadravyas should be made of gold, silver, copper, iron, ivory, buffalo's horn, various kinds of wood, tin or lead, and should be soft, cool, provocative of sexual vigour, and well fitted to serve the intended purpose. Vatsyayana, however, says that they may be made according to the natural liking of each individual.

The following are the different kinds of Apadravyas:

'The armlet' (Valaya) should be of the same size as the lingam, and should have its outer surface made rough with globules.

'The couple' (Sanghati) is formed of two armlets.

'The bracelet' (Chudaka) is made by joining three or more armlets, until they come up to the required length of the lingam.

'The single bracelet' is formed by wrapping a single wire around the lingam, according to its dimensions.

The Kantuka or Jalaka is a tube open at both ends, with a hole through it, outwardly rough and studded with soft globules, and made to fit the side of the yoni, and tied to the waist.

When such a thing cannot be obtained, then a tube made of the wood apple, or tubular stalk of the bottle gourd, or a reed made soft with oil and extracts of plants, and tied to the waist with strings, may be made use of, as also a row of soft pieces of wood tied together.

The above are the things that can be used in connection with or in the place of the lingam.

The people of the southern countries think that true sexual pleasure cannot be obtained without perforating the lingam, and they therefore cause it to be pierced like the lobes of the ears of an infant pierced for earrings.

Now, when a young man perforates his lingam he should pierce it with a sharp instrument, and then stand in water so long as the blood continues to flow. At night, he should engage in sexual intercourse, even with vigour, so as to clean the hole. After this he should continue to wash the hole with decoctions, and increase the size by putting into it small pieces of cane, and the wrightia antidysenterica, and thus gradually enlarging the orifice. It may also be washed with liquorice mixed with honey, and the size of the hole increased by the fruit stalks of the sima-patra plant. The hole should also be anointed with a small quantity of oil.

In the hole made in the lingam a man may put Apadravyas of various forms, such as the 'round', the 'round on one side', the 'wooden mortar', the 'flower', the 'armlet', the 'bone of the heron', the 'goad of the elephant', the 'collection of eight balls', the 'lock of hair', the 'place where four roads meet', and other things named according to their forms and means of using them. All these Apadravyas should be rough on the outside according to their requirements.

The ways of enlarging the lingam must be now related.

When a man wishes to enlarge his lingam, he should rub

it with the bristles of certain insects that live in trees, and then, after rubbing it for ten nights with oils, he should again rub it with the bristles as before. By continuing to do this a swelling will be gradually produced in the lingam, and he should then lie on a cot, and cause his lingam to hang down through a hole in the cot. After this he should take away all the pain from the swelling by using cool concoctions. The swelling, which is called 'Suka', and is often brought about among the people of the Dravida country, lasts for life.

If the lingam is rubbed with the following things, the plant physalis flexuosa, the shavara-kandaka plant, the jalasuka plant, the fruit of the egg plant, the butter of a she buffalo, the hastri-charma plant, and the juice of the vajrarasa plant, a swelling lasting for one month will be produced.

By rubbing it with oil boiled in the concoctions of the above things, the same effect will be produced, but lasting for six months.

The enlargement of the lingam is also effected by rubbing it or moistening it with oil boiled on a moderate fire along with the seeds of the pomegranate, and the cucumber, the juices of the valuka plant, the hasti-charma plant, and the egg-plant.

In addition to the above, other means may be learnt from experienced and confidential persons.

The miscellaneous experiments and recipes are as follows:

If a man mixes the powder of the milk hedge plant, and the kantaka plant with the excrement of a monkey and the powdered root of the lanjalika plant, and throws this mixture on a woman, she will not love anybody else afterwards.

If a man thickens the juice of the fruits of the cassia fistula, and the eugenia jambolana by mixing them with the powder of the soma plant, the vernonia anthelmintica, the eclipta prostata, and the lohopa-jihirka, and applies this composition to the yoni of a woman, and then has sexual intercourse with her, his love for her will be destroyed.

The same effect is produced if a man has connection with a woman who has bathed in the butter-milk of a she-buffalo mixed with the powders of the gopalika plant, the banu-padika plant and the yellow amaranth.

An ointment made of the flowers of the nauclea cadamba, the hog plum, and the eugenia jambolana, and used by a woman, causes her to be disliked by her husband.

Garlands made of the above flowers, when worn by the woman, produce the same effect.

An ointment made of the fruit of the asteracantha longifolia (kokilaksha) will contract the yoni of a Hastini or Elephant woman, and this contraction lasts for one night.

An ointment made by pounding the roots of the nelumbrium speciosum, and of the blue lotus, and the powder of the plant physalis flexuosa mixed with ghee and honey, will enlarge the yoni of the Mrigi or Deer woman.

An ointment made of the fruit of the emblica myrabolans soaked in the milky juice of the milk hedge plant, of the soma plant, the calotropis gigantea, and the juice of the fruit of the vernonia anthelmintica, will make the hair white.

The juice of the roots of the madayantaka plant, the yellow amaranth, the anjanika plant, the clitoria ternateea, and the shlakshnaparni plant, used as a lotion, will make the hair grow.

An ointment made by boiling the above roots in oil, and rubbed in, will make the hair black, and will also gradually restore hair that has fallen off.

If lac is saturated seven times in the sweat of the testicle of a white horse, and applied to a red lip, the lip will become white.

The colour of the lips can be regained by means of the madayantika and other plants mentioned above.

A woman who hears a man playing on a reed pipe which has been dressed with the juices of the bahupadika plant, the tabernamontana coronaria, the costus speciosus or arabicus, the pinus deodora, the euphorbia antiquorum, the vajra and the kantaka plant, becomes his slave.

If food be mixed with the fruit of the thorn apple (dathura) it causes intoxication.

If water be mixed with oil and the ashes of any kind of grass except the kusha grass, it becomes the colour of milk.

If yellow myrabolans, the hog plum, the shrawana plant, and the priyangu plant be all pounded together, and applied to iron pots, these pots become red.

If a lamp, trimmed with oil extracted from the shrawana and priyangu plants, its wick being made of cloth and the slough of the skins of snakes, is lighted, and long pieces of wood placed near it, those pieces of wood will resemble so many snakes.

Drinking the milk of a white cow who has a white calf at her foot is auspicious, produces fame, and preserves life.

The blessings of venerable Brahmans, well propitiated, have the same effect.

There are also some verses in conclusion:

'Thus have I written in a few words the "Science of love", after reading the texts of ancient authors, and following the ways of enjoyment mentioned in them.'

'He who is acquainted with the true principles of this science pays regard to Dharma, Artha, Kama, and to his own experiences, as well as to the teachings of others, and does not act simply on the dictates of his own desire. As for the errors in the science of love which I have mentioned in this work, on my own authority as an author, I have, immediately after mentioning them, carefully censured and prohibited them.'

'An act is never looked upon with indulgence for the simple reason that it is authorised by the science, because it ought to be remembered that it is the intention of the science, that the rules which it contains should only be acted upon in particular cases. After reading and considering the works of Babhravya and other ancient authors, and thinking over the meaning of the rules given by them, the Kama Sutra was composed, according to the precepts of Holy Writ, for the benefit of the world, by Vatsyayana, while leading the life of a religious student, and wholly engaged in the contemplation of the Deity.'

'This work is not intended to be used merely as an instrument for satisfying our desires. A person, acquainted with the true principles of this science, and who preserves his Dharma, Artha, and Kama, and has regard for the practices of the people, is sure to obtain the mastery over his senses.'

'In short, an intelligent and prudent person, attending to Dharma and Artha, and attending to Kama also, without becoming the slave of his passions, obtains success in everything that he may undertake.'

CONCLUDING REMARKS

THUS ends, in seven parts, the Kama Sutra of Vatsyayana, which might otherwise be called a treatise on men and women, their mutual relationship, and connection with each other.

It is a work that should be studied by all, both old and young; the former will find in it real truths, gathered by experience, and already tested by themselves, while the latter will derive the great advantage of learning things, which some perhaps may otherwise never learn at all, or which they may only learn when it is too late ('too late' those immortal words of Mirabeau) to profit by the learning.

It can also be fairly commended to the student of social science and of humanity, and above all to the student of those early ideas, which have gradually filtered down through the sands of time, and which seem to prove that the human nature of today is much the same as the human nature of the long ago.

It has been said of Balzac [the great, if not the greatest of French novelists] that he seemed to have inherited a natural and intuitive perception of the feelings of men and women, and has described them with an analysis worthy of a man of science. The author of the present work must also have had a considerable knowledge of the humanities. Many of his remarks are so full of simplicity and truth, that they have stood the test of time, and stand out still as clear and true as when they were first written, some eighteen hundred years ago.

As a collection of facts, told in plain and simple language, it must be remembered that in those early days there was apparently no idea of embellishing the work, either with a literary style, a flow of language, or a quantity of superfluous padding. The author tells the world what he knows in very concise language, without any attempt to produce an interesting story. From his facts how many novels could be written! Indeed much of the matter contained in Parts III, IV, V and VI has formed the basis of many of the stories and the tales of past centuries.

There will be found in Part VII some curious recipes. Many of them appear to be as primitive as the book itself, but in later works of the same nature these recipes and prescriptions appear to have increased, both as regards quality and quantity. In the Anunga Runga or 'The Stage of Love', mentioned at page 85 of the Preface, there are found no less than thirty-three different subjects for which one hundred and thirty recipes and prescriptions are given.

As the details may be interesting, these subjects are described as follows:

For hastening the paroxysm of the woman

For delaying the orgasm of the man

Aphrodisiacs

For thickening and enlarging the lingam, rendering it sound and strong, hard and lusty

For narrowing and contracting the yoni

For perfuming the yoni

For removing and destroying the hair of the body

For removing the sudden stopping of the monthly ailment

For abating the immoderate appearance of the monthly ailment

For purifying the womb

For causing pregnancy

For preventing miscarriage and other accidents

For ensuring easy labour and ready deliverance

For limiting the number of children

For thickening and beautifying the hair

For obtaining a good black colour to it

For whitening and bleaching it

For renewing it

For clearing the skin of the face from eruptions that break out and leave black spots upon it

For removing the black colour of the epidermis
For enlarging the breasts of women
For raising and hardening pendulous breasts
For giving a fragrance to the skin
For removing the evil savour of perspiration
For anointing the body after bathing
For causing a pleasant smell to the breath
Drugs and charms for the purposes of fascinating, overcoming, and subduing either men or women
Recipes for enabling a woman to attract and preserve her husband's love
Magical collyriums for winning love and friendship
Prescriptions for reducing other persons to submission
Philter pills, and other charms
Fascinating incense, or fumigation
Magical verses which have the power of fascination

Of the one hundred and thirty recipes given, many of them are absurd, but not more perhaps than many of the recipes and prescriptions in use in Europe not so very long ago. Love-philters, charms, and herbal remedies have been, in early days, as freely used in Europe as in Asia, and doubtless some people believe in them still in many places.

And now, one word about the author of the work, the good old sage Vatsyayana. It is much to be regretted that nothing can be discovered about his life, his belongings, and his surroundings. At the end of Part VII, he states that he wrote the work while leading the life of a religious student [probably at Benares] and while wholly engaged in the contemplation of the Deity. He must have arrived at a certain age at that time, for throughout he gives us the benefit of his experience, and of his opinions, and these bear the stamp of age rather than of youth; indeed the work could hardly have been written by a young man.

In a beautiful verse of the Vedas of the Christians it has been said of the peaceful dead, that they rest from their labours, and that their works do follow them. Yes indeed, the works of men of genius do follow them, and remain as a lasting treasure. And though there may be disputes and discussions about the immortality of the body or the soul, nobody can deny the immortality of genius, which ever remains as a bright and guiding star to the struggling humanities of succeeding ages. This work, then, which has stood the test of centuries, has placed Vatsyayana among the immortals, and on This, and on Him no better elegy or eulogy can be written than the following lines:

> 'So long as lips shall kiss, and eyes shall see,
> So long lives This, and This gives life to Thee.'

Also available . . .

KAMA SUTRA

THE ARTS OF LOVE

The *Kama Sutra* is the most famous book on the art and skills of sex and love ever written.

It gives a unique and poetic insight into a world of erotic pleasure, offering hundreds of sensuous techniques, exciting postures and creative ideas for enriching loving, monogamous relationships.

Much has changed since it was first written, but the human heart, mind and body remain the same – full of longing, romance and desire. The timeless magic of the *Kama Sutra* reaches far beyond any modern sex manual, so that you may find, as generations of readers around the world have done before you, that it creates profound changes not just in your sex life but in your life as a whole.

This beautifully produced edition is an abridged and annotated version of Vatsyayana's classic work, illustrated with over 150 stunning full colour photographs.

It is quite simply, the ultimate book for lovers.

THE ART OF

SEXUAL ECSTASY

The Path of Sacred Sexuality for Western Lovers

MARGO ANAND

This highly illustrated landmark book on human sexuality makes the sacred love-making techniques of the East available to Western readers. Margo Anand offers liberating practices that can immeasurably extend sensual experience for everyone.

She teaches a wide range of methods – massage, visualization, breathing, ritual, movement and fantasy – to enhance pleasure and deepen intimacy. Her sexual secrets include:

- prolonging pleasure by learning to remain aroused while fully relaxed
- expanding orgasm from a localized sensation to a full body experience
- healing a lack of sexual sensation
- recovering from sexual trauma
- using self-pleasuring to overcome sexual inhibition
- achieving multiple orgasm for both men and women
- discovering many innovative positions for versatility and compatibility
- learning the map of the sexual anatomy of the opposite sex
- increasing arousal and extending the sexual experience
- getting comfortable with safe sex
- transforming sexuality into a truly spiritual experience.

Far from being complex and esoteric, these simple techniques are accessible to anyone who wants to find a gentle and conscious way of bringing the spirit back into sex, of honouring sexual union as a bridge between body and soul, and of discovering a new sexual experience in which physical pleasure becomes a delight of the heart and an ecstasy of the spirit.

THE LOVER WITHIN

Creating Ecstasy in Relationships

JULIE HENDERSON

The Lover Within is a pioneering guide that teaches individuals and couples how to improve loving relationships. It represents 10 years of private research and public workshops on the theme of courting the 'lover within' – the inner pulsation of life and being.

Drawing on a wide range of techniques, including bioenergetics, drama, meditation and hypnotherapy, Julie Henderson describes in detail 63 practical exercises – to be done alone or with a partner – for the physical body, the 'energy body', the mind and the will. These exercises are designed to increase our capacity for drive, excitement, pleasure and intimacy.

This revolutionary work is a major contribution to helping us open our relationships to the play of energy. It raises sexuality to a new level and is an invaluable aid to anyone concerned with enriching their personal life.

Includes information on how to:

- challenge existing ideas about sexual activity
- stimulate energetic movement throughout the body
- dissolve old, useless boundaries between and within us
- experience limitless love and pleasure

WE TWO

Couples who have survived the '80s talk about working, living and loving partnerships for the '90s

ROGER HOUSDEN & CHLOE GOODCHILD

At a time when marriages are breaking down faster than ever and surveys reveal that extra-marital affairs are the norm, it may seem that monogamous, till-death-do-us-part relationships are a thing of the past. *We Two* sets out to explore whether there is a more satisfying alternative to unfulfilling marriages than moving restlessly from one relationship to another or living alone.

The eight couples here – all renowned as individuals for their insights into the human condition – are, perhaps, the new exception to the rule. Some are married, some are not, but all share a long-standing commitment to their relationship. Their intensely personal, affectionate, sometimes painful and often humorous accounts suggest some interesting answers to the questions that many people now face in the quest for intimacy.

- Are successful relationships a matter of destiny?
- Is the institution of marriage important?
- Do conflict and struggle necessarily mean the end?
- Can a relationship survive jealousy and betrayal?
- Is monogamy a key factor?
- How important is sex?
- What keeps a relationship alive?

This is not a book of theory but of personal experience. By sharing their stories these couples give us hope and inspiration in what has become one of the most confusing areas of modern life. They also give us a sense of what it is realistic to expect, because they do not gloss over the inevitable difficulties involved in sharing one's life with a partner while endeavouring to find individual self-fulfilment.

JOURNEY OF THE HEART

Intimate Relationships and the Path to Love

JOHN WELWOOD

Modern marriage has reached a critical point. Romantic ideals of courtly love have proved increasingly unworkable within the routines and stresses of contemporary life, yet we still long for a deep intimacy with a life partner on all levels – sexual, emotional, mental, and spiritual.

John Welwood shows that although the romantic ideal is partly based on illusion, there are real possibilities of fulfilment and growth within a long-term intimate relationship. Even after the honeymoon is over, the energy of passion can be maintained and new depths of intimacy discovered. The path is a razor's edge, but John Welwood is a discerning guide who shows us how to recognize and avoid the worst pitfalls.

This book does not provide easy options and instant answers. Rather, it provokes and encourages us to explore further, and to rise to the challenge of relationships in the modern world. It is hard work, but rewarding. Awareness, sincerity and commitment are required, to turn our relationships into an adventurous journey that can lead to understanding, personal growth – and even spiritual transformation.

A RETURN TO LOVE

Reflections on the principles of A Course In Miracles

MARIANNE WILLIAMSON

Marianne Williamson has for some time been the guru of many of the biggest names in showbusiness and recently catapulted to fame after officiating at the wedding of Elizabeth Taylor and Larry Fortensky.

Marianne lectures internationally in the fields of spirituality and new thought and with the publication of *A Return to Love* offers readers the chance to experience the uplifting and empowering teachings which are so evident at her personal appearances.

She has also established the Los Angeles and Manhattan Centres for Living, non-profit making organisations which provide services and hot meals for people suffering from Aids and other life challenging illnesses.

'Marianne Williamson displays in her writing the power and wit that she displays as a speaker. Her honest accounts of different periods in her life will motivate readers for a long time to come. *A Return to Love* makes for very powerful reading.' – LOUISE L HAY, author of *The Power Within You*.

'Marianne Williamson is a gifted interpreter of *A Course in Miracles* and is able to state its principles with simplicity and clarity. She sheds a unique light on its principles and brings love and forgiveness a little closer to home.'
– GERALD G JAMPOLSKY, author of *Love is Letting Go of Fear*.

A Return to Love is about the practical application of love as a daily answer to the problems that confront us, whether in the area of relationships, career or health. It is a spiritual journey, psychologically and emotionally, back to the truth we were born with. Let Marianne Williamson take you on this journey, where we surrender all preconceived notions of how we live our lives and accept back into our hearts the love we've been denying.

A LIVELY FLAME

Inspirations on Love and Relationships

EILEEN CAMPBELL

We all yearn for love and long to be in close relationships with others. Yet it is extraordinarily difficult to achieve this. Whilst our relationships can be a source of great fulfilment for us, they are also often the cause of our greatest pain and sorrow.

Largely it is our understanding of love which is at fault. A sense of oneness with what we love is what we are seeking, but too often our expectations are what lead us astray, and it is our perceptions which need to change. Our love is too often conditional, we do not accept people as they are, we do not love enough.

This anthology of quotations on love and relationships has been gathered from a wide variety of sources from both East and West. The quotations are loosely arranged in the following sequence: love and the nature of love, preparedness for love, falling in love, marriage and commitment, loss of love, love of God and universal love. It is hoped that it may prove helpful at those times when the mind is far from peaceful.